The Fundamentals of Workplace Learning

D1376087

The Fundamentals of Workplace Learning is a comprehensive guide to how people learn in the workplace, and the issues and challenges involved. Examining the essential aspects of workplace learning and unravelling the various influences which affect the success of work-based learners, Knud Illeris presents a holistic model to explain how diverse individuals can be encouraged and invited to learn at work.

Approaching workplace learning from the perspective of learners as human beings, with complex social and psychological needs, as opposed to resources to be managed, this book examines in detail the key issues surrounding workplace learning, including:

- the workplace environment as a learning space;
- workplace learning as competence development;
- a multitude of different kinds of workplace learning arrangements;
- job-transcending learning initiatives;
- the interaction between formal and informal learning environments;
- the challenges presented by specific groups: early school leavers, elderly workers and the new young generation.

Presenting conclusions on workplace learning and possibilities for the future this book focuses on a way forward while detailing the fundamentals of successful workplace learning. It will appeal to everyone involved in understanding and improving learning in the workplace including educationalists, business students, managers, personnel staff and educational leaders.

Knud Illeris is Professor of Lifelong Learning at the Danish School of Education, Aarhus University, Denmark. He is author or editor of numerous books, including *How We Learn*, *Contemporary Theories of Learning* and *International Perspectives on Competence Development*.

The Fundamentals of
Workplace Learning

Und
Lear

Knu

 Routledge
Taylor & Francis Group

LONDON AND NEW YORK

First edition published 2011
by Routledge
2 Park Square, Milton Park, Abingdon, Oxon, OX14 4RN

Simultaneously published in the USA and Canada
by Routledge
270 Madison Avenue, New York, NY 10016

Routledge is an imprint of the Taylor & Francis Group, an informa business

© 2011 Knud Illeris

Typeset in Galliard by Prepress Projects Ltd, Perth, UK
Printed and bound in Great Britain by TJ International Ltd, Padstow, Cornwall

British Library Cataloguing in Publication Data
A catalogue record for this book is available from the British Library

Library of Congress Cataloging-in-Publication Data
A catalog record has been requested for this book

ISBN13: 978–0–415–57906–3 (hbk)
ISBN13: 978–0–415–57907–0 (pbk)
ISBN13: 978–0–203–83652–1 (ebk)

Contents

Figures

Preface

This book has arisen out of my involvement in human learning in general and youth and adult vocational training and education in particular for almost four decades. My first book, on a comprehensive experiment in Danish teacher training, was published in 1972, and my dissertation in 1974 was an investigation of problem-oriented and participant-directed approaches to education and training, including a draft of a comprehensive learning theory, drawing mainly on the works of Jean Piaget and Carl Rogers (these books have been published only in Danish).

From 1976 to 1981 I was the research leader of a developmental project on the new Danish youth vocational training system that involved five researchers and some 20 teachers. Later my focus shifted to adult vocational training, and from 1987 to 1997 I was a consultant for the Danish Ministry of Labour in relation to the state programme on vocational training for unskilled and unemployed workers, including the direction in 1992–97 of the so-called generic qualification project (Andersen *et al.* 1992, 1996).

After this I was for some years mainly occupied with two international research projects. From 1997 to 2000 I was the research leader of the so-called Adult Education Research Project, which involved three Danish researchers and an international reference group consisting of Ari Antikainen (Finland), Jeanne Bitterman (USA), Thomas Leithäuser (Germany), Jessé Souza (Brazil), Robin Usher (UK/Australia) and Danny Wildemeersch (Belgium) (see Illeris 1998, 2000). Then, in 1998–2000 I participated in an EU project, Unemployed Youth and Social Exclusion, together with Wiltrud Giesecke (Germany), Theo Jansen (the Netherlands), Manuela Marinho (Portugal), Susan Werner Weil (UK) and Danny Wildemeersch (Belgium – project leader) (see Weil *et al.* 2005). These two projects gave me an important international insight and contribution to my understanding of learning, education and training.

Finally, during the period 2001–2004 I was the research director of the Consortium on Research in Learning in Working Life, which was established by the then new Learning Lab Denmark. The consortium undertook 16 very different projects and its members comprised 11 senior researchers, five PhD students and an international reference group consisting of Frank Blackler (UK), David

Boud (Australia), Per-Erik Ellström (Sweden), Karen Evans (UK), Silvia Gherardi (Italy), Henrik Holt Larsen (Denmark), Barbara Wasson (Norway) and Danny Wildemeersch (Belgium). For the final international conference of the consortium in December 2004 we published a general report, *Learning in Working Life*, of some 250 pages, to which we all contributed and of which I was the editor and the author of the majority of the content (Illeris and Associates 2004). However, only 180 copies of the English version of this report were printed, and these were mainly distributed to the non-Danish-speaking conference participants, so it is not very well known or easily available. But it has been a useful resource to me in the preparation of the present volume, and some chapters in this book contain updated parts of this report.

In addition to this record of the practical research background to this book, I should mention some other important points. First of all, I consider it equally important, indeed indispensable, that I have throughout my career combined practical research activities with continuous development of my theoretical understanding, which has also served as a way to structure, combine and make meaning of research findings. In 1999 this led to the publication in Danish of the book *The Three Dimensions of Learning* (English version: Illeris 2002), and in 2006 the extended and restructured *How We Learn* (English version: Illeris 2007). This theoretical work has also been a central part of the basis for writing and structuring the present book.

Another important aspect is the increasing impact of the issue of competences and competence development. There are weighty reasons why learning today, and especially workplace learning, should take the form of competence development, and in recent years I have taken a great interest in the questions of what is actually meant by competence, how learning can be said to take the form of competence development, and how this can be achieved in various forms and types of training and education (Illeris 2009a,b). I think that these questions constitute a very serious and important challenge to learning conditions, vocational training and workplace learning today. But I also think that a great deal of nonsense and unjustifiable propaganda has been adduced in this respect. I shall therefore, in this book, address this issue wherever it is relevant.

Further, I think it is important to emphasise that this is a book on *learning* at work and at the same time explicitly to emphasise that it covers management issues only to the extent that they influence the learning conditions. This is in clear contrast to other approaches that treat the issue and challenge of workplace learning as a branch of what is today generally called human resource management (HRM). In HRM learning is fundamentally dealt with as a means of optimising work efficiency, productivity and profit. No doubt it does so in general and in many specific cases, but in this book the basic issue is to optimise learning qualitatively and quantitatively. Learning is seen as valuable in itself, for the learner as well as for companies, organisations and nations – a value which is a part of human being and human development and thereby also a condition for human action, activity and work.

This also leads to an approach in which the learning of workers and employees at shop-floor level is viewed as just as interesting and important as the learning of leaders and managers. As a general rule, and one which has been verified time and again, the more educated a staff member is, and the higher his or her position in the organisation, the greater will be his or her opportunities for further learning and education. In this book the approach is rather the opposite: as the majority of employees are placed at the lower levels of the organisational hierarchy, it is their learning that is considered the most important issue, although I address the learning of all staff members.

In this connection, it is worth mentioning that, even from the economic viewpoint of a company, an organisation or a nation, there are some general indications that investment in learning, training and education offers the highest rate of return when applied to those at the lowest level, who have the most to learn. Of course, this is not so easy to prove, but for a Danish observer it is natural to refer to the fact that the Nordic countries, which have the highest rates of participation in adult education and training in the world, also did very well economically in the second half of the twentieth century despite having relatively few natural resources. We often attribute this to a high level of education, even among the low-skilled members of the workforce.

In any case, the workplace learning of the least educated members of staff is undoubtedly both a very big and very important challenge that is often not taken sufficiently seriously in the planning and distribution of training and educational opportunities, whether it be in organisations or at the national level – and thus there is the potential for companies as well as for nations to do better and at the same time contribute to an increase in the welfare and democratic standards of their entire staff or population.

In 2009 I reached the age of 70 and ended my career as a full-time university professor, and although I am still affiliated to the Danish University School of Education I now work mainly as a private consultant on learning and educational affairs (see www.simil.dk). This has given me the time to use my background, experience and viewpoints as outlined briefly above to write this book, *The Fundamentals of Workplace Learning*. I consider this title as sending two messages, which are equally important to me. First, the book will discuss what can be considered fundamental for good and rewarding learning processes at work or in direct relation to work. Second, the word 'fundamental' indicates that the learning of all workers and citizens is an important part of the basis of the quality of societies, organisations, companies and, not least, individual learners.

I especially thank my former colleagues Christian Helms Jørgensen and Niels Warring for their inspiration and contribution to my understanding and work on workplace learning, and also Vibeke Andersen, Pernille Bottrup, Bruno Clematide, Lone Dirckinck-Holmfeld, Bente Elkjaer, Steen Høyrup, Anne Marie Kanstrup, Henrik Nitschke and Kim Pedersen from the Learning in Working Life Consortium for input to various sections. Without the common work and experience of this consortium, the writing of this book would not have been possible.

I also thank all the aforementioned researchers throughout the world for their inspiring participation in the reference and research groups which have contributed insights into important trends and developments in the field of international workplace learning research.

Knud Illeris

May 2010

Part I

Basic conditions and theory

Chapter 1: Introduction

This chapter is a general introduction to the topic of workplace learning, stating the fundamental conditions and interests in the area. First, there is a short discussion of why learning at work in recent years has become such an important issue. After this, the various theoretical positions and approaches to workplace learning are pointed out and briefly commented on. Finally, the approach and perspectives of this book are described.

Chapter 2: How we learn

This chapter deals with the general features of learning, briefly repeating the main elements of the learning theory and overview model of learning which are developed and described in my book, *How We Learn* (published by Routledge in 2007). It is emphasised that all learning has three dimensions: the content dimension, which is about what is learned; the incentive dimension, which is about the motivation and emotions driving the learning processes; and the interaction dimension providing the social and content input for the processes. Finally, some important features characterising workplace learning are highlighted.

Chapter 3: The workplace as a learning space

In this chapter the general features of the workplace as a learning environment are discussed and a simple overview model of the main features of this environment is established, in line with the general learning model of the previous chapter. The most important point to understand in this context is that, alongside the dominant production-oriented element of the workplace environment, there is also an informal community element which is of great importance in terms of learning possibilities and motivation. As a consequence of this, the workplace learning environment has much more to do with workplace practice than with the concepts of management and human resources.

Chapter 4: Workplace learning as a whole

In this chapter the two areas of learning and the workplace are combined, and a general workplace learning model or framework is established and discussed. It is emphasised that the conditions of workplace learning always have this double nature in terms of learning as it is and can be performed in the workplace environment, and that both of these areas and how they are combined therefore must always be taken into consideration. Only with such a holistic view of workplace learning is it possible to determine the kind of learning which is actually taking place at work.

Chapter 5: Workplace learning as competence development

As a supplement to the general outlines of the structures and main elements of workplace learning established in the previous chapters, this chapter introduces the concept of competence development as the optimal tool in workplace learning. However, competence is a contested concept, there are a multitude of very different definitions, and the term is often used just to indicate smartness and modernity. If the concept of competence is to have any meaning and significance it must be made clear which qualities are necessary to separate competence from other kinds of skills and competence development from more ordinary learning. With this in mind, a crucial point is the potential to solve new and unexpected problem situations, and it is precisely this that makes it so problematic to measure competences.

Introduction

Why learning at work?

The aim of this book is to provide a comprehensive and up-to-date presentation of the issue of workplace learning, defined as all learning taking place in workplaces or in relation to workplaces. It is intended to unfold the topic of human learning and combine it with the multiplicity of learning possibilities at or in relation to work and in this way to try to give an impression and an overview of the totality and complexity of this field.

During the last two or three decades 'workplace learning', 'learning in working life', 'work-based learning' and the like have become popular slogans in the context of vocationally oriented education and personnel development. Considerable interest has arisen on many sides – in practice, in theory, in politics, locally, nationally and internationally – in placing increasing emphasis on the vocationally oriented learning and development that take places directly at or in relation to the workplace, and it is often assumed that such learning and development meets a number of current challenges to the competence development of staff better than learning on courses and in educational institutions, because it is more directly connected to the situations, challenges and problems as they actually occur in practical working life.

This situation is fundamentally paradoxical, because as a point of departure workplace learning has precisely been the general and obvious form of vocationally oriented learning and qualification ever since a distinction began to be made between working life and the rest of life. However, there has been a clear tendency for increasingly more parts of qualification to be transferred from the workplace to formalised types of school, education and course activity, as working life and the rest of society gradually have become more and more complex. And there have, of course, been important reasons for this. Expensive school and educational systems would not be established and developed if they made no difference.

This development got under way first and foremost with the breakthrough and spread of industrialisation and capitalism during the nineteenth century, and it seems to have its roots in the need for fundamental and gradually more and more differentiated socialisation and qualification for the requirements of wage labour, which at a basic level requires a certain attitude that is not inborn: selling one-self as labour and loyally performing work determined by others within certain time frames. Since then the requirements concerning wage labourers' qualifications, practical as well as personal, have grown and grown; they have become increasingly differentiated, and, as a result, it has become increasingly difficult for workplaces to undertake up-to-date training.

Originally, apprenticeships in Germany and the Nordic countries lasted for seven years and did not include any school activities. Gradually the duration was cut down to three to four years, and workplace training was supplemented by training at evening classes. From about 1960, it became common to spend one day per week at school (day release), and since the 1970s lengthy periods of schooling have been built into all types of apprenticeships, while time spent in training at the workplace has been reduced. Today we must accept the need for both vocational basic training courses and workplace training to be brought up to date by considerable supplementary training or direct retraining outside the workplace.

The development trend is absolutely clear: more and more schooling and less and less educational training in the workplace. Why, then, has there now arisen a significant countertrend to 'return' as much learning as possible to working life?

The reason should be sought primarily in the extensive and profound developments and changes in the structures of society that have been described as the transition to late modernity, post-modernity, the risk society, the knowledge society, the information society and so on, and which encompass the breakthrough of market management, globalisation and new technologies (see, for example, Giddens 1990; Beck 1992; Baumann 1998).

This process of change has resulted in two key development trends in the area of learning and education. First, there has been a shift away from the notion that education and qualification are something that essentially belong to childhood and youth, something that can be dispensed with once one has acquired a certain degree of vocational competence on which one can base a 40- to 50-year career, if necessary with occasional updating. This notion was well matched by a school and educational system that could deliver such vocational competences and could be expanded and differentiated in step with developments.

But it is clear that this situation no longer prevails. Everyone must be prepared for their working functions to change constantly and radically throughout the whole of their working lives. Therefore, what is needed today is what is typically called *lifelong, lifewide and lifedeep learning* (see, for example, EU Commission 2000; Illeris 2004; Jarvis 2009a), and how and the extent to which it takes place and the role the school and the educational system can play in this context are open questions.

Second, 'what is to be learned' has changed in nature. At one time the learning targets of the school and education programmes were referred to in categories such as knowledge, skills, attitudes or, more generally, qualifications. All of this is, of course, still necessary. But at the same time it must necessarily be updated, developed, reorganised and recreated constantly to fit new situations, so that it can quickly and flexibly be adapted to changed contexts that are not known at present but which we know with certainty will come. This is the essence of the current concepts of *competences* and *competence development* (see, for example, Raven and Stephenson 2001; Beckett and Hager 2002; Illeris 2009a). And it is undeniably a challenge to the school and education system to supply competences for the solution of problems and situations that are unknown at the time of learning. How is this to be done?

It is first and foremost these questions that have led to ideas about workplace learning gaining ground. Would it not be easier, less expensive and more efficient if such development and constant adaptation of competences were to take place in the workplace, where the competences are to be utilised and where there is always first-hand knowledge of what is new? In the case of vocationally oriented competences, this would mean that competences are acquired and adapted as part of working life, in workplaces, networks or partner organisations, and would ensure that the processes are always up to date.

And would this not also be more democratic? After all, in this way those who are directly affected would always know what is going on and play a part in deciding what is to take place and how. Is it not in the interest of society as a whole to ensure that decisions about up-to-date competence development are shared by workers and staff on all levels, thus ensuring that learning is far more wide-ranging and direct than when it takes place in schools and institutions that have their own agenda and modes of functioning?

There would seem to be many good arguments in favour of workplace learning from the point of view of learning theory, efficiency and democracy. This is why it also has attracted many strong adherents, including, not least, supranational expert organisations such as the OECD, the EU and the World Bank, which view workplace learning as a key element in the lifelong learning that leads to economic growth, individual personal development and increased social balance, nationally and internationally (see, for example, OECD 2000, 2001).

But there are other interests that cannot be disregarded if a full picture of the new trend is to be obtained.

First, it is clear that the steadily growing education requirements are expensive, and the state has, therefore, an obvious interest in removing some of the burden from institutions – but not all of it, because the state also has overall responsibility for the level of education and training of the workforce as a prerequisite for economic growth and global competitiveness. If vocationally oriented training is left completely to the labour market, qualifications could easily become too short-sighted and narrow. Thus, states will quite generally advocate interaction between institutionalised, vocationally oriented education and workplace learning and seek to get the business sector and participants to bear as much of the cost as possible.

Enterprises/employers will naturally be reluctant to do this, especially in countries where, traditionally, education is publicly financed, unless it is principally personal or enterprise specific in nature. On the other hand, workplace learning would give the enterprises more influence over what is learned and how, and much general education from which an individual enterprise achieves no direct benefit could be reduced in line with learning taking place directly at work. Attitudes to this could be positive or negative, but organisations would largely tend to welcome more learning being situated in working life, especially if it were linked with some type of financial compensation.

Workers would also be largely positive as there would be less need for them to 'go back to school': most people believe that they learn better in informal contexts and at their work than in institutionalised education (see, for example, Cedefop 2003). Trade unions would also find it easier to influence how education takes place. On the other hand, it is obvious that formalised education is in general better at ensuring a workforce with a good, well-documented level of education, and unions can perhaps exert more influence when the representatives of the state play a part in decision-making than can be achieved in direct interaction with employers.

Finally, it should not be forgotten that educational institutions and teachers have a strong self-interest in the maintenance of formalised study programmes. Although there is currently a trend for teachers to visit enterprises to take part in interactive courses, this can hardly make up for the safe incomes ensured by permanent courses in schools.

There are thus many and very different interests at play when it comes to workplace learning, and it is also part of late modern market society that one should not believe all one hears. Today goods, ideas and attitudes are marketed professionally on the basis of interests that are not always immediately visible.

Theoretical approaches to workplace learning

It is only within the last 20–25 years that reference has been made to any great extent and more systematically to the concept of workplace learning. Nevertheless, the development of the workforce has been in focus in many different ways since the 1920s at least, typically, for example, when it came to rationalising production or seeking ways to democratise work.

In classical industrial work under Taylorist management principles, removing the possibilities of the individual worker's independent opportunities for learning and development was a conscious wish. The subjective dimensions of the labour force were to be minimised, with the aim of making the work as uniform and efficient as possible, and processes requiring independent attitudes and planning were to be undertaken by leaders and superior technicians and planners.

However, research, mainly American, in the inter-war period gradually revealed the impact of social conditions on work efficiency, which resulted in the *human relations* approach to workplace management, which advocated that workers should be accepted and treated as individuals (see, for example, Mayo 1949).

Later, in the 1970s and 1980s, this led to the *human resource management* (HRM) approach, which is today the dominant approach to workplace learning, at least in the USA, and is sometimes called by the more learning-oriented term *human resource development* (HRD; see, for example, Swanson and Holton 2001). It is, however, important to make clear that, although this approach stresses the importance of human conditions and resources, it is fundamentally a management approach and not a learning approach. HMR and HRD are, in particular, oriented towards the way in which an organisation or enterprise is managed, and ultimately how it can yield profit, and therefore the issue of workplace learning tends to be viewed from management, organisational and financial perspectives.

Organisational learning, an approach launched in 1978 with the first edition of the book of the same title by Americans Chris Argyris and Donald Schön, which was considerably updated and expanded in 1996 (Argyris and Schön 1978, 1996), also tends to be mainly a management tool. But in this case learning has a much more central position: this approach recognises that it is the members of the organisation and not the organisation itself that learns, that there is often a big difference between what one says and supports and what one actually does, even when it comes to learning, and that to further appropriate learning in an organisation there must, therefore, be openness about the assumptions one makes about oneself and others, rather than defensive reaction.

This is to some extent in opposition to the approach of the *learning organisation*, as for instance described in 1990 by Peter Senge in his book *The Fifth Discipline* (Senge 1990). This concept has been widely disseminated, which takes the view that learning surpasses the individual and can also be thought of as taking place at organisation level. But in general these two approaches are rather close to each other, and many treat them as two variations of the same organisational approach (see, for example, Elkjær 1999).

Characteristic of the organisation-oriented approach is a special focus on how an organisation creates the best possible learning environment in terms of formal structures and the informal forms of interaction, with the specific learning initiatives playing a more peripheral role. Argyris and Schön, in their approach, also introduce the concepts of single-loop and double-loop learning and thereby offer a workplace-related contribution to learning theory as these concepts can be regarded as the vocational equivalent of the more general concepts of assimilative and accommodative learning, which are introduced later in this book.

Further, there seems to be a kind of *economic-administrative approach* to workplace learning inherent in the contributions of the supranational organisations and with an emphasis on modern international concepts such as 'knowledge management' and 'learning economy' (for example OECD 1996, 2000, 2001; EU Commission 2000). This can be understood as an extension of a broader lifelong-learning approach with a tripartite objective of economic growth, social balance and personal development. It should be noted here that these three components are always mentioned in this order, with the economic perspective seemingly becoming increasingly to the fore – partly because of the view that knowledge and learning have become crucial factors in the economy of modern societies and partly, and more concretely, as a result of the emergence of cost–benefit calculations of the way in which this knowledge economy can be handled.

Further, there is in this approach a certain tendency for the concept of knowledge to take precedence over learning and competence and for what is to be learned or developed to take on the character of something that can be delimited and handled like things or commodities, in contrast to learning and competence, which are more dynamic concepts. In relation to workplace learning, the orientation is otherwise in line with the organisational approach, especially towards the development of appropriate learning environments.

More or less in accordance with, or in contrast to, these approaches, the broad and not very specific approach usually called *work-based learning* or *workplace learning* has emerged mainly as a continuation of traditions and modes of perception prevalent in general adult education. It is distinct from the other approaches mentioned largely because of its broad societal perspective and its emphasis on learning from the learners' angle and interest in general personal development.

This approach has to some extent assumed the nature of a movement, and it has grown up simultaneously in several Western counties and in many different versions. A kind of a scientific breakthrough came in the USA with the book entitled *Informal and Incidental Learning in the Workplace* (Marsick and Watkins 1990), which highlights the extensive learning that takes place 'incidentally' through work and how it can be qualified by improvements to the learning environment of the workplace. This approach was later developed further, in Australia among other places (for example Garrick 1998; Boud and Garrick 1999; Beckett and Hager 2002), and most concretely in Stephen Billett's book, *Learning in the Workplace*, which sets the stage for a curriculum for learning in the workplace (Billett 2001). Subsequently, the most important contributions seem to have come from the UK (for example Evans *et al.* 2002, 2006; Rainbird *et al.* 2004; Evans 2009). But there are also several contributions from other countries and in other languages.

Two ideas are common to these approaches: first, learning is fundamentally a social process, something that takes place between people and not only in people; and, second, as an extension of this, the learning culture or environment is decisive for the learning. The cultural context and practice are both a prerequisite for and the objective of learning in the sense that a better cultural environment promotes the quality of work and participants' personal development.

Somewhat different, but largely in line with the broad range of these approaches, are the works by Americans Jean Lave and Etienne Wenger, relating to the concepts of 'situated learning' and 'communities of practice' (Lave and Wenger 1991; Wenger 1998). However, these contributions have also attracted considerable criticism. For example, they seem to suggest that merely entering a community of good practice is sufficient for learning to take place. In Lave and Wenger's book, in particular, there is no close consideration of what takes place in this community, the individual side of learning is only touched on, and there is also very little consideration of the importance of management and power structures. In Wenger's later book the introduction of the concepts of meaning and identity remedies this to some extent.

It is notable that it is the concept of learning environment, in its broadest sense, that in one way or another is central to all the approaches mentioned, whereas more concrete learning processes generally play a more modest role. The differences between the approaches are to a higher degree in points of departure and ideas of objectives. For this reason, in practice it is not very difficult to cut across the different approaches, but at the same time the fundamental differences should not be overlooked.

The approach and perspective of this book

It is clear that this book is closely related to the workplace learning tradition as outlined above. However, as already mentioned in the preface, the point of departure and the central issue throughout the book is the complex processes of human learning and how they take place and may be influenced and improved at work or in direct relation to the workplace. Fundamentally this book is written from a learning perspective.

This learning perspective implies a tendency to prioritise the learning needs as they are interpreted by the learners themselves, and this is an important point as literature on workplace learning has a tendency to view learning needs and processes from the perspective of the company or the management, deliberately or inconsiderately – just as most writings on school learning tend to deal with the topic from the point of view of the teacher, the school or the authorities.

However, this fundamental commitment to the learners' perspective certainly does not prevent or hinder the involvement of other perspectives too, and, as every teacher or instructor has experienced, learners quite frequently have no clear conception of their own needs and interests or, if they do, this perception can be very one-sided and unsuited to achieving the various goals of the learning process.

Of course, it is not possible to take a completely neutral view when writing a book on a topic that is so central to today's political and cultural debate as workplace learning. On the other hand, the starting point in the learning perspective can form a frame of reference for the way in which the different possibilities are viewed and in this way to some extent make the book free of the many different interests in the field and give it a professional and democratic legitimacy.

The intention is to discuss and explain what can successfully be achieved by means of workplace learning, the principles for how such learning could be organised, and what it is important to take into account under different circumstances. Naturally, no clear, precise, thorough and final answers can be given to all these questions. Much depends on, for example, what the learning is about, who is to learn and under what conditions. But it is usually possible to arrive at some general perceptions and guidelines, to point out the most significant differences and their consequences, and to explain openly the background and the arguments for various standpoints and advice.

The book is arranged in three parts. Part I is concerned with arriving at a general overview and general understanding of matters to do with learning, workplaces as a learning environment, the interaction between learning and the workplace and the issue of competence development. In Part II a broad range of different practical ways of dealing with workplace learning are presented and examined, ranging from incidental and informal learning to all kinds of organised learning measures, activities and arrangements. Finally, in Part III, some important cross-cutting topics and problems in relation to workplace learning are taken up, attention is drawn to low-skilled learners and other groups with special problems, and some general conclusions are drawn and discussed.

How we learn

What is learning?

As a starting point to investigate the issue of workplace learning, this chapter will briefly present the definition and main features of learning which I have developed over a period of almost 40 years and finally unfolded in the book *How We Learn* (Illeris 2007) and in various shorter versions (e.g. Illeris 2006a, 2009c).

Traditionally, learning has been defined as the process through which an individual acquires knowledge, skills and possibly also attitudes and opinions, and professionally it has been considered as belonging to the field of cognitive psychology, together with areas such as perception, thinking and memory. However, in recent decades, several commentators have called this view into question.

First and foremost, it has been maintained that learning is fundamentally to be viewed as a social process that takes place in the interaction between people, for instance in various communities of practice (Lave and Wenger 1991) or, more generally and exclusively, within the so-called social-constructionist view (Gergen 1994; Burr 2003). From this arises the question whether the ability to learn is the exclusive ability of individuals, or whether it might be said that groups, corporations, organisations and perhaps even nations also have the ability to learn.

However, both the traditional view that learning is an inner psychological process within the individual, as maintained by classical learning psychology, and the view that learning is exclusively a social process, as maintained by the social constructionists, lead to erroneous conclusions. On the contrary, the point is that human learning always involves both elements at once: through the social interaction between the individual and his or her environment, the individual receives influences or impulses which he or she may absorb through inner psychological elaboration and acquisition processes. Only if both the interaction processes and the acquisition processes are active does learning take place.

This means that there is always a form of direct or indirect interaction, sociality, fellowship or collectivity involved in the learning processes. Even when an individual is alone in a current situation, the influences received from the environment are socially co-determined, and if the influence is mediated through reading, electronic media, images, architecture, etc., one or more specific influences are also indirectly present.

Therefore, one might say, in agreement with Lave and Wenger (1991), that all learning is situated, i.e. it takes place in a specific situation or context that co-determines both the learning process and its outcome, and, therefore, that it also makes perfect sense to refer to social learning or the social dimension of learning.

On the other hand, one might consider collective learning to occur only in very special contexts, if collective learning is defined as several individuals in a given situation learning the same thing. This is because the individual psychological acquisition process is a combination of the current impulses and the results of previous learning, and even though the impulses may be the same for all participants in a tuition situation, there will be individual differences in what has previously been learned, unless the group of people in question have highly similar prior knowledge (for instance, members of a religious sect or adherents to a certain ideology may share knowledge about areas crucial to their defining tenets).

However, it is not possible on the basis of the explanation of learning outlined to speak of 'the learning organisation', or to use similar expressions. The social interaction processes and the psychological acquisition processes which learning includes involve some capacities which living beings, and especially humans, have acquired and refined through millions of years, and which, for example, not even the most advanced computers are able to replicate, because human learning is much more than mere functional acquisition and processing of information (see, for example, Dreyfus and Dreyfus 1986). Human learning also involves complicated patterns of motivation, understanding, meaning, emotions, blockings, defence, resistance, consciousness and subconsciousness, and it is something entirely different from the incorporation and application of information and functions of which a computer or an organisation is capable. (However, the computer is able, for example, to process vast quantities of data in a short space of time, and an organisation may, with the cooperation of many people and the use of tools, perform tasks on a scale and of a magnitude that an individual would never be able to match.)

In summary, learning involves specifically human processes that include both social interaction and individual psychological processing and acquisition. Joint or social learning processes may well exist, but only in special cases will the outcomes be the same for all involved to an extent that permits the use of the term 'collective learning'.

Furthermore, fundamental premises are that both rational and emotional elements, in the broadest sense, are involved in learning and that psychological phenomena such as barriers, distortions, defence, resistance and similar factors may play an important role in the learning process.

A general learning model

To illustrate the basis of the view of learning outlined above I have developed a model or graphic illustration, which was presented first in my book *The Three Dimensions of Learning* (Illeris 2002) and has since been elaborated further (Illeris

2007). This model includes the two basic processes, three dimensions and a situ-ated position that are the fundamental elements of all human learning.

First, the social interaction process is depicted as a vertical double-headed arrow linking the individual and his or her environment. The environment is placed at the bottom (at the social level) and the individual at the top (at the subjective level). Next, on the subjective level a horizontal double-headed arrow depicts the psychological acquisition process between the content and the incentive, which are the two necessary elements of any learning acquisition. Content is essential because there is no learning without some content: learning always means learn-ing *something*. And incentive is necessary because the acquisition of knowledge, like any other brain process, demands a mobilisation of mental energy: there must be motivation, interest, some emotions, feelings or volition to make the process work. This model is shown in Figure 2.1.

As can be seen, the double-headed arrows mark out a triangle with one angle downwards to the social level and two angles at the top, at the subjective level, which represent the content and the incentive elements of subjective processing and acquisition. Finally, the circle framing the triangle indicates that all learning is situated and that the nature of the situatedness is ultimately determined by the society in which the learning takes place. Figure 2.2, 'the learning triangle', shows the basic three dimensions of learning.

The message of the model is thus that human learning is always composed of two co-determinant processes and includes the three dimensions of content, incentive and interaction. In the following each of the three dimensions will be examined and discussed separately.

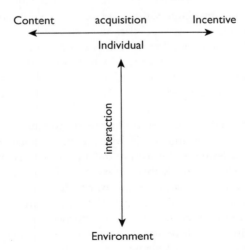

Figure 2.1 The fundamental processes of learning (after Illeris 2007, p. 23).

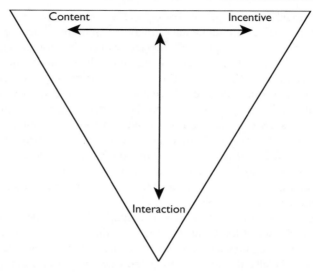

Figure 2.2 The three dimensions of learning.

The content dimension of learning

Whenever learning is described or discussed, it is nearly always the content dimension that assumes the main focus. What was learned or what should be or could be learned, but was for some reason not learned? Learning content is traditionally thought of as factual knowledge, skills and, possibly, attitudes and qualifications. However, such a definition is one-sided and much too narrow to fully describe the content of learning in working life today. What is learned may also encompass, for example, sensibilities, preparedness, modes of perception, forms of consciousness, identity, ways of acting and reacting, relations or strategies, and it is also through learning that we are able to develop the complicated and complex functions that today are referred to as competences, and which are in demand everywhere in society (see Chapter 5). From this wide range of learning areas it becomes apparent that learning is something that relates not only to reason and skills, but also always to emotional and social factors.

As already mentioned, learning takes place by combining new impressions and information we receive in the interaction with our environment with the results of previously acquired learning in the area in question. This has an impact on both the new input and what is already there. If we know or are able to do something in a certain area, and we learn something new, which we ascribe to the same area, the previous situation or understanding is changed by the new impact that is added, and the new input is at the same time influenced by being integrated into some already established contexts and structures. If, for instance, we are travelling to a country we have not visited before, we often try to acquire some information on that country before going there. We form some pictures and opinions.

Once we arrive, we find that our impressions are expanded, nuances added and, perhaps, pictures and opinions altered. At the same time, the new impressions are influenced by the perceptions we had beforehand. Furthermore, our preconceptions may contribute to determining what we notice and how we perceive it.

The learning we acquire is stored in some psychological structures, patterns or 'schemes' in the brain and the central nervous system. We call it the memory, and imagine that it is some sort of archive or storage facility in which all the different inputs are stored, and whence they may be retrieved when we need them, similar to the hard disk in a computer. However, the matter is, of course, much more complicated than that, specifically because it involves not only storage of data, but nuanced human functions that are interconnected and influence each other in innumerable different ways. Modern brain research can tell us much about this, even though there is much that is still unknown and perhaps may never be understood in detail (see Illeris 2007).

It should be mentioned that the understanding of acquisition of learning content that has been outlined here refers to a *constructivist* learning approach, which suggests that it is the learner who actively builds or constructs his or her knowledge and other capacities. Further analysis reveals four different ways in which learning may be acquired, and which have an impact on its character and possible applications.

Cumulative learning

Sometimes, but especially during the first few years of life, we find ourselves in the situation in which we, so to speak, 'open' a new learning area for which no scheme has yet been established, but the learning possibility consists of a congenital psychological disposition. This learning is thus isolated in terms of content; it is not connected to anything at all. This 'ground-breaking' phase takes place through a mechanical or 'cumulative' type of learning that involves no 'comprehension', but only a linking of an impulse and a learning product.

We probably know this best from what we call dressage or training of animals, the aim of which is to produce a highly specific reaction to a specific impulse. But this is, for instance, also the aim of what one might call classical military training. The intention is that the trainee acquires the ability to obey mechanically without 'thinking' or trying to understand an order as anything other than an order. However, to humans this is typically a 'dissatisfying' experience, and our cumulative learning at the same time involves a possibility for, and an urge in the direction of, moving on by extending the isolated learning.

Adults may, for instance, have to practise cumulative learning when they are to learn a new PIN. In this situation we must acquire and memorise something that has no meaning in itself, is not related to any other known context, and as such is incomprehensible, because to 'understand' means exactly to establish a context. So, what do we do? We may attempt to learn the four digits by heart by repeating them to ourselves, or perhaps writing them down so that we can return to them time after time. Alternatively, we may develop a mnemonic technique, impose a meaning on the digits by, for example, relating them to a birthday or other memorable number or date, or find what is often an entirely home-made system in the number combination, in order better to remember it and 'recall it to mind' when we need to.

This example describes what is characteristic of cumulative learning. Its weakness is that it is isolated in terms of content, it can in itself only be learned, not understood, and therefore is difficult to remember and can be used only in situations that psychologically recall the learning situation. Its strength is that we are able to build on and develop this learning, we can hardly help it, and thereby we have established a point of departure for what may eventually develop into a gigantic scheme that holds massive volumes of knowledge and options of action.

Assimilative learning

However, this already takes us to the next type of learning, additive or 'assimilative' learning. It might also have been called ordinary learning, for this is the type of learning we employ all the time in our daily lives when we encounter new impressions and add the new impulses to what has previously been learned in the area in question.

It is also this form of learning on which schools and education programmes are typically based when we employ the approach of gradually extending our knowledge, skills and comprehension by constantly adding new elements to what has already been learned in each subject.

In working life there may similarly take place extensive amounts of assimilative additive learning, to the same extent as workers or employees encounter new impulses and impressions. However, the work may also be strongly characterised by routine and without new impulses and therefore also involve very little learning.

Most of the assimilative learning takes place 'of itself', so to speak. We encounter something new, do not reflect much on it, but merely take it in by adding it to the scheme to which we 'think' it belongs. Sometimes, however, we take a more focused approach when the subject is something we would like to learn or must learn, for some reason.

When learning becomes more goal oriented, it also becomes more demanding: we must invest more psychological energy in it. In most cases, this does not cause problems, but there may be contexts in which it is difficult, either because we have difficulty understanding the content to be learned or because we are not sufficiently committed to mobilising the necessary concentration and effort.

Generally, as the years pass, all people build extensive knowledge and skills and capacities through assimilative learning, and this learning is widely applicable because we are, as a rule, able to recall it exactly when we need it, because it is attached to a scheme that makes it coherent with everything we know and are able to do and understand within the area in question, in the way we ourselves have defined and expanded it through our learning.

The limitations appear when, once in a while, we need to use what we have learned in a context in which some other schemes hold our attention, i.e. when we are in a situation where we are not used to applying the knowledge, skills and comprehension in question. We could all think of many examples of this. If, for instance, we encounter a person with whom we are only superficially acquainted in an unexpected context, it may often be difficult to recall who he or she is and the person's name. At schools, physics teachers often complain that students are not able to apply the relevant mathematics, because to them this skill is attached to another subject on which their awareness is not focused. In the workplace, it can be difficult to remember if, for some reason, one has promised to call one's aunt, because one does not associate her with working life.

As a result of such limitations, assimilative learning may be vulnerable in certain contexts, and in modern society, where everything is in constant change, we actually encounter this to an increasing extent. What we learned yesterday does not apply today, because the context of our knowledge has changed, so we get stuck in some 'obsolete routines', and if we are unable to adapt we are perceived as 'inflexible', which is almost the worst term of abuse found in today's working life. Thus, it is important that there is a form of learning that is more far-reaching, and which is exactly the basis for flexibility, creativity, innovation, adaptability and the like.

Accommodative learning

This form of learning is termed transcendent or 'accommodative' learning, and it is typically activated when we find ourselves in a situation which we cannot immediately comprehend or experience events to which we are unable to relate. What we experience does not match the modes of comprehension or functioning that we have developed in advance, so we are not able to connect it with the schemes we have in this area through the application of assimilative learning. If, in this situation, we are willing to make the effort nonetheless to comprehend and acquire what is going on, we are able to decompose part of the relevant scheme or schemes and restructure them so that the new impulses may be absorbed. It is this decomposition and reconstruction that is called *accommodation*.

Accommodative learning is, however, considerably more psychologically demanding than assimilative learning. It requires going against a reluctance to decompose already acquired modes of understanding, and it requires a creative effort to make a restructuring. Therefore, we tend to evade the challenge, either by blocking out the situation or by slightly distorting the experience so that it fits into our existing schemes or prior understandings and can therefore be acquired by assimilation. This is, for example, the way in which prejudice typically works: we see what we *want to* see, instead of what actually takes place.

However, if the situation is concerned with something we would very much like to acquire correctly, either because we need it or because it is something that we find significant and interesting, that is, if it involves a suitably high degree of motivation, then we are able to mobilise the necessary psychological energy and carry out the accommodative learning process. It may in some cases take place suddenly and spontaneously, what in psychology is called an 'aha' experience: all of a sudden we grasp the nature of the matter at hand. In other cases, it requires more thorough processing or 'reflection': we turn the matter over in our head, we wrestle with it, perhaps we even dream about it at night, and gradually 'the pieces start fitting into a larger picture'. In both cases, the accommodation carried out is associated with a certain feeling of relief, and the learning outcome is typically something that is highly durable in memory, and which we are able to 'recall' and apply within a broad spectrum of relevant contexts. We have achieved a new structural comprehension of something, and this is exactly the basis for us to be able to use it more freely; it is no longer 'trapped inside' a scheme – we have become more flexible and creative in the area in question.

Accommodative learning is thus exactly what is needed when in working life there is a demand for employees who are more flexible, creative, independent of thought and ready to adapt, and learning initiatives aiming at accommodative learning must offer impulses that are new, challenging and problem oriented. However, at the same time educators and others must be aware that these qualities are not so easily 'tamed', i.e. that people whose thinking is flexible and creative are less prone merely to do as they are told.

Transformative learning

Finally, the works of various researchers over the past 10–15 years have made it clear that there is a still more demanding and extensive form of learning, which they have identified by various terms. I shall here use the term 'transformative' learning, which was introduced by the American Jack Mezirow (1978, 1991), but I might also have chosen the term 'expansive' learning, which was coined by the Finnish psychologist Yrjö Engeström (1987).

This form of learning has, however, been known for a long time within psychotherapy; for example, in the late 1800s, Freud used the term 'catharsis' to describe a favourable outcome of a psychoanalytical treatment that is concerned exactly with a transformative course (Freud and Breuer 1956), and it was another psychotherapist, the American Carl Rogers, who with his concept of 'significant learning' was the first to link such a course with a perception of learning (Rogers 1951, 1969).

With respect to learning, the term refers to the decomposition of several schemes in a coherent process and their restructuring into a new coherent understanding and experience in relation to one or more significant areas of life, often involving the self or the identity of the learner, a new understanding or a fundamental tenet. This is a highly taxing process that possesses the character of undergoing a personal crisis, and when this happens the learner will usually experience some sort of release.

However, it is no mere coincidence that the transformative processes that were previously connected with psychotherapy have today become an area of interest in connection with learning and education. The reason for this is partly because the ever-changing and unstable nature of modern existence brings an increasing number of people into situations that can be surmounted only through transformative courses and partly because the ability to adapt which society increasingly imposes as a demand on its members in many cases can be gained only in this way.

This type of learning is typically a necessary result of the involuntary unemployment that ensues when an employer reduces its workforce, for example as the result of a merger, closes down operations altogether or relocates production to other countries where labour is cheaper, and workers find themselves unable to find other employment doing work of a similar type. The result of such a scenario is more than just the need for retraining, the necessity for the unemployed individual to learn something new. For instance, a person who has been a well-functioning and appreciated banking employee for many years also has a work identity connected with his or her ability to handle this work, earns enough to support the level of consumption to which he or she has become accustomed, and is generally used to receiving reasonable recognition and appreciation of his or her efforts.

Such an identity typically involves a corresponding identity defence, and an individual is unlikely just to surrender this as a matter of course between one day and the next. We may, for instance, in adult education programmes today encounter many people who constantly relate to the working life they came from, and who therefore also have great difficulties looking forward to the job they are supposed to orient themselves towards. It goes without saying that this is an impediment to learning.

The need for transformative learning may also be due to other crises, such as divorce, serious illness or death of a close relative, or problems with substance abuse, and very often a crisis in one area brings about crises in other areas, so that the situation becomes even more complicated.

The novel development is thus the greatly increasing frequency with which situations that require difficult and demanding transformative learning arise, to the extent that such matters need to be taken into account in workplace learning or work-related education, despite the fact that there is neither the time nor resources to apply psychotherapy; instead the crisis must find its resolution through 'learning' in the more general sense and under conditions which, as a rule, involve considerable societal pressure and the threat of being relegated to the margins of society, socially and financially.

The incentive dimension of learning

Above, I have described four different types of learning in relation to the content dimension of learning. It is characteristic that through these four types of learning in general we constantly strive to understand, give meaning to and become able to function expediently in our existence and environment. This endeavour, however, does not function only cognitively in relation to the learning content. The acquisition process as well as the learning outcome also depend on the incentive, i.e. the mobilisation and the strength and nature of the mental energy that is driving the process. Knowledge, skills, insights, thinking, bodily functioning, ways of behaviour, identity – everything we learn always also has a psychodynamic or emotional side, which is concerned with how we feel about these functions, how we perceive them, what we want to do with them and how committed we are to them.

The content and the incentive dimensions have, both phylogenetically (in man as a species) and ontogenetically (in the individual person), developed from a common basis, and only gradually and partially have separated and gained their relative independence. They are always in close interaction; both dimensions always play a part in the learning process and are involved in the learning outcome. Our reason and motor nervous system are always to some degree influenced by our motivation and feelings, and what we learn cognitively is also always influenced or 'obsessed' by the character of the feelings we attach to the learning. If learning produces enjoyment or we have a strong will to complete it, what is learned will bear the imprint of this, and thereby, for instance, tend to be easier to 'recall' in relevant situations; we will also be more inclined to apply and extend the learning in new situations. Conversely, if the learning is characterised by reluctance and lack of interest, the learning outcome will tend to 'appear' to us only in situations that to a higher degree remind us of the learning situation, and learning will be more likely to fade into oblivion.

We have all experienced this in countless situations and contexts in our daily lives, in connection with school and education, and of course also in working life. If our work is a dull routine, or if we are stressed or feel that we are being controlled, this will have a limiting impact on the possibilities for learning. Conversely, if our work is challenging, driven by interest and meaningful to us, we learn both more and better.

However, it is not only that cognitive learning is obsessed by emotion and motivation. Learning in the incentive dimension, including our emotional, conative and motivational patterns, is also influenced by our knowledge and ability in the cognitive dimension. For instance, although we may harbour some negative feelings towards certain people or groups of whose behaviour we disapprove of, this may change if we gain better insight into why they act the way they do. Similarly, romantic feelings for a person can vanish in the blink of an eye if we suddenly learn something about the object of our affection that we find entirely unacceptable.

Some of the background underlying the interaction between reason and emotions has in recent years been discovered and investigated by modern brain research (see, for example, Damasio 1994, 1999). Whenever our senses receive any kind of stimulation, messages are transmitted simultaneously, via two different channels, to the 'working memory' in the frontal lobes of the brain, which is the vital coordination centre that directs our learning, thinking and decision-making processes – sometimes termed 'the executive brain' (Goldberg 2001). One channel passes through the central part of the brain, which contains the most important emotional centres, while the other bypasses these centres. In this way the working memory receives impulses that reproduce the 'pure' sensory impressions and impulses that transmit the sensory impressions together with the emotions activated by the event. Thus, our elaboration of the impressions relates to both the impressions themselves and the emotions that they evoke (and only a very rare and serious brain damage that severs the connection between the emotional centres and the working memory without influencing any of them can prevent this).

As far as learning in schools and education programmes is concerned, there is a strong tendency to disregard the emotional side and concentrate attention on the content – educational activities are usually defined exclusively in terms of the material and skills to be learned. The same tendency is largely true of workplace learning, when the main concern is the objective of work, and how workers and employees feel about it is regarded as a private matter. But in both areas such traditional attitudes have been challenged for some time, because many have realised, and extensive research has shown, that people both learn better and work better when a measure of commitment and enjoyment is involved and the learner feels comfortable and unforced by outside compulsion.

However, the problems surrounding the incentive dimension often run deeper. Freud was the first to demonstrate how psychodynamic factors at a deep and subconscious level can have an impact on the way humans function that the individual cannot control. If there is something faulty in the content dimension, it may lead to wrong learning, misunderstanding or no learning. It may, of course, be deplorable or disqualifying for the individual , but in most cases the faults may be corrected through new learning processes if necessary. In contrast, problems in the incentive dimension are more serious and more difficult to cure. In connection with learning, there may be two more general types of such matters that have an impact on learning, i.e. defence and resistance against learning.

A common reason why possible and intended learning does not take place is various forms of *psychological defence*. These are usually quite different from the defence mechanisms enlisted when faced with personally threatening impacts, which were pointed out by Freud and more systematically described by his daughter Anna Freud (Freud 1942). Of course, such defence mechanisms also have a strong impact on learning by individuals. But, today, in the extremely complex and ever-changing globalised market society, some far more general kinds of psychological defence have to be developed by all of us to protect ourselves against the absolutely overwhelming flood of incoherent and often forceful impulses and influences to which we are constantly and unavoidably exposed. Just consider the cacophony of news, information, documentaries, advertising/commercials and entertainment that unfolds without ceasing on a myriad of channels on our television screens.

The German sociologist and social psychologist Thomas Leithäuser has described such a defence system as a central element of our *everyday consciousness* which, in terms of learning, functions such that in various different thematic areas we develop some general preconceptions through which we filter the many inputs. Impulses that are not in accordance with these preconceptions are then, often entirely automatically or subconsciously, either rejected or distorted so that they are made to harmonise with the preconceptions, and in this way we avoid learning anything from them, and we also avoid psychological overload. However, at the same time we forfeit many opportunities for learning that might be both relevant and enriching.

The everyday consciousness also, of necessity, functions in the contexts of education and work, and often poses opaque obstructions to our learning and changing, even though there is no shortage of opportunities and encouragement, and even though it could also be in our own best interest. It requires great commitment and psychological mobilisation to scale the ramparts and penetrate the defences of everyday consciousness (Leithäuser 1976; Illeris 2007).

Another form of psychological defence that has acquired increasing significance, not least in working life, is the aforementioned *identity defence*. It is characteristic of modern man in the Western world that through the years of our youth we endeavour to develop an individual identity, an adequately stable perception of who we are and would like to be, and how we experience other people's perception of us. Psychologists and others have typically considered it something highly positive that a person should develop a mature and stable identity (Erikson 1971; Giddens 1991).

In working life, a significant element of such an identity has traditionally been professionalism or pride in one's profession: I am a carpenter or nurse or engineer, something that I am good at and which puts food on my table, which means something to me, is an integral part of my personality and self-perception, and therefore is also very important to me, and something which I am ready to defend if anybody were to try to change anything about it.

The novel characteristic of today's society is that 'somebody' causing a serious tectonic shift in our lives is something that happens quite often. The cause is not, as in the past, denigration of our performance, but structural and fundamental change resulting from, for instance, the introduction of new technology that takes over our work tasks, transfer of jobs overseas to other countries where labour is cheaper, downsizing, restructuring after mergers, or simply termination of the work because it is unprofitable.

There is nothing one can do to protect oneself against such events, but if a person has performed satisfactorily in a trade over a number of years and through this has built a strong professional identity, it is not only a financial and social problem if that individual all of a sudden, and through no fault of his or her own, finds himself or herself unemployed. Then we just stand there, all dressed up with our professional identity and our identity defences, but with nowhere to go.

The younger generation has reacted to this and other uncertainties with a tendency to develop less stable, and therefore also less vulnerable, identities, something which may then cause other types of problems: employers do not much like labour that is 'unreliable' and 'unstable', but they appreciate 'readiness to adapt', and it is exactly this readiness to adapt that is difficult to muster when a person has strong identity defences. This makes it difficult to accept the need to rebuild one's professional competence and work position more or less from scratch, of being someone other than the person one is.

In economic and political terms, employees are merely labour that must be retrained, but psychologically people are, for example, carpenters, nurses or engineers, who are then to metamorphose into computer operators, home helpers or whatever the case might be, and this is not so easy. In the education programmes in which the metamorphosis is to take place, we meet many who face serious difficulties handling these matters and constantly talk about and on the basis of the identity they are to shed instead of the identity they are supposed to build. The problem is a fundamentally societal one, but it is up to the individual to create a personal solution. This requires transformative learning, and the identity defences become a barrier to be surmounted.

In practice, it can often be difficult to distinguish between what is learning defence and what is caused by another common complication of learning, that is, learning *resistance*. However, the distinction is important, because where defences are general and function more or less subconsciously and automatically, resistance is directed against specific learning opportunities and involves active and usually also conscious decisions: adults typically react with learning resistance when they are faced with, or perhaps directly pressured or forced into, learning courses of which they subjectively cannot see the point, or which they have no interest in, or when other subjectively unacceptable conditions apply (Illeris 2007).

Such resistance may arise in response to trifles that perhaps one 'ought' to be able to disregard, for instance an instructor's personality or style. However, there may also be somewhat deeper causes concerning attitude or interest. In some cases, the resistance may be connected with an ambiguity or ambivalence, such as when a person refuses to learn about a new technology because it appears threatening and alienating, but at the same time people are well able to understand with their reason that such skills may give them advantages or perhaps even be absolutely necessary.

In this connection, it is important to be aware that learning resistance can also be a strong driving force for other learning of major importance to the individual in question, and perhaps also for others. Decisive personal and professional developments often spring from psychological resistance. An individual, when faced with something that he or she cannot or will not accept, and actively opposes, may resolve his or her motivations and find alternative possibilities, moving ahead both personally and with the matter concerned. Both in education programmes and in workplace learning, resistance may seem annoying and irritating in one situation, but it often involves a potential that may be of great value.

More generally, the more difficult and complicated the learning demands placed upon adults, the greater is the likelihood or risk that they will put up incentive barriers against the learning programme, in the shape of either defence

or resistance. This also often plays a part in cases involving competence development, which is a form of learning that poses great demands on participants, as
concerns both content and personal character. At the same time, the rapid pace
of development and continual change of modern society often places adults in
situations in which specific competence development is the only way forward.

In many cases, the individual experiences pressure to engage in learning, something which cannot be avoided, but which at the same time is most demanding
and taxing. In such contexts, we have seen, in connection with retraining and
vocational education, how people react by more or less consciously developing
certain learning strategies through which they attempt to maintain their identity and self-respect, while at the same time they try, to the extent they are able
to muster the capacity, to meet the demands and move ahead. More generally,
their approaches typically aim at keeping the unwanted input at arm's length by
not getting more involved than absolutely necessary. More specifically, this may,
for instance, involve defences built with irony and humour, with irritation and
petulance, excessive attention to irrelevant detail and perfectionism, or sheltering
behind superficial openness (Illeris 2003).

All this, without doubt, applies also to learning in working life. The Australian
adult education researcher David Boud has documented how employees resist
being positioned as learners or as persons who have a need to develop (Boud
2003). However, more generally, emerging research on workplace learning has
often shown the same slightly naive attitude that traditionally has prevailed in
research oriented towards pedagogy and education, that is, an implicit assumption that if learners are just placed in suitable and expedient situations, and they
are given the right sort of challenges, learning will take place as a matter of
course.

However, the incentive dimension of learning cannot be overlooked. It influences and plays a part in all learning and is able to amplify powerfully both positive
and negative tendencies. When work is perceived as something exciting and positive, it strengthens the learner's motivation to learn something and become even
better at it, but, if it is not so, or if the learner has no job or is unable to see how he
or she may get a job, it can very easily result in a corresponding downward spiral.

The interaction dimension of learning

The interaction dimension of learning is distinguished from the other two learning
dimensions by being concerned not with the individual psychological acquisition
process, but with the interaction process between the learner and the social and
societal environment. It is inherent in this dimension that the contents and emotional impulses of learning are always mediated through this dimension, but that
they are, on the other hand, always acquired through the two other dimensions.

It is important to emphasise that this mediation bears a social and societal
imprint, even in cases where other people are not directly involved (see Giddens
1991), not only in cases of mediation by media, where a sender is indirectly

present, e.g. the author of a book or the composer, the musicians and various technicians at a radio or TV concert, but also in our interaction with the material environment. Because there is nothing in the world today which does not in one way or another reflect social and societal influence. Even when we are alone in nature, social and societal perceptions and assumptions influence what we perceive as, for instance, beautiful or useful or dangerous; and even if we stand in the wilderness and contemplate the stars, we perceive them in terms of social and societal figures, and we take part in scientific knowledge of dimensions and distances.

The interaction process itself may take place in an infinite number of ways and be described from many different angles. In this chapter I shall consider the interaction on the basis of a learning perspective that is concerned with the learning-related character and various possibilities involved in the interaction processes. From this point of departure different types of interaction can be identified, which in various ways have an influence on learning and are characterised by the fact that this learning is involved in different ways (see Illeris 2007, p. 100f.).

In its simplest form, the interaction process consists of what in psychological terms is called *perception*, i.e. that the impulses enter the learning process as unmediated sense impressions. It might be said that this takes place all the time, that we receive a constant flow of impressions through our senses, many of which we do not notice at all, but others we absorb without much or even any conscious reflection. This is also the way things often function in workplace learning, but the volume and character of the sense impressions may be very different. There is, for instance, monotonous and repetitive work, which is characterised precisely by the fact that sense impressions are very few and contain nothing new, and there is other work, which overwhelms us with the sheer volume of continuous impressions. Both of these extremes may be very psychologically taxing, but between them we find a broad field of working contexts that mediate many sense impressions that we receive.

It is somewhat different when the interaction has the character of some form of *transmission*. In that context, somebody makes a more or less focused attempt to direct certain specific sense impressions or messages to somebody else. The recipients may then be more or less interested or attentive, or they may be dismissive or just not care. In working life, there is, as a rule, a certain number of messages that employees are expected to receive and thereby learn, but this number may vary greatly depending on what and how much the expectations involve, ranging from a defined body of knowledge and rules that employees are to learn once and for all to a steady flow of messages, instructions, explanations and impressions that constantly demand attention and decision. When we consider workplace learning, receiving transmitted information is often an important part of it, but rarely the only one.

Experience may also hold much perception and transmission, but when we use this term it usually makes reference to a particular commitment characterising the particular type of learning in question, something on which it has a special focus and relates to in an active way. An experience may be either positive or negative, but it lies more or less outside the ordinary. To many people, it is important that their work also contains experiences, that sometimes something special takes place that reaches beyond the daily routines.

A special form of interaction which also may have great importance in workplace learning is *imitation*. In classical apprenticeship, a major part of the learning process consists exactly of the apprentice's imitation of the more experienced craftsman's way of working, and imitation is still of great importance in many contexts, for example imitating a skilful salesman handling a sales situation or a technician executing a certain detailed task. However, much of what was previously learned through imitation has today been built into machines and technologies, and it can make learning difficult and more abstract when the learner cannot directly observe what takes place and how it is done.

The two forms of interaction most significant in terms of learning and in which theorists of learning have taken a great interest in recent decades are termed participation and activity.

Participation is the most general of these two terms. It has especially been used as defined by Jean Lave and Etienne Wenger in their book on situated learning (Lave and Wenger 1991), which emphasises the learning that takes place through participation in a community of practice for an extended period of time, in which all the previously mentioned forms of interaction may be present and it is exactly the total sum of them that produces the broad result, but, on the other hand, it is fairly unclear what it is that mediates learning and therefore also difficult to identify possible approaches to optimising the learning process.

The term *activity*, on the other hand, views things from the learner's perspective and is concerned with commitment in goal-oriented activities, i.e. the characteristic that the learning process pursues specific goals is what promotes and qualifies the learning. This term has especially been used with reference to the so-called cultural-historical (or activity theoretical) psychology that was first developed in Russia during the period between the First and Second World Wars, especially by Lev Vygotsky (1978, 1986) and Aleksei Leontyev (1981), and which in recent decades has been developed further, not least with a consideration of learning in working life, by, among others, the Finnish psychologist Yrjö Engeström (1987, 2009).

The many different shapes and structures of working life thus arise from, among other things, the fact that the conditions for the interaction dimension of learning are highly variable, and this may be decisive not only for the work itself and the employees' situation, but also for the extent and character of the learning that takes place.

Learning, identity and working life

In summary, the interaction that constantly takes place results in a continuous flow of impulses through which workplace learning is generally achieved, for instance opinions, explanations, behavioural patterns, impressions and perceptions, which workers and employees may receive in a number of different ways. The pivotal point of learning thus lies in the way in which the impulses of working life or the community of practice are handled in the individual acquisition process. If we return to Figure 2.1, this handling lies in the transition between the vertical double-headed arrow, which represents the interaction process, and the horizontal double-headed arrow, which represents the acquisition process.

Through an elaboration of the learning model in connection with the formation of identity, which may also be viewed as a learning process, it can be pointed out that it is exactly in this intersection between interaction and acquisition that the formation of identity takes place. The word 'identity' itself derives from the Latin *idem*, which means 'the same' and has to do with the experience of being the same or recognisable both to oneself and to others in changing situations. This also points to the duality in the identity so central to Erikson's original conception (Erikson 1971), namely that one is an individual creation, a biological life, while simultaneously being a social and societal being. Thus, identity is always an individual biographical identity, an experience of a coherent individuality and life course, at the same time as being a social, societal identity, an experience of a certain position in the social community. Therefore, as shown in Figure 2.3, identity is located at the intersection of the two double-headed arrows in the middle of the line that represents the individual level of the figure and down towards the environment or social level.

When considering workplace learning, we are very specifically looking at our *work identity*, which is a partial identity, concerned with our experience of ourselves as working individuals and as members of a working community (see Andersen *et*

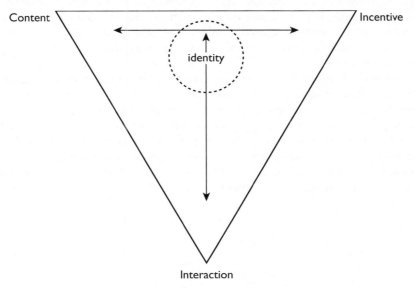

Figure 2.3 The position of identity in the structure of learning (after Illeris 2007, p. 139).

al. 1994, p. 46ff). As can be seen, on the one hand, the work identity is mediating the influences of the interaction between the learner and the environment, which is in this case the workplace, and, on the other, the workplace environment and its learning possibilities are perceived through the individual work identity.

It should be noted here that other researchers would use the concept of 'habitus', developed by the French sociologist Pierre Bourdieu (1977, 1998), rather than 'identity'. This applies to, among others, considerable parts of British research on learning in working life (e.g. Hodkinson *et al.* 2004). However, I have chosen the concept of identity for several reasons.

First, the word 'identity' is more immediately known and used in ordinary everyday language, whereas 'habitus' is a rather less easily accessible academic concept.

Second, identity is a predominantly psychological concept, which is concerned with the way in which the individual perceives him- or herself and perceives being perceived by others, whereas habitus is a sociological concept, concerned with the way in which the cultural and societal matters with which the individual has been confronted are deposited in the individual. Figure 2.3 specifically refers to a concept located on the individual, subjective level.

Third, the concept of identity also corresponds and relates to the concept of identity defence, which was introduced and explained above as an important matter in relation to learning, and it is only one example among others that learning processes are often related to the concept of identity (see also, for example, Wenger 1998), whereas the concept of habitus, as mentioned, is used more in relation to cultural and societal matters. There is a tendency to refer to identity as something on the basis of which we actively think and act (and learn), whereas habitus is to a greater extent used to refer to something that is done to the individual and which lies outside the individual's control (which may of course also have an impact on learning).

However, there would actually not have been anything preventing me from using the concept of habitus – I shall later consider the relationship between identity and practice somewhat along the lines of Bourdieu's treatment of the relationship between habitus and practice – if it were not for the wish exactly in connection with learning to treat the interaction between the individual and the workplace as an interaction between two equivalent elements, whereas the concept of habitus rather aims at focusing on the individual from the perspective of the social and societal environment.

The workplace as a learning space

Learning dimensions in the workplace

What is special about workplace learning – viewed in relation to learning as a whole – is that it takes place in a certain learning space. This chapter deals with the fundamental features of the workplace as a learning space and offers an overview model in line with the learning model in the previous chapter. It shall be mentioned that in dealing with these matters I have found great inspiration in the work of two of my colleagues, Christian Helms Jørgensen and Niels Warring (Jørgensen and Warring 2003, and several papers in Danish), and part of the following is, directly or indirectly, taken from their contribution to our common book *Learning in Working Life* (Illeris and Associates 2004).

When considering learning possibilities at work it is, first of all, very important to remember that work-related learning increasingly takes place not only in the physical workplace, but also, for example, on courses, in networks and exchange schemes, in contact with customers, users and suppliers and trade unions, in industrial organisations, and in more private work-related contexts. In this book the term 'workplace learning' includes the work-related learning that can take place in all such work-related connections (in the same way as the concept is used by Evans *et al.* 2006).

It must also be taken into account that there are great differences between different types of work with regard to the possibilities of work-related learning both inside and outside the workplace. For instance, Vibeke Andersen and Christian Helms Jørgensen found that the opportunities for learning were very different for industrial workers at a bread factory and graduate employees in a public agency (Andersen and Jørgensen 2002).

Fundamentally, workplace learning takes place in the encounter between the *learning environment* of the workplace and the workers' and employees' *learning potentials*. The concept of learning environment refers to all the opportunities for learning contained in the material and social surroundings. The concept of learning potential refers to the life of the individual as a continuous learning process that builds on the complex experiences of the previous life course and which is given direction by the forward-looking perspectives. Learning potentials are decisive for the readiness for learning with which the individual and groups meet and exploit the opportunities for learning in the learning environment.

The encounter between the learning environment and the learning potentials is in principle the workplace-related part of the general interaction between the individual and the environment which in the previous chapter was described as one of the two basic processes of learning and which in the learning model was depicted as a vertical double-headed arrow. In the same model, the other basic process of learning, the individual acquisition process, was depicted as a horizontal double-headed arrow linking the content and the incentive elements, and in the same way the learning environment of the workplace can be depicted as a combination of two basic elements. On the one side there is the content of the workplace, i.e. primarily the activities of *production* – of articles, commodities, service, knowledge or whatever output or performance it may be – and the related administration, sales promotion, etc., all of the work tasks that have to be executed. On the other side is the workplace *community,* i.e. the totality of all human relations and connections and the communications, feelings, emotions, workplace culture and spirit and all the actions which are not primarily part of the production.

The distinction between these two fundamental elements of the workplace learning environment is important because different dynamics determine the impact of each. In the case of production, it is primarily market forces and technological and organisational changes that determine the learning conditions. In the case of community, it is, in particular, cultural and social orientations that are important for learning possibilities. It could be remarked that this distinction corresponds to the distinction between Jürgen Habermas's concepts of the system world and the life world (Habermas 1984).

Thus, workplace learning fundamentally takes place in a dynamic relation between learners' learning potentials and the production and community elements of the workplace environment. On this background a triangular model can be set up, similar to the learning model, but with the difference that the horizontal double-headed arrow of the learning environment must be placed at the lower end of the vertical double-headed arrow, i.e. at the social or environmental level (Figure 3.1).

It is worth mentioning that these three elements are analogous to the elements of the situatedness of workplace learning that Evans *et al.* describe as 'the sociobiographical features of the learners' life', namely 'practical activity' and 'the culture and context of the workplace/learning environment' (Evans *et al.* 2006, p. 13).

However, the learning environment constitutes only the framework for learning: it is in the interaction between the individual worker or employee and the learning environment that learning occurs. Thus, workplace learning, like any other type of learning, is fundamentally an individual process, and a smaller or larger group of workers or employees will undergo the same learning only to the extent that there is a corresponding homogeneity in the learners' situations, positions, backgrounds, experiences and mental structures.

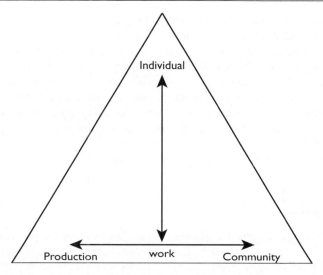

Figure 3.1 The fundamental elements of workplace learning.

In the following I shall consider in more depth each of the three dimensions of workplace learning.

The production element of the workplace learning environment

The production-related part of the workplace learning environment depends on the content of the work, how the work is organised and the technology that is used. This has been dealt with in detail within work and industrial sociology as a question of the relation between technology, work organisation and qualification requirements, and different approaches have pointed to different important aspects of this general relation such as, for example, the room for manoeuvre provided by technology (Kern and Schumann 1984), the power and conflict dimension of learning possibilities and qualification distribution (Knights and Willmott 1990) and the importance of dialogue and communication (Toulmin and Gustavsen 1996).

Interest in such approaches to workplace learning conditions arises primarily from the requirements of management and the system – and this is even more true when it comes to the approaches of the learning organisation (e.g. Senge 1990; Easterby-Smith *et al.* 1999) and human resource management (e.g. Swanson and Holton 2001; Tyson 2006; Boxall *et al.* 2008), which since the 1980s have to some extent taken the lead in these areas. However, these approaches are at the same time largely oriented towards the experiences and possibilities of the workers and employees as a source of productivity and profit.

In any case, it seems today to be broadly accepted that with regard to conditions for workplace learning a top-down perspective is insufficient and must be supplemented by concepts and categories describing the experiential qualities for those who live and work within the environment. This means, among other things, the possibilities it gives the workers and employees for experiencing their work tasks, and thus themselves, as meaningful, and the extent to which the work gives the workers and employees possibilities for developing a work identity by using their qualifications and influencing the content and methods of the work.

Obviously, the most immediate conditions for workplace learning have to do with the *contents* of the work and the basic organisation, which is the *division of labour.*

Work content

Work content is important for learning possibilities in many ways. For example, work with living people calls for other types of competences and typically has a different subjective significance from industrial work with dead products. The emotional engagement in the work, and thus the dynamic forces in the learning processes, is different.

The content of the work is decisive for the meaning that the work has for the worker or the employee. On the one hand, the meaning depends on the importance accorded the given work by society. The work of doctors, educators and cleaning assistants is accorded different importance, which is reflected by, among other things, how the work is remunerated. On the other hand, work has a unique meaning for the individual by virtue of his or her socialisation, individual life course and experience.

The content of work also has an element of societal utility. Work content is not just about the position and status conferred by one's occupation, whether that be an architect or bricklayer. It also has to do with the importance of the work to others. Even subordinate and routine assembly line work is experienced as meaningful by most workers, but at the same time can be experienced as meaningless and attrition. Producing good, useful things of which one can be proud is a meaningful activity, which can provide an important motive force in workplace learning. This implies that workplace learning also includes learning about one's position and role in society by virtue of the position of the work in the larger societal division of labour.

But the content of work often has requirements that can be experienced as contradictory and therefore may produce ambivalences in relation to learning possibilities. For instance, factory workers often must meet standards of quality and quantity that can be difficult to reconcile. The work of a civil servant is formally assessed on the basis of professional criteria, but informally it may be assessed on the basis of political demands that are in opposition to professional demands. Being able to handle such contradictory demands in the workplace often means learning how to adapt oneself without being squeezed or ending up in unpleasant positions.

Division of labour

Division of labour is an overall concept for analysing the form of organisation. Vertical division of labour concerns the relationship between managers and subordinates, or more precisely the relationship between the planning, decision-making, coordinating and controlling and the performing work functions. There is a current trend to delegate parts of the management competence concerning daily work to units or individuals at shop-floor level while at the same time transferring more strategic decisions further away from the individual workplace.

Horizontal division of labour concerns the extent to which the individual stages in the chain of production are separated or integrated. Taylorism, which was a dominant form of management (and mythology) for most of the twentieth century, advocates that the work process in both of these dimensions is subdivided as much as possible, resulting in very poor possibilities for learning.

In contrast, skilled work is often regarded as the ideal of an integrated work process, in which the same person carries out planning, execution and evaluation. It is generally assumed that the more subdivided a work process is, the poorer are the learning possibilities. This is partly because the individual worker does not have the opportunity to experience the consequences of his or her own efforts.

Alongside the formal division of labour there exists also a division of labour between men and women, between natives and immigrants, among different professional groups, between the young and the old, and other socio-cultural forms of labour division. Learning possibilities are created when the established division of labour is broken up, for example when women enter an area that traditionally has been reserved for men. But here, as in other contexts, it is the case that learning *possibilities* do not in themselves result in learning. Contradictions and breaks can just as well create conflicts that promote entrenchment and strengthen hostilities and psychological defence mechanisms.

However, in addition to these two basic issues of relevance for workplace learning there are also some more specific issues of great importance. As long ago as the 1970s some of these were taken up in German industrial sociology and formulated in a seminal article by Ute Volmerg (1976), who pointed to the possibilities for decision-making, for utilising one's qualifications and for participation in social interaction as areas that strongly promote learning motivation and possibilities. (Later her sister, Birgit Volmerg, was the leader of a very interesting empirical project investigating the importance of the so-called 'crevices' in everyday working life for the experiences and learning of floor-level staff – but this important study has only been documented in German; Volmerg *et al.* 1986.) Here I shall take up the three categories mentioned.

Possibilities for making decisions

This describes the degrees of freedom or autonomy of work. The degree of autonomy depends on both the form of management and the organisational structure
of the enterprise and on the individual's position in the organisation. Enterprises
can have a more or less centralist, hierarchical organisation, or a flat, decentral-
ised structure. There are large differences among trades and types of enterprises.
A small, innovative, pioneering company with close contact with its customers
affords its employees greater possibilities for making decisions than a large, hierarchically structured industrial enterprise producing standard goods.

In the traditional bureaucratic organisation, decision-making possibilities are
closely related to position in the management hierarchy. The lower the position,
the less the autonomy. In Taylorist mass production, the lowest placed workers
have very few possibilities for selecting new methods of work, changing the pace
of work or the order of work tasks, or choosing whom to work with and the way
in which it should take place. In contrast, the work of management contains a
great deal of room for individual prioritisation and making decisions about work
tasks – and thus learning possibilities. The assumption is thus that the greater the
autonomy that exists in the work, the better are the learning possibilities that the
work contains (see, for example, Ellström 2001).

Possibilities for using one's qualifications

These depend on, among other things, the enterprise's production technology,
products and division of labour. There are more possibilities for applying and further developing qualifications in highly trained and skilled jobs than in unskilled
ones. It has generally been assumed that work that requires a high level of qualification also has greater possibilities for decision-making, i.e. salaried workers
and skilled workers have a higher degree of independence than the unskilled. But
the advent of information technology has opened new possibilities for subjecting
qualified knowledge work to detailed, central management control and thus has
reduced its decision-making possibilities (Bechtle 1994).

Two opposite trends in the labour market can be discerned. On the one hand,
qualification requirements are growing – there are more 'knowledge workers'.
On the other hand, there is a tendency to rationalise service work by imposing
from above more detailed demands as regards work performance and methods.
These trends are pulling in opposite directions in relation to learning possibilities
at work.

Possibilities for social interaction

Possibilities for social interaction at work are also important for the learning
possibilities. Learning takes place as a social process when the employees have discussions or reflect on or exchange experience, ideas and assessments with each other.

For instance, Donald Schön (1987) has pointed out how interaction between an experienced coach and a student can stimulate the student's reflection-in-action.

It is not least through the contradictions in the meeting between different professional groups – for instance operatives, technicians, production planners and salespersons – that fruitful learning environments can be created, but such interactions may also have the effect of cementing mutual myths and hostilities. In contrast, a workplace with stringently maintained lines of communication and one-way communication does not provide a suitable environment for stimulation and the open exchange of ideas.

This dimension of the production element of the learning environment is important for the communities that arise at the workplace, and which will later be described as part of the community element of the learning environment of the workplace.

Stress and strain

Finally, the spread during recent decades of concepts such as the learning organisation, human resource management and new public management (see, for example, McLaughlin *et al.* 2002) has in many organisations gone hand in hand with an increasing emphasis on personal independence and responsibility for the individual work organisation and achievement for self-directed teams. This has led to positive changes for many employees, for example flexible working hours, the opportunity to work at home, individual wage negotiations, bonus possibilities and many other arrangements, which give an immediate experience of freedom and individuality, but has also, in many cases, increased stress and strain.

Stress and strain certainly also affect learning possibilities, because frequently affected individuals have less time and energy for learning, and especially for the more energy-demanding learning processes of accommodation and transformation. Learning presupposes, on the one hand, that jobs provide challenges and contain tasks and problems that encourage learning. On the other hand, a high degree of work strain tends to reduce experimentation and the development and testing of new ideas.

The six categories of conditions for workplace learning that I have described relate to one side of the learning environment. They set part of the framework for learning processes at the workplace both by making demands and by providing possibilities, and in some situations they also counteract workplace learning. They are to be understood as analytical categories, which typically in practice are closely tied together, as indicated in the above exposition, and they constitute both resources for and limitations on learning.

It should be emphasised that the various categories may influence but do not determine the way in which workers and employees meet the various conditions and exploit possibilities. Workplace learning is dependent on the importance of the technical and organisational changes for the individual employee or for groups in the workplace. Therefore, the analysis of the production side of the learning environment says something only about the learning possibilities and nothing about what the employees in fact learn. Workplace learning is also influenced by the individual processing of previous experience and of the collective interpretation and negotiation of meaning that occurs in communities at the workplace. It is this last topic that will be taken up in the next section.

The community element of the workplace learning environment

As already stated, the workplace always encompasses more than just what is related to production. The workplace is also always in some way a community of the people who work there, and if more than a few people are employed there will also be 'subcommunities' of various kinds. To workers and employees these various communities will often be as important as the concrete work or production, and seen in relation to learning, which is also always a very personal matter, the communities may very well be decisive for what is learned and not learned, and how it is learned and thus the attitudes and feelings of learners towards the learning outcome.

In practice, everybody somehow knows that this is the case, and, in the critical theory of the so-called Frankfurt School, Jürgen Habermas (1984) and several other German researchers have dealt with this issue as an obvious extension of the general interest in the topic of socialisation. The study by Birgit Volmerg *et al.* (1986) mentioned above makes this aspect crystal clear. But in more traditional studies of workplace learning there often is a strong tendency to focus on the production side of the learning environment and to some extent neglect the community side.

A very important exception to this in the English-language literature is, however, the approach of 'situated learning', which was launched by Americans Jean Lave and Etienne Wenger in 1991 (Lave and Wenger 1991) and since then has continued in two somewhat different directions, with Lave stressing the concept of 'practice learning' (see Chaiklin and Lave 1993; Lave 2009) and Wenger focusing on 'communities of practice' (Wenger 1998, 2009; Wenger *et al.* 2002). The latter is today the most significant approach to the community element of the workplace environment. Wenger fundamentally regards workplace learning as a negotiation of meaning in the various communities of practice at the workplace, and considers that learning takes place not just in the mind of the individual but in association with the social groups and processes in which the learners are involved and with which they identify. Traditions, norms and values in the informal communities at the workplace are of decisive importance for learning possibilities, the learning processes and the learning outcome.

In this connection it is important to realise that there are different types of workplace communities that exist in parallel, and which deal with different aspects of working life, have a different status and are more or less formal or informal in their position, function and ways of communication. In Denmark, Christian

Helms Jørgensen and Niels Warring have described three main types of workplace communities: communities of work, political communities and cultural communities (see Jørgensen and Warring 2003).

The communities of work are created around the performance of common work tasks. The point of departure for industrial sociology was the discovery in the 1930s of these informal communities in which workers and employees give each other personal support and recognition. Such communities, for example a work group, are primarily structured by the enterprise's formal organisation, management hierarchy and the technological and administrative structure. However, it is important to emphasise that communities of work are not the same as the formal organisation. Workers standing side by side at an assembly line often have no community of work because they do not directly cooperate. Usually, learning in communities of work is about becoming better and more efficient at one's job, producing higher-quality work and making fewer mistakes in accordance with joint criteria in the community. But such learning depends on the extent to which the workers or employees experience a common meaning in the work and develop personal relations via proximity and identification. If the workers do not experience the work as meaningful, they have no reason to become engaged and involve themselves in any improvement, and in such cases their learning may just be about how to be involved as little as possible.

Political workplace communities are established around the struggle for control, power, status and influence at the workplace (see, for example, Knights and Willmott 1990). There is a political rationale behind the organisation of the different professional groups which constitute the basis for the trade unions' communities across enterprises and are personified in an elected shop steward or safety representative. Viewed from this rationale, the workplace is a power structure concerning the direct and indirect control of the work process as 'contested terrain' (Edwards 1979). At traditional workplaces with authoritarian forms of management, struggles often take place as open confrontation, but at modern workplaces the external control of the work process has been more or less replaced by the employees' own internal control, and conflicts are about cultural control dealing with the employees' loyalty and engagement. Learning in the political communities is traditionally about solidarity, the norms and language of the community, and about avoiding exploitation and oppression. At modern workplaces it is more often about personal possibilities, development and career – and sometimes these two tendencies exist side by side in constant ambivalent mutual struggle.

Finally, cultural workplace communities are created on the basis of common values, norms and ideas that link groups at the workplace and which may have the nature of workers' culture (Willis 1977), corporate culture (Schein 1986) or just personal friendships and interests. The cultural community is the precondition for direct mutual understanding, and fundamental cultural patterns are linked to gender, generation, ethnicity and social background. Thus, there are also at most workplaces cultural differences, which often form the basis for division of labour, so that certain work functions or departments primarily consist of women or certain ethnic groups, and which may be the basis for subcultures or countercultures in opposition to the dominant corporate culture. For a new employee at the workplace, learning consists, among other things, of decoding the cultural patterns. Workplace cultures contribute to employees' adaptation to the prevalent working conditions as well as to the development of resistance and counter-images to those conditions.

It is important to stress that the differentiation between the three types of community described and the concept of the community element of the workplace learning environment are here taken up as an attempt to understand how various groups and relations affect the workplace learning processes. The individual worker's or employee's learning typically occurs in the interaction with the established communities, and in relation to the collective experiences, norms and values that exist there. Learning often takes place in the meeting between the different communities in connection with contradictions and conflicts that can lead to new ideas and patterns of action.

Workplace learning and practice

As already stated, workplace learning is fundamentally individual because learning always is related to the learners' background and experience from their previous life course and their hopes and expectations for the future. In particular, workplace learning is influenced by learners' fundamental attitudes to work as they have been formed through socialisation in the family, in the school and education system and in later experience at work.

Further, as most learning theory has been developed on the background of children's learning, it is important to realise that learning in youth and adulthood is in several respects qualitatively different from learning in childhood (Illeris 2004, 2006b, 2007). In childhood learning is basically unlimited in the sense that children try to learn whatever they meet in their environment, so it is also essentially uncensored, and finally it is confident, as the child must 'assume' that the environment includes what it is important to know and to understand.

For adults this is all different. Today we are living in a world that is so far developed and differentiated that it is without doubt impossible for anyone to learn everything that can be learned. This situation has reached a state in which we are all constantly confronted with more learning possibilities than we are able to take in. So there must somehow be a selection of what we try to learn and what we reject. In the case of matters which are subjectively important, we want to make our own conscious decision about what to engage in, but we cannot engage in everything – just think of all the information we are bombarded with on television or in the newspapers. Thus, every one of us has to create a semiautomatic selection function, so that – for instance when we are watching the television news – we are able to select what we take in and what we do not. It is semiautomatic because we have equipped it with some guidelines (personally I take no interest in sports, weather forecasts or commercials), but it is handling all the details, and after the news we usually sit back with three or four points that we have taken in or learned, some more that we can recall if there is a need to do so, and a majority of possible learning that we have, unconsciously, rejected.

So adult learning is fundamentally selective, and as we grow older we tend to become ever more selective – seen from a learning point of view, it is, then, in youth that we develop the semiautomatic selective system. This has been termed by German sociologist and social psychologist Thomas Leithäuser (1976) our 'everyday consciousness' – it is part of our identity, as it is our understanding of who we are, who we want to be, and how we want to be perceived by others, which during youth gradually develops the criteria for the semiautomatic selection system.

In order to understand how workers and employees meet workplace learning opportunities, it is important to understand that workers and employees as adults in their everyday learning are guided and directed by their everyday consciousness, which is a kind of mirror of their life history, the social and cultural conditions that have formed their environment, the upbringing and educational processes they have experienced, the persons and institutions they have met, and also experiences and life situations that have been significant in their past, as well as their fundamental understanding of the world and the plans and hopes they have for their future – or, in short, their total identity and subjectivity (see, for example, Alheit 2009).

Of course, a very important part of all this in relation to workplace learning is the individual work experience, and the personal course and experience of working life have a decisive influence on the way in which we meet new learning opportunities in the workplace.

The early analysis of German industrial sociologists Kern and Schumann included detailed studies of workers' attitudes to their work (Kern and Schumann 1970). They concluded, among other things, that workers adapt their general attitudes and expectations concerning work to their specific work situation. This adaptation is not only a passive conveyance of expectations, but an active process in which subjective needs for meaning, recognition and self-realisation are linked to the work. Workers perceive themselves by means of interaction with colleagues and management, with tools and products, and through the meaning they attribute to their work. As later pointed out by Becker-Schmidt (1982) and Volmerg *et al.* (1986), this conveyance takes place even in relation to work with very limited autonomy, but in this case it is a conflictual process, in which the workers develop their own oppositional work and professional identity at the same time as they adapt to restrictive work conditions.

To put it simply, the development of the work identity takes place in interaction between the socialisation *to work*, which mainly occurs in the family, in school, and in any vocationally oriented education taken, and the socialisation *in work*, which takes place after education is completed, in the vocational biography.

Professional identity is a special type of work identity that is typically developed through a combination of vocational education and work.

With the rapid changes in production and work organisation, individuals today are often faced with challenges to reorient themselves in relation to the professional identity they have built up (Olesen 2001). Technological development removes the basis of certain professions and trades and radically alters the content of others. This leaves the employee faced with the choice of trying to maintain a professional identity in spite of the development in the production side of the workplace environment or redefining his or her professional identity. The process whereby existing professional identities are subjected to the pressure to change can be described as a transformative learning process, as explained in Chapter 2.

The rapid changes in modern flexible production systems create, on the one hand, many learning possibilities, because they force workers and employees to constantly relate to the new conditions. But the lack of stability and cohesion can also undermine the possibilities for learning. As the American sociologist Richard Sennett has emphasised, flexible capitalism tends to reduce workers' opportunities to attach themselves to their work and to experience it as meaningful and thereby to develop a strong and stable work identity (Sennett 1998).

In summary, just as the work identity in the last section of Chapter 2 was pointed out as the central individual instance in the complexity of workplace learning, the corresponding central social instance can be seen as *work practice,* which is the totality of the workplace environment as it functions in everyday working life and thereby constitutes the outer framework of the social learning conditions. Here the concept of practice is in accordance with the use of this

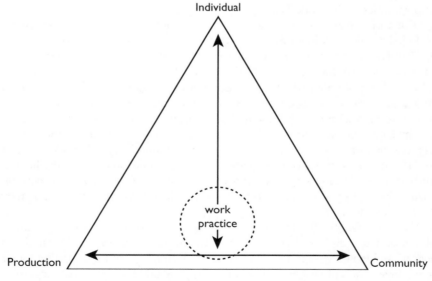

Figure 3.2 The position of work practice in the field of workplace learning.

concept that has been widely developed in many contexts over the last few decades (see, for example, Bourdieu 1998; Lave and Wenger 1991; Chaiklin and Lave 1993), and which not only refers to what takes place 'in practice', but also takes into account that this practice is a constituent instance for, *inter alia*, human consciousness, identity and learning.

In relation to the workplace learning model in Figure 3.1 and similarly to the position of the work identity in Figure 2.1, the position of work practice can be illustrated as in Figure 3.2.

The model shows how work practice integrates the influences of the production and community sides of the workplace learning environment and thereby also occupies the position as the central instance of the workplace learning conditions as they are experienced by the workers and employees as they are participating as learners in the concrete daily work.

Workplace learning as a whole

The advanced workplace learning model

This chapter rounds off the fundamental consideration of workplace learning by introducing a holistic model that can form the basis for analyses and reflections in the subsequent parts of the book and by accentuating the fact that learning always takes place on both a social and an individual level.

In the two previous chapters I have dealt with workplace learning first from a general learning perspective and then from a workplace perspective. This has resulted in two general models (Figures 2.2 and 3.1) and two models which have introduced work identity and work practice as the central elements of the individual and the social side of workplace learning (Figures 2.3 and 3.2). These two models have deliberately been worked out in a similar way, which makes it possible here to unite and integrate them into an advanced holistic model covering the main features of workplace learning as a whole (Figure 4.1).

The joint model is elaborated in such a way that the two triangular models from Figures 2.3 and 3.2 have been superimposed on each other. The first of the two models depicts the individual learning and therefore has its baseline on the individual level at the top of the model, while the third angle, which has to do with the interaction dimension of learning, points down towards the social level. The second model depicts the workplace as a learning environment and therefore has its baseline on the social level at the bottom of the model with an angle pointing up to the learning potentials on the individual level.

It is thus a fundamental condition that the model tries to both distinguish between and connect the individual and social levels of workplace learning. When captured in a model, the impression can be that the connection between the two levels is of an external and mechanical nature, but that is certainly not the case. It is therefore important to emphasise that in the real world it is a matter of a dialectical whole between the subjective and the objective, i.e. an interaction between two connected levels that mutually contain and presuppose each other. The objective environment is present in the subjective experience and understanding and is simultaneously marked by subjective perceptions and actions. It is a matter of integrated processes of subjectivisation and societalisation in a continuous

Individual level

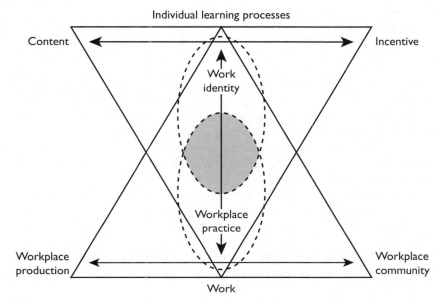

Social level

Figure 4.1 The advanced model of workplace learning.

interaction that can be disentangled only analytically (see, for example, Berger and Luckmann 1969).

The model captures this dialectic in the areas of overlap between the two triangles, and especially between their central elements: work identity in the first model and work practice in the second model. It is precisely in the area of overlap of these two elements that the decisive interaction happens. Learners' work identities, which are a combination of the totality of their workplace learning potentials, and of their work practice, which includes everything that has to do with the workplace and working life as a social and societal learning space, ranging from the production side to the community side of the learning environment, overlap in the darker area in the middle of the model. And it is precisely here that important and transcendent accommodative and transformative workplace learning can take place.

This means that, no matter what influences are present in the learning space, whether they are linked to the performance of the work itself, or to the workplace, or to working life more generally, they are marked by the work practice that the learners experience and are part of, and they are filtered through the individual learner's work identity before they become something that he or she processes and acquires as learning. At the same time they influence learners' individual and common perceptions and relations to everything that takes place at the workplace, and thereby also the way in which it functions and develops as a learning space and as a place for work, production and community.

In the figure I have therefore chosen to emphasise this central overlap between work practice and work identity by shading it. It is here that learning obtains its special character of being workplace learning, here that the learners' identities influence and develop the practice of the community, and the community's practice forms the individual work identity. Phil Hodkinson *et al.* emphasise that it is not sufficient to understand the relationship as 'two separate entities, "mind" and "social world", which are logically separated but inter-related', but it is (quoting Brown *et al.* 1989) the case that 'learning is not merely separated in practice – as if it was some independently reifiable process that just happened to be located somewhere; learning is an integral part of generative social practice in the lived-in world' (Hodkinson *et al.* 2004).

At the same time it should also be noted, and as can be seen from Figure 4.1, that more peripheral workplace learning can also take place by circumventing the central common field. In this case the learning will be more general and less work related in nature. The model has carefully been drawn up so that the practice and identity fields do not extend to the sides of the triangles to indicate that workplace learning processes can take place by routes which to a lesser extent, or even not at all, are influenced by these central factors.

The content side of individual learning and the production side of the workplace learning environment have both been placed on the left in the model to show that in workplace learning there is also room for acquiring, for example, technical-practical understanding and skills that are not specifically linked to work practice and work identities, such as general methods of calculation and general technical or mathematical modes of understanding.

Correspondingly, the incentive side of individual learning and the community side of the workplace learning environment have been placed on the right of the model, so that there is room for more general learning about personal, social and cultural matters that are not necessarily particularly related to the workplace in question or to working life in general.

Direct vertical connections are not possible on either the right or the left of the model, because even if learning does not affect the very nature of work practice or work identities, all workplace learning will to a certain extent be marked by the fact that it is precisely in the workplace that it takes place, that it is situated. And if the learning is more cross-cutting in nature, involving both sides of the model, of necessity it will also come in over the central fields.

The status of the model

In the above I have given an account of how the model in Figure 4.1 was thought out and constructed. But what is the intention of such a model and what can it be used for?

A model such as this must be understood first and foremost as a simplified and systematised way of providing some overview of what may be regarded as the most central elements, fields and processes that are at play in connection with workplace learning and their mutual connections. Learning, the workplace and working life are very complicated areas to which to relate, and when they are brought together the result is a very high degree of complexity, which one can try to 'manage' or obtain an overview of in many different ways.

Any method will of necessity have the character of adopting a certain perspective, a certain point of view that will draw certain matters into the foreground. A trend in current societal and political thinking and exercise of power is a one-sided focus on economic viewpoints, and as a result, *inter alia*, attempts to also control the organisation and content of research from these viewpoints.

With this model I primarily wish to illustrate a learning-oriented perspective on workplace learning and working life. But this can be done in many different ways and is, naturally, a choice on my part – a choice which can be substantiated on the basis of learning theory and understandings of working life – that I do so because I regard the dialectics between the individual and the social spheres as the most central. As I see it, the economical rationales that mainly form the basis of management and organisational theory are inadequate in this area because they do not incorporate precisely the individual and social conditions that are of crucial importance in connection with both learning and working life. For example, matters connected to motivation typically have much more impact on learning than economic incentives.

The perspective from which the model has been worked out also implies that it does not directly depict the societal and economic framework conditions that apply to workplace learning. Of course, these matters are very important, but the task here has primarily been to examine issues to do with learning, and learning is only indirectly dependent on the economy.

Thus, in general the model should principally be understood as a way of providing an overview while at the same time indicating what may be considered as the most important elements, features and relations in the field. The model is in the nature of a map, and like a map it can be used to indicate different elements in relation to each other but also to manoeuvre by.

The three double-headed arrows in the model indicate key lines of connection or interaction. The vertical double-headed arrow illustrates the central dialectical interaction between the individual and the social level. The uppermost horizontal double-headed arrow indicates the interaction on the individual learning level between the content side and the incentive side, or, as it is often expressed, between cognition and emotion, in the individual acquisition process. And the double-headed arrow at the bottom indicates the interaction between the production and the community sides of the learning environment.

However, if one examines a concrete learning process – whether it be in connection with analysis and discussion of a specific course or event, or in connection with planning various measures – many connections can be drawn in all directions in the model. In this context the model can function to provide an overview as a kind of checklist of different key factors that are at play, and as a guide pointing out the areas one comes through and the elements to which one must relate.

But one should not read more into the model than was intended: it was drawn up as an auxiliary tool. It can be used to support one's perception in the context of planning, implementing and evaluating workplace learning processes, undertakings and measures precisely to the extent that one thinks it can be of help in the specific case. And it does not postulate that matters *are* so, but only that one can choose to view them in this way.

At the same time the model is a declaration of the way in which, in this book, a number of fundamental issues to do with workplace learning are regarded. It could be useful for the reader to keep this in mind in connection with what follows. But I shall not in the following constantly refer back to the model. This will happen only occasionally, and for the most part the various issues will be dealt with on more concrete levels, with the model considered as a background figure to which one can relate if the specific issue is to be understood or dealt with in a more general context.

A holistic view of workplace learning

It is important here in connection with the general and holistic model of workplace learning to make explicit what I have already mentioned several times: that the model and the descriptions which are offered here take a different – and in my opinion a more balanced – view of the nature of workplace learning from what appears, directly or indirectly, in most of the literature on the field.

In the first place, in the model learning is regarded as an individual and a social process at one and the same time and to similar degrees. As mentioned previously, this contrasts with both the traditional, individual-oriented and the modern social-constructionist perception of learning, each of which only or mainly relates learning to one of the two levels involved.

And this is not merely an oversubtle point of learning theory. It also extends to the more concrete issues of workplace learning, which is here regarded similarly as an interaction between, on the one hand, workers and employees, with all their backgrounds, interests and life perspectives, and, on the other hand, work and all its dimensions, including environmental conditions and power relations. This contrasts with all the contexts in which the viewpoint, often as a matter of course and without any further deliberation, is that workers and employees must learn something specific that is believed to be needed for their work, thus making them objects of an externally given learning project.

But life is not that simple. Adults do not just allow themselves to be made into objects. One can, naturally, force certain teaching or other influences upon them, but whether or not they internalise them as learning depends on many things, as I have attempted to illustrate in the model. This is why learning initiatives for adults that come from the outside frequently fail, or only have limited success. This is rarely because the adults in question are so 'stupid' that they cannot learn what they are taught, but far more often because they do not feel engaged or allowed to influence what they have been told to learn.

Thus, it is not just that the balanced approach to learning that is advocated here is more democratic and humanistic than approaches which to a greater or lesser degree make workers and employees into objects for the learning desired. It is also because this approach is simply a more realistic and, ultimately, a more efficient way of understanding and relating to learning, even if it can also imply that both the content and form of the learning become different from what was intended at the outset. Contemporary psychological, sociological and brain research indicates that learning becomes qualitatively better when participants are engaged in it (e.g. Damasio 1994, 1999; Jarvis 2006, 2009a; Illeris 2007, 2009c). In most cases, involving learners in decisions about and the direction of workplace learning activities will also result in improvements in learning measures that are externally defined, quite simply because as a rule the learners have some shop-floor experience – which others have no part in – and because they have better knowledge of what functions in a problematic manner in their day-to-day work and what could be better. In addition, workers' and employees' perspectives of learning are seldom in direct opposition to what the management would like to see; rather they are an expression of another, more down-to-earth and often more realistic way of doing things.

Learning *is* both an individual and interpersonal matter that cannot simply be regulated like a mechanical process. It needs the involvement of both the learners and those who are responsible for the workplace as a learning environment.

Workplace learning as competence development

The need for competence development

In the previous chapters I have dealt with the basic structures and elements of workplace learning. However, before going on to consider learning at a more concrete and practical level, it is necessary to address the general question of the kind and quality of workplace learning that is needed today. As a central concept for this discussion I shall take up the issue of 'competence development'. This is an important concept, and one currently much in vogue, because, when used correctly, it encompasses the most important qualities that workplace learning needs to include to be up-to-date not only in working life, but in modern life in general.

It is not so very many years ago that the concept of competence was mainly a formal and legal matter, something that gave a person a legal right to make decisions in a certain area, especially in terms of public administration. However, over the last two decades, the use of the word has permeated the areas of education, working life, management and politics as a modern expression for what a person should be able to do or achieve.

During the 1990s, this led to a pronounced change in language usage in relation to the intended results of education and the human resource demands of the labour market, implying that the concept of competences to a great extent was being substituted for that of qualifications. Moreover, this was not just an incidental or trivial language renovation. It should rather be understood as an attempt to recognise the full consequences of the change in the types of abilities that were demanded.

The concept of qualifications has its roots in industrial sociology and fundamentally relates to labour demands for concrete knowledge and skills. Most significantly, it was used in relation to the so-called de-qualification of labour demands as a result of industrialisation (see Braverman 1974). However, this was gradually accompanied by a trend towards an increase in demand for a range of personal or generic qualifications such as flexibility, reliability, responsibility, creativity and independence.

Conversely, the concept of competences was first taken up in organisational psychology and modern management. Here, the point of departure is on the personal level, particularly an individual's ability and readiness to meet the changing challenges of a job. Precisely such competences as the above-mentioned personal and generic qualities are needed for this purpose, while the more formal qualifications become something that can be called upon to contribute to implementing the competences in specific situations.

This could also be expressed by saying that the concept of competences attempts to include different types of qualifications in an understanding which spans a person's potential and practical abilities, i.e. a holistic concept integrating all that is necessary to manage a given situation or challenge: concrete qualifications are integrated into the personal competence in relation to a specific task. Whereas the qualification approach started with single elements and gradually developed in the direction of a more coherent understanding, the competence approach starts with the whole – such as the type of person who will be able to manage a certain task – and, from this position, eventually identifies different qualifications that must be available or acquired.

Definition and important qualities of competences

When dealing with the concept of competence, however, it soon becomes very apparent that there is great uncertainty about and great variety in interpretations of what precisely is meant. Very many different definitions have been proposed, and none of them can be said to be authoritative or generally accepted. A typical and generally accepted definition is the following, which was formulated by the Swiss Dominique Rychen and Laura Salganik as a result of their intensive work for the OECD (Organization for Economic Co-operation and Development) on the topic:

> A competence is defined as the ability to successfully meet complex demands in a particular context through the mobilization of psychological prerequisites (including both cognitive and noncognitive aspects). This represents a demand-oriented or functional approach to defining competencies.
>
> (Rychen and Salganik 2003, p. 43)

However, I shall also mention another definition – proposed by Per Schultz Jørgensen, a Danish Professor of Social Psychology and leading member of the Danish National Competence Council – because this definition explicitly includes the central condition that competences involve the potential to deal appropriately with future and unforeseen situations:

> The concept of competence refers [...] to a person's being qualified in a

broader sense. It is not merely that a person masters a professional area, but also that the person can apply this professional knowledge – and more than that, apply it in relation to the requirements inherent in a situation which, in addition, may be uncertain and unpredictable. Thus competence also includes the person's assessments and attitudes, and ability to draw on a considerable part of his/her personal qualifications.

(Jørgensen 1999, p. 4)

As an extension of these definitions, I shall here draw attention to some of the most important qualities of competences that make this concept more comprehensive and up to date than, for example, qualifications, knowledge, skills, attitudes and other concepts that deal with the outcome of learning and education.

Competences relate to the application in specific situations

As mentioned in Jørgensen's definition, competences can be applied in relation to the requirements inherent in specific situations. It is not sufficient that a person commands a professional area. To be competent the person must also be able to apply his or her professional knowledge and other attributes, such as insights, techniques and methods, in practice.

The competent person is able to act appropriately in specific areas or in specific kinds of situations, and this must be emphasised because it is a demand that clearly exceeds prevailing understandings of knowledge as the central aim of learning and education and to some extent also the concept of qualifications, which does not always include the dimension of application. In contrast, it is an integral feature of the concept of competence that specific knowledge and professional qualifications are necessary but not sufficient for competence: it does not automatically follow that knowledge and qualifications can be applied in all the many situations of practice. For example, in learning psychology the well-known concept of transfer of knowledge implies precisely that students and learners are often unable to activate what they have learned in relevant situations that are different from the learning situation (see, for example, Illeris 2007, 2009d).

Competences are situation related in the sense that they clearly include the ability to handle specific kinds of situations, which can be defined with respect to, for instance, a job or certain groups of people. So competences are not expressed themselves and do not achieve their concrete form until they are applied in appropriated situations. And competences are also related to action, i.e. they express themselves through the relevant and appropriate actions they release when required.

In this way competence is a concept which, more than other concepts in the field, is in line with today's dynamic and changeable society, in which new challenges and situations are constantly arising.

Competences have the nature of potentials

Jørgensen's definition of competences also explicitly states that the competent person is able to use his or her competences in future situations, which 'may be uncertain and unpredictable'. This is, as I see it, one of the most important qualities of competences in comparison with qualifications. Competences have the potential to be further developed or deployed in future unknown situations. Another Danish definition pays special attention to this:

> A competent person [...] is a person, who is in possession of certain quali-
> fications and also commands the exercise of these qualifications in a specific
> situation which may be unknown to him or her. [...] Competence is something
> which is practiced in situations when the results are not known in advance.
> This implies that it is possible to be well qualified, but not competent.
>
> (Jensen 2000, pp. 126 and 136)

To be competent in a certain area implies that the person has acquired the prerequisites or potentials to handle both well-established situations and new situations, something that in our late modern society happens regularly and demands understanding, attitudes, handling, taking a stand and solving problems.

The fact that potentials are central to competences is probably the most decisive quality that makes the concept of competence so important today. We live in a world and at a time in which the conditions are constantly changing and nobody knows in advance exactly what the changes will be, only that they will occur frequently. Change ranges from small changes in everyday matters to fundamental changes in conditions, and it can take place from one day to the next. Thus, 'flexibility' and readiness to change have become key capabilities, and which potentials are at one's disposal when a new situation or challenge occurs is of decisive importance.

This is also why the greatest and most important challenge to schooling and education today is to help develop students' potentials, i.e. to prepare them to handle problems and situations that are not yet known and cannot be predicted. In working life, the potentials that workers and employees possess and are able to draw on when needed are clearly crucial. At the same time, both in education and in working life, this implies abilities which fundamentally cannot be described or measured fully, because they include reactions to challenges which are partly or totally unknown and unpredictable.

Competences include insight, empathy and structural understanding

An important aspect of potentials is that they include insight into how an area is structured and related to other areas, which incentives, balances and power conditions are at stake, which criteria are decisive in determining what is good and bad practice, why things are as they are and, not least, a familiarity with the subject, meaning not only an intellectual but also an emotional and social engagement, including well-substantiated opinions, preferences and a conscious attitude as to one's own position and views.

All these qualities must be so well established that they work together as a whole so that they function even when conditions are changing or strained. Competences should be acquired and developed so that they allow changes, flexibility and remodelling. It is not enough just to know and understand the principal structures and criteria in the area, it is also necessary to adopt a personal, conscious and deliberate attitude and to have the ability to react frankly and at the same time critically to new trends and changes that constantly arise and demand a reaction and often well-founded support or opposition.

Thus, taken seriously the concept of competence implies quite extensive demands for flexible insight and empathy in relation to the reality in which it is to be displayed.

Judgements and decisions are central elements of competence

Another essential and crucial element of competences – one which again is more than just qualifications – is that they, when used in practice, to a great extent imply the ability to make qualified judgements and appropriate decisions in relation to the area in question. When applying one's competences one must, especially in relation to the continuous stream of new situations, be able to decode what is at stake, judge its impact and make relevant and workable decisions about what to do, and all of this often has to be done immediately and under time pressure.

These special conditions and qualities of competences have primarily been pointed out and emphasised by the Australian educational researchers Paul Hager and David Beckett (Hager and Beckett 1995; Beckett and Hager 2000, 2002; Beckett 2004, 2009). As stated by Beckett:

> judgements-in-contexts are at the heart [...] of competence. [...] By this I mean that in these postmodern times, those who can 'read the moment' (or the situation in general) for its particularities and opportunities, are probably those most likely to identify a niche, a hybridity, or an innovation which serves and may even extend prevailing circumstances, thereby reaching new understandings of workplace practices.
>
> (Beckett 2009, p. 71)

Beckett and Hager strongly emphasise the importance of what they term 'the inferential understanding' in connection with judgements and decisions:

> the reflective action of making a 'judgement' is central. Workers do this all day, every day, and I have claimed [...] that these adult education experiences are central to a new concept of holistic competence. Frequently, what

humans find themselves doing [...] is making decisions (judgements) about what to do next. Workplace learning is increasingly shaped by this sort of fluid experience ('knowing how' to go on), but it needs to be made explicit. [...] The 'making explicit' is what the best adult teachers and trainers can do, in facilitating, even revealing, adults' experiences for educational purposes.

(Beckett 2009, p. 76)

Although many writers share this largely rational and cognitive approach to the concept of competence, there are also other voices attaching more importance to empathy and intuition, as, for example, the American Dreyfus brothers in their five-step model of 'human intuition and expertise', which claims that human intelligence will always be superior to any computer in certain vital areas (Dreyfus and Dreyfus 1986). The relationship between the cognitive and the emotional is altogether a psychological topic, and one which for quite some time has been very much in focus (see, for example, Damasio 1994; Goleman 1995; Illeris 2007); it also has a gender dimension (Baron-Cohen 2003), but I shall not explore that further here. I shall only draw attention to the fact that, not least in connection with judgements and decisions that have to be made immediately in an unexpected situation, it is very difficult or almost impossible to distinguish between what is due to cognitive reasoning and what must be referred to empathy and intuition. Both elements will nearly always be involved in a combination that cannot be unravelled in any way.

What is essential, and what is also the central message for Beckett and Hager, is that judgements and decisions are central matters in connection with the application of competences in practice.

Competences exist and can be displayed at all levels

A last general point about competences to mention here is that they in a sense have a certain democratic quality, because it is possible to have and display competences in all possible connections at all levels. For instance, in the Scandinavian countries we use the expression 'real' or 'de facto' competences for anything people have learned informally outside the school and educational systems and we have, like in many other countries, formal systems to validate such competences (see, for example, Skule 2004; Lucio et al. 2007; Parker and Walters 2009).

Competence is found everywhere and is relevant and necessary in all activities at all levels. Thus, everybody possesses some competences, because we have all been involved in some activities which we have learned to handle. One of the most popular Danish books on developmental psychology, which has been translated into several languages, has the title *Your Competent Child* (Juul 2001), and another is called *Children's Competences* (Cecchin 2000). We also talk, in general, about, for instance, social competences, personal competences, professional competences and even key competences (Rychen and Salganik 2003; Rychen and Tiana 2004).

Competence is not necessarily elitist, i.e. limited to a few specialists in the same way as, for instance, expertise (see, for example, Dreyfus and Dreyfus 1986; Herling 2001; Jarvis 2009c). We all develop competences in relation to what we deal with and in particular to what we are absorbed in or committed to. There are many television programmes in which members of the public compete against each other to test their competence in a particular area – this can be seen as a contrast to the many television experts who are constantly explaining and commenting on everything.

Of course, competences are also concerned with learning, developing and improving, but always starting at the level and position one has already reached. Thus, competence, like learning and development, is something common and general – and only when somebody wants something from us might it take on an elitist aspect.

Problematic ways of using the concept of competence

In the above I have highlighted and discussed five specific and important qualities of the concept of competence, and I hope that this has made it visible and understandable why I find this concept an appropriate and agreeable term to use in relation to the qualitative side of workplace learning. I do believe that this concept is well qualified and quite precise in relation to what is needed for the individual to function appropriately and be well integrated in today's complicated and ever-changing society and working life. It seems to cover the whole range and complexity of the very comprehensive challenges we face both individually and as a society. It reaches far beyond both what public education has traditionally aimed at and to a great extent also what industrial and organisational psychology have taken up. And, finally, it should be able to maintain that what is at stake are human capacities in their totality and mutual connectedness, and not just some more limited qualifications.

Nevertheless, there are also important reasons to be cautious about using the competence concept, because it has been greatly misused and involved in tendencies leading to an overload and sometimes even impoverishment of human resources. Competence has been and is still one of several buzzwords that have contributed to press human labour and capacity to the edge, and sometimes even over the edge of what human beings can endure. The concept has been an integrated element in some tendencies, which for many have led to stress, burnout, mental breakdown and other symptoms of a serious overexertion. Two tendencies, in particular, in their different ways, have played a part in this.

First, the concept of competence in the current sense was launched by the trend that in general is known as human resource management, or HRM (see, for example, Tyson 2006; Boxall et al. 2008). This is a way of managing, leading or directing human resources, i.e. other people, a kind of modern management that fundamentally regards workers and employees as resources to be treated in ways that make them function as effectively as possible, ultimately with regard to the earnings and profit of the company – or, as more directly expressed by the South Korean Professor of Lifelong Learning, Soonghee Han, as a 'commodification of human ability' (Han 2009). But it is a modern trend, and it tries to achieve its goal not, as in the early days of industrialisation, by compulsion or coercion, but rather by positive incentives, self-direction and responsibility.

However, there are very many and very different practices that could be called or understood as HRM, but which do not necessarily lead to radical exploitation – and many people today prefer to speak about human resource development (HRD), to stress the developmental element and not so much the management (see, for example, Swanson and Holton 2001). In any case, in relation to competences, there obviously is a risk that HRM and also HRD in practice will encourage or lead to an uncritical ability to direct oneself to do what is expected by the management without being able to set any limits. And this is often encouraged by an unmistakable tendency of HRM and HRD to stand for everything that is regarded as trendy and modern – it may be more important to follow the newest trend than to know where it will take you.

Second, the most far-reaching misuse of the concept of competence is actually taking place in the public sector, related to the approach which has been named 'new public management' (see, for example, Lane 2000; Horton 2006; Hjort 2009). This approach was introduced in the 1980s in the USA and the UK in the time of Ronald Reagan and Margaret Thatcher and later spread to many other countries, mainly in the West, strongly supported by supranational organisations such as the EU, the OECD and the World Bank. In general new public management is about strict economic government and regulation, especially through detailed objectives, budgets, rules, measurements and incentives and strong autocratic leaders of large organisations created by merging existing institutions.

As to competence, the extensive and uncritical use of this concept in the legislation and administration, particularly of educational systems, has in many respects made it unclear what is actually meant and referred to. There does not seem to be any limits as to the number of competences that should be developed, and at the same time it can be quite unclear what is actually required. For instance, in the official regulations of the education of nurses in Denmark (Danish Ministry of Education 2008), the word 'competence' appears 51 times, and the interminable enumeration of competences that the nurses are supposed to acquire includes everything that they might possibly come across. Among many other competences, nurses are expected to be able to:

- practise independent, responsible and well-founded, patient-directed nursing;
- observe and document patients' health conditions, health risks, disease symptoms and treatment results;
- describe the chemical and anatomical composition of humans and human development through the course of life in the interaction with the environment

and micro-organisms; and
- act professionally in an interdisciplinary, societal, cultural and organisational context.

The reader is inevitably left wondering what all these high-faluting demands really mean in practice.

Perhaps this is part of the reason why the Ministry has also been very eager to join the OECD project, which was originally launched in the late 1990s, and has the aim of establishing so-called national competence accounts. Later, in the early 2000s, the focus was changed to measuring and comparing so-called key competences in a broad range of areas including, for example, literacy, numeracy, social competences, learning competence, communication competences, self-management, political competence, ecological competence, cultural competences and health competence (Trier 2001). And gradually the ambitions have then been downscaled to the current so-called PIAAC project (Programme for the International Assessment of Adult Competencies), which, as a parallel to the highly discussed PISA project (also an OECD project), shall include adult competences in the more measurable areas of (OECD 2010, p. 6)

- problem-solving in technology-rich environments;
- literacy;
- numeracy;
- assessment of reading components.

After some delay the first results of this are now scheduled to be published in 2013.

It is obvious that the extensive and unclear use of the concept of competence and the somewhat doubtful measuring and comparing of key competences have resulted in a devaluation and blurring of the concept and totally disregard the special qualities that I have dealt with above. The reason for talking about competences rather than qualifications disappears to the same extent that its content is treated precisely as what Soonghee Han (2009) has critically termed the 'commodification of human abilities', i.e. as goods which can be produced, weighed, measured, declared, quantified, priced and bought and sold on the (labour) market. This is exactly the opposite of what I regard as the most fundamental strength of the idea of competences: that they refer to human qualities which cannot be produced but only developed, which cannot be regarded quantitatively but only qualitatively, which cannot be described as mechanical functions but only as potentials, and which cannot be declared precisely but only in relation to certain challenges and tasks.

I have in my own practice heard many nursing teachers and teachers in other areas with similar kinds of regulations question the meaning and implications of these lists of competences. And when the results of the PIAAC are published, there will, no doubt, be a renewed discussion about what has been measured and how this deflects attention and effort from all other areas to those narrow functions which are measured – just as we have seen in relation to the PISA outcomes.

If the competence concept is to be taken seriously it must be understood that it fundamentally refers to the application of potentials, the ability to deal with unknown future situations, challenges and problems – and this cannot be measured. To try to measure the least complicated of many relevant competences and draw some far-reaching conclusions is to devalue the very concept of competence, which is distinguished precisely by its relevance to the present realities in all their multitude and complexity.

In addition, it is worth mentioning that one outcome of the application of new public management has been that some of the most negative aspects of HRM have been transferred to the public sector in a very unfortunate way, such that stress and burnout have been joined by a strong demotivation as a result of the constant changes and reorganisations forced on the workers and employees by autocratic leaders, very often in direct opposition to the professional norms and attitudes in the area. The mixture of stress and demotivation causes extreme mental strain, and the consequence tends to be a personal depression that may result in being both worn out and unemployed. In Denmark there has been, during the 2000s, a large increase in this kind of syndrome among public servants (Prætorius 2007).

Competence development in practice

In this last section of Part I of this book some general features of competence development in relation to workplace learning shall be lined up – before the more specific discussions of different kinds of workplace learning are taken up in Part II.

Competence development, school and education

First, I believe that it is important to state that the development of work competence cannot be achieved by schools, courses or educational programmes unless they are in some way combined with work practice, for example in the form of apprenticeship, trainee service, alternating school and practice periods or school practice projects. This is because competences, as stated previously, are closely related to application in specific situations, and if the kinds of specific situations in question are work situations the competence development must at least to some extent include such situations.

However, this certainly does not mean that schooling and education are not relevant for competence development in general or for work competence development in particular. On the contrary, it is only in very special cases that school or educational learning is not relevant or necessary for work competence development, either as an indispensable precondition or as an integral or parallel part.

When the nature and quality of competences are taken seriously, it is a huge challenge to schools and educational institutions to take part in goal-directed competence development. In a nutshell, it could be asked how it is possible for a school or other educational institution to develop potentials to cope appropriately with situations and problems that take place elsewhere and are not known and cannot even be foreseen. This is actually a question that undermines a great deal of traditional educational thinking that takes as its starting point the formulation of precise objectives and then tries to deduce educational measures from these.

On the other hand, in principle, the role of schooling and education has always been to prepare students for something which is placed outside in time and space. And in today's society it is hardly possible to think that the highly qualitative work competences that are demanded at almost all workplaces can be developed without comprehensive contributions from the school and educational system. It is obvious that the school and education system will also in the future be the 'state apparatus', which is constructed to be the fundamental public means of providing the major contributions to the competences demanded. Moreover, it will inevitably – even in the future – be in the practical and economic interest of both the private and the public sector that as much competence development as possible takes place outside the workplace so that it does not strain the economy and daily working conditions of companies and organisations.

So the proper question to ask is, rather: how can schools and educational institutions be geared to optimally develop competences which are relevant for further competence development at workplaces and elsewhere outside the educational system? And the answer obviously must meet demands in the areas of both content and ability to perform activities.

As to content, schooling and education must still include essential general skills such as literacy, numeracy, information technology and foreign languages, a basic grounding in subjects such as biology, health, history, natural sciences, social studies and the arts, as well as the general prerequisites for further competence development in one or more professional areas. All this must be thought through from the perspective of what is relevant and necessary today, but it is unlikely to be much different from what we are already used to.

The more important changes needed to strengthen schooling and education in the direction of competence development will be related to the organisation and practice of school and educational activities: traditional teaching must be supplemented by, and there must be much more emphasis on, participation in decision-making, social relations, responsibility, planning of processes and projects, interdisciplinarity, individual and social reflection and the like. It is obvious when looking back on the important qualities of competences described earlier in this chapter that achieving such qualities will require something like a revolution in schooling and education that is carried through right down to the roots of how it is practised. This again will require a good deal of serious experimentation and research and, probably the most important, difficult and decisive point, an open-minded and dedicated attitude by all the many politicians, professionals, students, parents and people from working life who need to be involved. (In this connection a good piece of advice could be to consult some literature presenting a comprehensive and up-to-date understanding of human learning such as, for example, Illeris 2007.)

Conditions for competence development programmes at work

Competence development at work is different from educational competence development, not least because it is to a greater or lesser extent integrated into the very activities in which it can be utilised, so the borderline between competence development and competence application is often hardly visible. This is probably also part of the reason why the conditions for competence development at work is a topic which in itself and systematically has not been researched very much. However, recently, the Swedes Per-Erik Ellström and Henrik Kock have attempted to survey the literature in the area and give a systematic overview of 'What characterizes successful strategies for competence development in organizations?' (Ellström and Kock 2009, p. 48ff.). Their main conclusion is that the effects of competence development depend on an interplay between four kinds of factors.

The first group of factors concern the prior experiences of the participants, i.e. previous experience of education, self-confidence, motivation and already developed competences. Ellström and Kock, in this connection, primarily refer to the well-known condition that the higher an individual's social background and the educational level, the more likely it is that he or she will participate in further educational activities, and this also seems to be the case in relation to programmes and activities that aim at competence development at work. From this can also be drawn the conclusion that, if such programmes or activities are to involve workers or employees with a lower educational level and social background, special measures and considerations should be taken (Illeris 2005, 2006d; see also Chapter 12).

The second group of factors comprise the planning, content, design and implementation of programmes and activities. Here Ellström and Kock emphasise that the motives for engagement should be problem oriented, i.e. that the competence development should be viewed as part of a specific strategy or activity in which the company is involved, for instance a new work organisation or a new production, and that the staff should be involved directly, or indirectly through representatives, in the planning and direction.

The next group of factors have to do with the relationship between programmes or activities and internal organisation and company culture, for example recruitment, counselling, design, job extension, proportions of time and personnel involved and supervision. In all such dimensions it is important that there is an agreement and relation to the internal norms and understanding and if possible that deviances, extensions or changes are made open, substantiated and discussed – so that there are no grounds for suspecting that managers are trying to follow some hidden agenda.

Finally, there are factors related to the external environment, such as the competitive situation, the labour market and the rate of technological development in the field. According to Ellström and Kock these conditions can be assumed to be related mainly indirectly to the effect of investments in competence development. However, as shown by the world developments that have occurred since 2009, it is difficult to accept that they can be ignored. Rather, a situation of stability in the external context must be regarded as out of reach so that the risks and changes must be openly faced and taken into account.

However, overall, Ellström and Kock seem to draw a very useful and reliable picture of the general conditions in which important and sustainable competence development in the workplace needs to take place.

Guidelines for the process of competence development at work

As to how the competence developmental processes can be thought of and arranged as learning courses on the social and individual levels, some guidelines can be drawn from the special qualities of competences as described above in combination with learning theoretical and educational considerations.

As competence development implies important and demanding learning processes, a first requirement must be that the participants are personally committed to the idea and the process which are set up. *Commitment,* engagement and motivation are needed to mobilise the mental energy which can make learning a deeper process than just the acquisition of new knowledge (Illeris 2007). Another prerequisite on the personal level is, of course, that participants have a reasonable level of professional knowledge, skills, insight and understanding in relation to the area(s) in which the competence development is supposed to take place. These requirements can be seen as a practical utilisation of the first group of factors concerning the prior experiences of the participants in Ellström and Kock's overview, and in relation to their special concern about the low-skilled it should be observed that any competence development programme that includes this group must be effected in ways that meet the positive motivations and also the concerns they may have (see Chapter 12). It is a waste of energy and resources to offer competence development opportunities and programmes that do not correspond with and respect the motivational conditions and prerequisites of the participants. Thus, representatives of the participants should also be involved at an early stage.

Next, competence development activities in workplaces must to some extent be integrated with or involve the daily work *practice*, and in most cases also intended future practice. This is well in line with what Ellström and Kock have observed. Seen from the participants' point of view this is because work practice – as shown in Figure 4.1 – is the area that overlaps with work identity, and serious competence development must be anchored in and influence participants' work identities. In effect, this means that serious competence development processes cannot exclusively be activities that do not involve participants' work practice.

They cannot involve only teaching, exercises, discussions, explanations, demonstrations, excursions or the like. All such activities have a part to play, and can be very important elements, but practice cannot be left out and must in general play the principal part and must always be referenced in other kinds of activities.

Finally, and I think my advice here goes beyond the points of Ellström and Kock, it is of fundamental importance that competence development activities include *reflection*. It is through reflection that experience can be turned into potentials for the future, and this is also the deeper reason why the concept of reflection has gained a very central position in contemporary learning theories, especially in relation to adult and workplace learning. There are many slightly different interpretations and understandings of this concept, but they can be summed up in two main categories. One category is what the American psychologist Donald Schön has called reflection-in-action (Schön 1983, 1987), indicating that such reflection takes place as an integrated part of action – actors reflect, individually or in groups, on what they are doing when they are doing it in order to make the best out of their actions. This is certainly very important in relation to competence development, but it refers to what can and should always be part of the nature of goal-directed activities, and so it is rather a general requirement of the work culture and not something that can be specifically planned. If it is planned and scheduled as a special element of competence development arrangements it is no longer reflection-in-action, but reflection-on-action, and this is what most researchers have pointed to – not least the American adult educator Jack Mezirow in relation to his concept of 'transformative learning' (Mezirow 1990, 1991, 2009) and the British-American adult educator Stephen Brookfield in relation to his concept of 'critical reflection' (Brookfield 1987, 1996) – and what is essential for the planning and practice of competence development programmes. Systematically including and practising individual and shared reflection activities as a kind of evaluation and adjustment of programmes leads to a high probability of genuine competence development.

So as a sort of general formula for the planning and practice of workplace learning as competence development I can recommend the simple triad of

commitment–practice–reflection

This is, of course, an oversimplification of a very complex topic, but I have found that it is a handy rule of thumb to keep the arrangements on the right track. Commitment is a necessary point of departure for all who are involved. Including practice ensures that activities do not lose relevance. And reflection is the way in which experience can be turned into potentials – which is the same as turning more ordinary learning into competence development.

Competence development and the learning triangle

As a last point in relation to competence development I shall return to the learning triangle developed in Chapter 2 (Figure 2.2) to point out the theoretical basis of the qualities that learning should possess in order to obtain the nature of competence development. I shall do this by referring to the three learning dimensions:

1   The content dimension concerns what is learned. This is usually described as knowledge and skills, but many other elements, such as opinions, insight, meaning, attitudes, values, ways of behaviour, methods and strategies, may also be considered learning content. The endeavour of the learner is to construct *meaning* and the *ability* to deal with the challenges of practical life. An overall personal *functionality* can thereby be developed.

2   The incentive dimension provides and directs the mental energy that is necessary for the learning process to take place. It comprises such elements as feelings, emotions, motivation and volition. Its ultimate function is to secure the continuous *mental balance* of the learner and thereby it simultaneously develops a personal *sensitivity*.

These two dimensions are always initiated by impulses from the interaction processes and integrated in the internal process of elaboration and acquisition. Therefore, the learning content is, so to speak, always 'obsessed' with the incentives at stake, e.g. whether the learning is driven by desire, interest, necessity or compulsion. Correspondingly, the incentives are always influenced by the content, e.g. new information can change the incentive condition.

3   The interaction dimension provides the impulses that initiate the learning process. This may take place as perception, transmission, experience, imitation, activity, participation, etc. It serves the personal *integration* in communities and society and thereby also builds up the *sociality* of the learner. However, this building up necessarily takes place through the other two dimensions.

In Figure 5.1 the signal words from the above have been placed outside each of the learning triangle angles which show the three learning dimensions. The words that signify what the learner is aiming at are written in regular type and the words that signify the general outcome are written in italics. Thus by accentuating in italics the qualities of the learning outcomes in each of the three dimensions this figure highlights what are also the three necessary and crucial components of all competences.

It should be noted that these qualities are in principle the qualities of all learning, but in relation to competence development it is particularly important to emphasise that precisely these three qualities – functionality, sensitivity and sociality – are the basic building blocks, and it is the strength of these three qualities that is decisive for the extent to which learning takes on the nature of competence development. The holistic demand that this concept implies can adequately be specified into a claim that functionality, sensitivity and sociality must be involved with considerable weight in relation to the area in question. Therefore, for learning to have the quality of competence development it must include all three

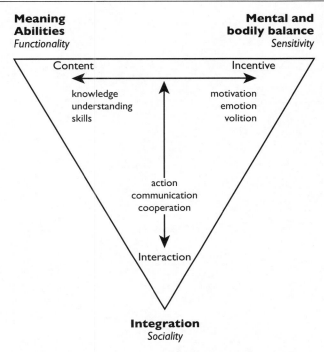

Figure 5.1 Learning as competence development (after Illeris 2007, p. 28).

learning dimensions in ways that are important and relevant in relation to the required competence.

Part II

Workplace learning in practice

Chapter 6: The workplace as a framework for learning

The second part of this book concerns the many different ways in which workplace learning can be dealt with in practice, and this chapter addresses some of the most important general features of the workplace in relation to learning. First, it is emphasised that learning is always a secondary matter in the workplace and that, especially in demanding circumstances, the production of goods and services will inevitably take priority. Next, the concepts of incidental and informal workplace learning are introduced, the significance of the learning environment is accentuated, and the use of information and communication technology (ICT) in connection with learning is discussed. Finally, attention is drawn to the concept of organisational learning and 'the learning organisation'.

Chapter 7: Learning initiatives in connection with daily work

This chapter is about learning initiatives in connection with daily work. Most important in this context are initial guidance and general instruction at ground level. Other everyday arrangements of importance for workplace learning are informal and formal meetings, conversations, workshops and seminars, and special attention is given to ICT-mediated learning processes. In addition, interviews of various kinds may support learning, and finally some more specific possibilities are introduced, such as history workshops, future workshops, experience groups and internal networks.

Chapter 8: Sparring and support schemes

Another and usually more individually oriented type of workplace learning concerns various kinds of sparring and support schemes, which are explored in this chapter. More or less informal guided learning is very widespread, but seems today to be overtaken by the formal schemes of mentoring and coaching, the difference between the two essentially being that mentoring functions from the perspective of the mentor whereas coaching should take place from the perspective of the coachee. Organised support by colleagues, sometimes called ambassadors, super-users or gardeners, in connection with the use of ICT, is another rapidly growing possibility, and an external consultant may also be employed.

Chapter 9: Job-transcending learning initiatives

More radical or renewing workplace learning which transcends existing job structures may take place by such organisational means as self-directed groups, projects, action learning, job exchange, job rotation or external networks, which are discussed in this chapter. In all such arrangements, the learners have possibilities and are expected to transcend the limits of their jobs and develop into new fields and contexts. This is likely to encourange, to a much higher extent than has been described in previous chapters, the kinds of learning which rightly deserve to be called competence development.

Chapter 10: Interaction between workplace learning, courses and education

In this chapter the limits of not only jobs but also workplaces are transcended by addressing the interaction with providers of work-oriented courses and education. This may be done simply by offering employees a variety of courses. However, this leads to the classic problem of transfer between different learning environments with different learning rationales. Therefore the learning outcome can often be dramatically increased by closer cooperation and interaction between the workplace and the external provider. Such arrangements are costly, however, and are therefore often only undertaken in ways which are insufficient to realise the vast potentials they may entail.

The workplace as a framework for learning

Learning as a secondary matter

What is special and significant for workplace learning is, of course, first of all, that it takes place in or in direct relation to a specific type of learning space with specific conditions. It is fundamentally important that workplaces have certain specific purposes and conditions of existence that are not primarily related to a learning perspective, but nonetheless inevitably are of importance for the learning that can take place. The framework conditions are unlike those found in schools and educational institutions, which are primarily directed towards learning, being instead directed towards the production of the goods and/or services that the organisation supplies, and ultimately, in the case of private sector organisations, towards the maximisation of profits, and, in the case of public sector organisations, maximising politically formulated goals within a given financial budget framework. It is inherent in this that submission to quantifiable efficiency and effectiveness parameters is a fundamental condition for workplace learning.

In addition to this, workplaces contain power structures that may be organised in many ways, but which usually mean that there are managers who make decisions and have the right to supervise and distribute tasks, to hire and fire employees, and ultimately to discontinue operations and move, merge, restructure and generally make decisions on all issues pertaining to the existence and conditions of the workplace.

No matter how employee- and learning-oriented managers believe a workplace to be, it is always these fundamental conditions, the efforts to achieve efficiency and effectiveness and the privilege of management, that constitute the fundamental conditions for learning. The learning that is the objective of more or less focused efforts must of necessity directly or indirectly serve the interests of the workplace as defined by management, and the incidental learning which also always takes place among the employees outside, and in some cases contrary to the interests of management, is also necessarily influenced by the fact that it takes place under these conditions (see, for example, Volmerg *et al.* 1986; Leithäuser 2000).

Learning in the workplace thus encompasses both a large volume of learning that is in accordance with the intended functions of the workplace, and which ranges from acquisition of the necessary skills and insights in connection with mastering the various work processes to a personal and identity-related development in accordance with the aim and practice of the workplace, and at the same time learning concerned with ways in which employees individually and collectively are able to handle their own situation in the workplace in a way that is manageable and satisfying to themselves.

The second type of workplace learning may in some cases be in direct opposition to the interests of management. There is, however, also a more adaptation-oriented form of 'counter-learning', concerned with developing routines and modes of perception directed towards ways in which employees may satisfy their own needs and attitudes while at the same time discharging their work duties in an acceptable manner. This is the way in which employees develop what, for example, the American organisational theorists Chris Argyris and Donald Schön, in their books on organisational learning, call 'defensive routines', and which they consider to be the most significant obstacle to the development of appropriate learning in accordance with the need of the workplace. Thus, organisational learning is, among other things, concerned with breaking down the defensive routines and developing some modes of functioning that may be more appropriate from the perspective both of management and employees (Argyris and Schön 1996).

In the following discussions on various initiatives that may be relevant to workplace learning, it is therefore of key significance to remember that this learning is always related to the primary purpose and power structures of the workplace but also to be aware that employees themselves contribute with their own perspectives and interests, which may be in accordance with, or more or less in opposition to, the primary purposes and power structures.

It is the same fundamental tension between the workplace-rational perspective and the subjective perspective of learning that is central to the model for workplace learning set up in Chapter 4. It is essential that the parties involved recognise, accept and acknowledge this tension – something that is in clear opposition to most management-oriented literature in the area, which more or less exclusively considers workplace learning from a workplace-rational management perspective.

At the same time, it is important to emphasise that this dual perspective is not just assumed on the basis of ethical and democratic viewpoints, but that it also accords better with reality and therefore is better suited as the basis for rational reflection.

Incidental learning in the workplace

One very important form of learning in the workplace, and presumably also the most widespread, is the unplanned learning that takes place in connection with and as part of the discharge of an individual's daily duties and daily contact.

The understanding and significance of this was brought centre-stage in the book *Informal and Incidental Learning in the Workplace* by Victoria Marsick and Karen Watkins, which was published in the USA in 1990. The book defined 'incidental learning' as 'a by-product of some other activity, such as task accomplishment, interpersonal interaction, sensing the organizational culture, or trial-and-error experimentation' (Marsick and Watkins 1990, pp. 6–7).

Incidental learning thus involves both the professionally oriented learning of work methods and procedures for implementing the various activities specific to the work of that particular workplace and, at least in equal measure, the input of perceptions and attitudes – or workplace socialisation – that takes place if not automatically then at least without any consciously planned aim.

The fact that this learning is not intentional or planned also, of course, makes it difficult to direct it towards a specific goal. Once it is accepted that incidental learning is very important and therefore worthy of consideration, either attempts should be made to modify it, in which case it is no longer incidental, or there must be a general effort to change the learning environment of the workplace to improve conditions for the more desirable forms of incidental learning and thus make it more likely to occur (which was the essence of Marsick and Watkins's book).

However, the concept of incidental learning itself is not without problems. This is partly because the character of the learning environment can have a significant impact on the relative likelihood of various types of incidental learning, and partly because the background and preferences of the individual employee also have a major impact on what this individual takes note of and thereby learns. Incidental learning is thus not as random as a cursory glance might suggest, but is generally dependent on both the learning environment and who the employees are.

It is also against this background that the Australian John Garrick has raised serious objections to this concept (Garrick 1998, p. 11), and later suggested that 'incidental learning' should be viewed as informal learning (a concept which will be considered in the next section), but that we might in special cases talk of 'accidental learning' when for some reason an entirely fortuitous event takes place: an unpredictable coincidence or an episode from which someone may learn a lesson (Garrick 1999, p. 219).

In summary, it shall here first and foremost be maintained that in any workplace much incidental learning takes place without planning or explicit request, but which may nonetheless have a great impact on both the function of the workplace and the individual employee. This type of learning can, however, be influenced only indirectly and at a general level, and thus it overlaps to a great extent with informal learning, which shall therefore be dealt with in the following section.

Informal workplace learning

Informal learning encompasses everything that is not formalised, e.g. teaching, instruction, debate, meetings or other organised activities, but it may well be intentional, as when an employee asks for advice from another employee, or when employees discuss approaches to dealing with a situation that has arisen. More extensive forms may involve self-directed or group-directed learning, in which the learner or learners without any formal framework orientate themselves in various ways towards learning something they need or in which they are in some other way interested.

In recent years it has become common, for example when discussing 'lifelong learning', to distinguish between informal learning and non-formal learning (e.g. the EU Commission 2000), the latter typically taking place in associations, projects or movements or through specific initiatives in workplaces that do not make use of institutionalised training, while the former can take place in all sorts of contexts that do not involve any organised endeavour.

However, the terminological practice for reference to informal, non-formal and formal learning has been made the subject of research in England and published as a report by Helen Colley, Phil Hodkinson and Janice Malcolm. The authors conclude that, although it is possible to some extent to distinguish between formal learning and informal or non-formal learning, it is virtually impossible to maintain a clear distinction between informal and non-formal learning. It may thus make a certain measure of sense to use the terms formal and informal learning if it is kept in mind that there may well be formal elements in informal learning, and that there are almost always informal elements in formal learning, whereas non-formal learning is a category so vague that it is hardly expedient to use it generally (Colley *et al.* 2003).

These questions are not merely of academic and linguistic interest, because underlying the use of these concepts is usually an assumption that informal learning in a number of contexts is better than formal learning and, furthermore, it is common in political circles to believe that with some effort much of the learning that predominantly takes place in educational institutions could successfully be transferred to other contexts, notably the workplace. Jean Lave and Etienne Wenger's work on situated learning (Lave and Wenger 1991) and communities of practice (Wenger 1998) has provided an important contribution in this regard. Important arguments in favour of informal learning included the belief that motivation is generally higher in informal contexts and that informal learning overcomes the so-called transfer problem, i.e. the difficulties involved in applying what a person has learned in one context, e.g. an education programme, in another context, e.g. in a workplace (see, for example, Tennant 1999).

There can be little doubt that these arguments are not without substance and that there is much to be gained from learning through practice, learning through experience, workplace learning, self-directed learning, and other types of informal learning. However, there are also powerful opposing arguments, in particular that institutionalised learning affords greater opportunity for considering a subject in depth, especially when that subject consists of complex and theoretical perceptions; informal learning, in contrast, tends to focus exclusively on the immediately apparent and more superficial level, and there is often insufficient time, space and qualified input in informal contexts to go into depth. Learning-oriented initiatives in the workplace may in many contexts have a disturbing effect, and neither public nor private organisations seem generally to be interested in taking on interns and apprentices to an extent commensurate with need in any particular area. At the same time, it should not be overlooked that the discussion on where learning may best take place may also involve underlying financial issues such as who is to pay for which part of the qualification and competence development of the workforce.

Thus, it is clear that the argument placing more emphasis on informal learning is both important and justified. However, at the same time there is a need for a realistic weighting of the pros and cons, and not least for a qualification of informal as well as formalised learning and the interaction between the two. This weighting and qualification will be a key issue in the rest of this book.

The significance of the learning environment

In all cases, the learning environment is of crucial importance for both the extent and character of the workplace learning. In Chapter 2 the intricate character and most important elements of learning environments were discussed, and in Chapter 5 the documentation by Per-Erik Ellström and Henrik Kock (2009) on the importance of the environment for competence development was mentioned. Here I shall take a closer look at the significance of learning environments for learning possibilities.

It has in many contexts been pointed out that different types of workplaces offer very different learning environments with very different learning opportunities. David Beckett and Paul Hager have claimed that the most significant factor affecting the quality of a workplace as a learning environment is *the variety* of opportunities and situations it offers the employees (Beckett and Hager 2000, 2002). This may be compared with the previously mentioned basic sociology of consciousness analysis by the German Ute Volmerg, who contends that the central dimensions of such variety depend on employees' opportunities for disposition (i.e. the opportunity to make decisions about their work), their opportunities for interaction (i.e. for interacting and communicating with others) and their opportunities for applying their acquired qualifications (Volmerg 1976, p. 21f.).

The Swede Per-Erik Ellström has also made important contributions to our general understanding of these issues and pointed to the significance for the learning environment of both external factors, such as competition, quality demands and fluctuations in the macro-economic environment, and internal factors, including a combination of individual-oriented and company-oriented learning strategies, employees' involvement in initiation, planning and implementation of learning initiatives, time schedules, management's motives for and commitment to learning initiatives and management pressure and support for learning in the workplace (Ellström 2004).

The mentioned contributions are adequate for illustrating both the breadth and complexity of the factors that have an impact on the character and quality of a workplace as a learning environment. It also makes it clear that both management's attitude to these issues and the employees' attitudes play a crucial role, while external factors may also have a decisive impact.

It is part of modern management endeavours that many workplaces make extensive and determined efforts to live up to all these challenges in ways which, especially from management's point of view, appear expedient in relation to the learning environment. However, in practice, it is not always so straightforward. On the basis of a survey carried out by a well-known Danish organisation that is in the vanguard in this area, Mette Morsing concluded that in an open learning environment it is competition and conflict that particularly drive development and learning forward, and the important issue is 'to get competition and co-operation to coexist, to balance between change and stability [...] it is the fractured surface between different "types of reason" which in practice holds the potential for innovation' (Morsing 1995, pp. 22 and 26).

It is, of course, true that both competition and conflict may motivate learning, but the impact on the character of this learning may be such that learning efforts have the opposite effect from that intended. In Denmark a young researcher, Jesper Tynell, has documented this in detail. He spent some time observing work in a modern Danish IT enterprise with super-modern HRM strategies. He found that the extent of employees' independence and responsibility was so great as to be described as exploitation leading to extensive colonisation, i.e. there was little room for much else in their life, and even to mental breakdown and illness (Tynell 2001). In a similar study, psychologist Nadja Prætorius described how modern management strategies, including those applied in the public sector, are causing an increasing number of employees to seek help from psychologists to relieve stress and burnout (Prætorius 2004).

Tynell's example may be extreme, but Prætorius's observations suggest a significant trend, one that may serve as a reminder that issues involving the learning environment and learning in working life are not simple and one-dimensional, with more and more meaning better and better. Like everything involving interaction between humans, the learning environment has many facets and presents both great development potential and huge risks.

ICT as a constituent part of the learning environment

One element in the workplace learning environment that today demands particular attention is the deployment of ICT.

A Danish professor in this field, Lone Dirckinck-Holmfeld (2004), has described how ICT as a learning tool is to a very great extent gaining a strong position in European workplaces, and, indeed, e-learning has been proposed as a form of mass education that can reach all categories of employees on a large scale and more or less replace other forms of work-related learning:

We see many different examples of how ICT is involved and how ICT is able to contribute to the learning processes. From more traditional courses, in which ICT is primarily used for training the employees in relatively limited skills, to new forms of collaborative and project-oriented courses, in which ICT is used as a communicative and collaborative infrastructure for building bridges between the need for learning in the workplace and theories and methods from the institutions, to radical forms of virtual learning environments that are operated by self-directed learners, and which build on motivation structures and dynamics imported from informal learning environments.

(Dirckinck-Holmfeld 2004, p. 28)

One of many very positive examples comes from a global company with employees throughout the world which has been able to implement a continuous programme of upgrading skills via e-learning, with great benefits in both financial and learning terms. Audiovisual communication offers numerous advantages including a reduction in travel costs, the ability to extend courses over longer periods of time, the simultaneous development of digital competences of both instructors and students, and the ability to develop cooperation and other 'soft' competences through collaborative and project-oriented courses.

However, as Dirckinck-Holmfeld points out, the greatest focus is still on the design of the technical tools, whereas, if the learning is to be up to date, the starting point should be the learning processes and the situation and motivation of the learners. A Swedish survey of two major initiatives aimed at low-skilled workers, one in the automotive industry and the other in the timber industry, found that e-learning was inexpedient and that the results were disappointing (Thång and Wärvik 2004). And the evaluation of a major Norwegian project in the graphic industry concluded that 'in summary, we can say that the project made obvious the chasm that separates the expectations attached to net-based learning in the workplace and the outcome which is actually realisable today' (Lahn 2004).

There seems to be broad agreement that there are great possibilities in using ICT as an important tool in workplace learning. However, it is not enough just to introduce PCs and learning programmes that the employees may use. Like all other learning, e-learning forms part of a complicated interaction that encompasses the workplace conditions in the broadest sense, learners' prior qualifications and motivation, the nature of the programmes used (including opportunities for learning with others rather than as individual PC users), as well as the opportunities for using the tools in accordance with the employees' working rhythms and needs.

More generally, it might be said that the main issue involved is that of making ICT learning an integrated part of the daily learning environment. Swedes Carina Åberg and Lennart Svensson (2004) have, on the basis of a number of broadly conceived projects, formulated a model of what will be required (Figure 6.1).

Figure 6.1 shows the many factors that influence the learning that takes place in the direct interaction between the individual employee and the computer, and Åberg and Svensson (2004) provide a detailed account of these different factors.

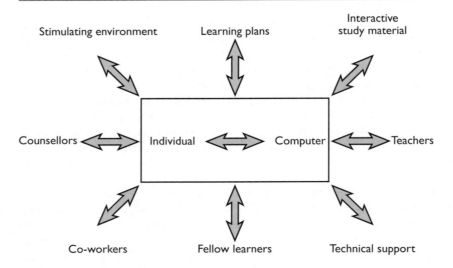

Figure 6.1 E-learning in the workplace (after Åberg and Svensson 2004, p. 80).

However, the figure does not show what in this context is probably the most important issue, which is that, if e-learning is to deliver the learning possibilities necessary for it to become a significant and active element in workplace learning, the interaction between the individual and the computer can be only one element in the workplace learning environment. The point of departure for the development of this environment should be not computers and programs, but employees and the learning they need and are motivated to undertake.

It is easy enough to see the huge learning potential of e-learning. However, experience to date unanimously shows that, if this potential is to be realised, technology must be an integral element of a supportive learning environment and a culture of education rather than being implemented because of a fascination with technology or the desire to achieve cost savings, although cost will, as a rule, provide some of the impetus.

E-learning requires, of course, up-to-date technology, programs that enable interaction between learners and their instructors as well as among learners, easy access to who can solve the technical problems that unavoidably arise (see the section on 'gardeners' and 'super-users' in Chapter 8) and, not least, management that puts wholehearted efforts into the development of such an environment, makes available the necessary time and financial and technological resources, and understands that technology must be developed and offered on the basis of the needs of the employees. If these conditions are not met, e-learning will in general have very limited functional scope for professional instruction, and there will be many frustrations and conflicts attached to more extensive use of ICT in workplace learning.

Organisational learning and 'the learning organisation'

More generally, the discipline and study of education encompasses a field called 'organisational learning', which lies in the twilight zone between management and organisational psychology and is much concerned with development of the learning environment and the learning possibilities in organisations and in the workplace, and the concept of the development of 'the learning organisation' has become a powerful and penetrating brand for these endeavours (see, for example, Elkjær 1999).

Two key figures in this area are the Americans Chris Argyris and Donald Schön, already mentioned a couple of times. They have worked in this field for many years, and in 1996 they published *Organizational Learning II*, which has assumed the dominant position in the field (Argyris and Schön 1996). In the book, the authors explain organisational learning as follows:

> Organizational learning occurs when individuals within an organization experience a problematic situation and enquire into it on the organization's behalf. They experience a surprising mismatch between expected and actual results of action and respond to that mismatch through a process of thought and further action that leads them to modify their images of organization or their understandings of organizational phenomena and to restructure their activities so as to bring outcomes and expectations into line, thereby changing organizational theory-in-use. In order to become organizational, the learning that results from organizational inquiry must become embedded in the images of organization held in its members' minds and/or in the epistemological artifacts (the maps, memories, and programs) embedded in the organizational environment.
>
> (Argyris and Schön 1996, p. 16)

The quotation pinpoints a key issue concerning organisational learning. Argyris and Schön maintain that it is in fact individuals who learn, and their learning can only be called organisational if it leads to development in the organisation. Furthermore, even though the work of Argyris and Schön contains some significant and fundamental learning psychology reflections, it is clear, in their work and more generally in connection with organisational learning, that it is the organisation and its development that take centre-stage, while individuals act and learn 'on behalf of the organisation'.

At the psychological level, Argyris and Schön are occupied by the difference that they have very often encountered in practice between the theories of the organisation expressed by employees and management ('espoused theories') and the rationales that provide the basis for practical action ('theories-in-use'). If such a difference is to be overcome so as to make actions rational given the intended aim, there must be so-called 'double-loop learning', which, as opposed to the ordinary 'single-loop learning', not only leads to changes in 'strategies of action or assumptions underlying strategies in ways that leave the values of a theory of action unchanged' (Argyris and Schön 1996, p. 20), but also 'results in a change in the values of theory-in-use, as well as in its strategies and assumptions' (Argyris and Schön 1996, p. 21). This requires a preparedness to transcend the established 'defensive routines' (as mentioned in Chapter 5). The learning concepts used are highly similar to the learning types accommodation and assimilation, as explained in Chapter 3, but there is the significant difference in that Argyris and Schön's concepts explicitly are related solely to organisational learning, which means that the modes of definition underlying their work are constantly related to the organisation.

It is also worth noting that these fundamental psychological reflections occupy only a minor part of Argyris and Schön's work. As in the other literature on organisational learning, the main emphasis is on the organisation and the development of the learning possibilities it offers. Thus, there is no clear distinction between the field of organisational learning and the concept of 'the learning organisation' (see Elkjær 1999), except for the discussion on what exactly it is that an organisation learns.

The account of 'the learning organisation' generally considered the most qualified is that of American Peter Senge, in his book *The Fifth Discipline* (Senge 1990). His approach is probably the most comprehensive and extensive attempt to describe and understand the development of workplaces as places of learning, but it remains peripheral to the field of interest of the present book specifically because it is not primarily concerned with employees' learning and development. As mentioned above, employees tend to be viewed as agents acting 'on behalf of the organisation', i.e. they are of interest merely to the extent that they are bearers of learning in the organisation in question.

There is generally a huge degree of interest in organisational development, which in many ways overlaps with the field of workplace learning, but which I shall not examine any further in this context. It can be studied in many sources, a few of which are Harvard Business Review (2001), Easterby-Smith and Lyles (2003), Nicolini *et al.* (2003), Evans *et al.* (2006) and Billett *et al.* (2008).

Conclusion and perspectives

This chapter has focused on the general prerequisites for learning in the workplace. It has been pointed out that the workplace is a special learning space with certain specific qualities, including first and foremost that learning is not the primary aim of the workplace, but takes place in relation to certain rationales and power structures anchored in other intentions. At the same time, the workplace is undoubtedly an arena for extensive and significant learning processes of both a work-oriented and general nature.

Much learning in the workplace has an informal and partially incidental character, but it is nonetheless influenced by being subjected to the conditions of workplace learning. At the general level, workplace learning that is not related to specific learning-oriented initiatives can be influenced only by development of the learning environment of the workplace, which is a very complicated and multifaceted matter that may lead to considerable gains for society, the organisation and its employees, but which in extreme cases may also lead to critical 'overload'.

Generally there are considerable interests and perspectives attached to a development of workplaces as a learning environment, an endeavour that in a professional context has especially been the focus within the field called 'organisational learning' and the notion of 'the learning organisation'. However, this endeavour shows a tendency to be predominantly disposed to view learning and learning possibilities from the perspective and interests of organisations.

It is important for employees, as well as for the quality and versatility of the learning, that this learning is based on an understanding of the interaction between organisation-related and employee- or individual-related rationales. If workplace learning is to contribute to competence development, it is crucial that the prerequisites, interests and motivations of learners are considered just as important as the interests of the organisation. In the case of low-skilled learners, in particular, there is an obvious risk that attempts to strengthen workplace learning solely through a general development of the workplace learning environment, without special learning-directed initiatives, will not be enough.

In the following chapters a broad range of possible special workplace learning initiatives will be described, examined and discussed, beginning with more traditional initiatives in the form of instruction, tutorials, exchange of experience, and the like, followed by different counselling-oriented initiatives and then, subsequently, by initiatives that transcend employees' current job situations. Finally, the last part of the book considers learning arrangements that combine formal learning in courses and institutions with learning at work.

Learning initiatives in connection with daily work

Instruction and initial guidance

The most common and least formalised form of goal-oriented learning in the workplace takes place through the instruction that workers and employees receive from colleagues, superiors or external instructors or teachers concerning the different activities involved in the work. Instruction delivered by a co-worker of the same position but perhaps with more experience can often take place in a rather unstructured fashion on the basis of the problems that arise in daily work. However, it can also be more formalised, for instance when a new employee more or less systematically is shown the ropes, when a supplier of a new machine sends an agent to the workplace to provide instruction, when an employee takes over a new function, or when, for instance, a shop foreman, engineer or internal computer operator gives instruction to rank and file employees.

As regards learning, instruction, initial guidance by co-workers and other similar forms of training are apparently relatively unproblematic. It is, as a rule, immediately apparent what is to be learned and why. However, not everyone is a good teacher. For example, those who teach computer skills may not be able to provide a comprehensible explanation of what takes place and why users are supposed to do certain things. In addition, learners may have a personal dislike of, or scepticism towards, their teacher, for instance if the teacher is a superior. On-the-job training may also have the effect of passing on misunderstandings, bad habits, unintended perceptions and inappropriate attitudes. It is essentially a conservative form of learning, and may not meet the need for modernisation and new development that could be relevant from the perspective of both the workplace and the employee.

Often, when training a new employee in a particular function or a new technology, some of these less fortunate consequences can be avoided by making the instruction more formal. This may, for instance, assume the form of a more detailed training plan with a time schedule and indication of different instructors, written material or computer programs to support the instruction, or a subsequent evaluation or other form of ascertaining whether the learning intended has actually taken place.

Instruction and initial guidance by co-workers not only constitute cognitive, professional learning, but to a large degree also contribute to the general socialisation process, for instance with respect to the language of the workplace, attitudes and behaviour vis-à-vis colleagues of the same or superior rank, what is emphasised and similar general matters.

Generally, these forms of learning have the great advantage that they are relatively naturally absorbed into daily work. This makes it possible to avoid the experience of 'going back to school' or feeling denigrated by being defined as a 'trainee' (see Boud 2003; Illeris 2003); feelings of inferiority and bad experiences in school have often been known to provoke defensive reactions, not least among low-skilled employees, whose school experience is often largely negative.

On the other hand, these types of learning can be relatively limited, especially at the practical-technical level. A good instructor who has sufficient time may take things a bit further, for instance by placing the instruction in a larger context, process-wise in relation to other work activities, structurally in relation to what is special and important about the subject with which the instruction is concerned, socially by pointing out ways in which the new learning can become part of the interaction in the workplace, and from a historical-societal perspective by touching on the background of the subject of the instruction, why this new subject has emerged, and what future perspectives may be involved.

However, there is rarely time for or interest in these things, and the more common scenario is that the practical-technical learning is embedded in communication of the existing workplace culture. This may in and of itself be reasonable and appropriate for addressing immediate concerns, but it also, as previously mentioned, offers the opportunity to perpetuate misapprehensions and prejudice. In relation to competence development short instructions usually have no room for special consideration of the learners' commitment and interests, and neither for objections, discussions or reflection.

As a rule, instruction and initial guidance by co-workers will be something employees appreciate, and they prefer to have exhaustive and broad instruction. There is a well-known tendency that the less formalised education employees have, the more they think that learning that is integrated in the work is by far the best and most important form of learning, and at a general level it is important for these forms of training that there is a good learning environment in the workplace, and that learning does not serve as a limited and constricted function. However, if learning is to reach further in its perspective in the direction of competence development, instruction, initial guidance by co-workers and other similar forms soon become too limited in the possibilities they offer.

Meetings, seminars, internal courses, etc.

Another common way to learn as part of daily work is through meetings and other formalised forms of interaction within the framework of the workplace. The primary aim of such meetings is rarely to convey learning to the participants, but there is an exchange of information, various matters are discussed, plans and agreements are made, and the totality of this is that a considerable amount of learning actually takes place. Such learning is promoted if the meeting is well structured, the atmosphere is informal and focused, information is communicated in a clear and friendly manner, and first and foremost the participants are given the opportunity for stating their views and exchanging viewpoints and ideas concerning the issues raised. More often, however, meetings have an entirely different agenda concerned with efficient exchange of information or views or making necessary decisions, with the result that existing perception patterns are reinforced and learners experience boredom when the same people just say the same things they usually say.

Meetings structured specifically for the purpose of learning with specific goals will usually be called seminars, internal courses, internal training, education, or similar. These may be one-off events based around a particular topic, or a series of meetings or multiple sessions or seminars may constitute a coherent course of learning.

Internal training can have many advantages as regards learning. It will, as a rule, be concerned with matters in which the participants have an immediate interest and which they need to learn, something that involves their experience. At the same time, it provides the opportunity for learners to get to know each other, perhaps see each other from new angles, and to benefit from other participants' contributions. There may be especially good learning opportunities if the activities involve exchange of knowledge and ideas, problem-solving or planning, in which all participants feel involved in a positive way.

The decisive factor for learning in such internal educational activities is that participants can clearly relate the activities to their daily work. It is specifically the opportunity to establish this connection clearly and directly that is the greatest advantage of internal learning; clearly there are also good opportunities for competence development. Even when learning takes the form of tuition, it is experienced as less school-like when it takes place in the familiar and, as a rule, more secure environment of the workplace, and when the teacher or instructor is a colleague or another employee in the organisation.

The relevance to daily work can be reinforced if the course involves practical tasks or projects that may be solved in the workplace and as part of the normal functions of the employee or employee group. In the case of an extensive course with multiple sessions, a helpful structure is to alternate between course tutorials and practical work in the form of assignments or projects to be completed between sessions. Such activities may range from limited assignments to be completed on an individual basis and defined entirely or partially by the employee him- or herself to extended group projects with the teachers acting as counsellors.

In this connection, it should not be forgotten that many employees learn a great deal by being placed in the role of teacher or instructor. In some workplaces, it is possible to set a goal of all employees taking their turn training others, and this offers very powerful learning opportunities, both professionally and personally. In any event, although the teacher may perhaps not acquire much new professional knowledge, having to teach others results in a clearer professional understanding and structuring, while having to organise and be responsible for the course is for many a great personal challenge from which they can learn a great deal – and it will almost inevitably be the case that the learning has the quality of competence development.

Of course, internal training courses are likely to experience the same problems that occur in other educational contexts, but which in some cases can be magnified in an internal environment. For example, the teacher's competence may be inadequate to the task, professionally, pedagogically or organisationally, and if this inadequacy is exposed in front of a group of colleagues, it is even more embarrassing than it would be in an educational institution, because the fiasco lives on in the internal relations. Thus, organisations should not 'commandeer' employees for internal teaching duty, but rather seek to 'build them up' by offering them support and good advice, and possibly by giving them the chance to act as a supporting teacher before they are charged with complete responsibility for teaching.

A compromise between internal and external training may be holding seminars and courses outside the workplace, for instance at a training facility. This can have several advantages. Not only do employees get the opportunity to go away together, ideally to somewhere new and attractive, and put some distance between themselves and the workplace, but ties with daily work become weaker and, indeed, the course may assume the character of an isolated experience without any direct connection with the daily work. Therefore, there is reason to be highly conscious of where the training is to take place and why, if the situation offers a choice.

In general, there are many good reasons for preferring an emphasis on internal training. It can strengthen both professional and the social learning as well as interaction among employees, it is less likely to be associated with a feeling of going back to school and, when it takes place in the workplace, participants will to a higher degree than in the case of external training psychologically connect it with the functions and activities of their work.

In organisations with many low-skilled workers and employees, it is also possible to arrange internal courses on more general subjects, for instance reading and writing, mathematics or computer skills, and thereby to achieve some of the advantages offered by having training take place in the workplace.

ICT-mediated learning processes

Many workplace learning initiatives that have traditionally taken the form of instruction or courses, as described in the two previous sections, are today delivered as various kinds of ICT-mediated learning. This may often be entirely appropriate; for instance, a good video can often be very useful and has the advantage that it can be viewed several times as the need arises. However, as already mentioned in Chapter 6, certain special factors apply when ICT is used in connection with workplace learning. Here I shall review some of these factors as they seem to apply in connection with the use of learning/training-oriented programmes.

An obvious advantage that these programmes have is that they can be administered at precisely the time when the individual employee or group has the need. However, this can also be a disadvantage, because there is then no specific time when it has been determined that it must be done. The example taken from the Swedish automotive and forest industries referred to in Chapter 6 (Thång and Wärvik 2004) shows that it is not enough just to have available computers loaded with relevant training programs ready for use when both the need is urgent and time can be freed up from other work. Experience shows that such facilities are used to only a very modest extent because this form of training presupposes a level of motivation that does not exist as a matter of course (as is also true of ICT-mediated training in contexts outside working life).

Switching on a computer and opening a training program 'off one's own bat', so to speak, i.e. when the time is available and the urge arises, is in practice a rare occurrence indeed. Volmerg et al. (1986) have described how we (almost) all try to make small pauses and breathing spaces in our work in order to establish small islands of 'living space' in the midst of 'system space', that is, in order to avoid being consumed by activities determined by others. So the individual is, as a rule, in sore need of any pauses that might arise and allow the pursuit of something other than work-oriented learning, and such pauses are already likely to be rare because of work intensification and work rationalisation.

However, the more fundamental problem with most computer training programs is that they are based on the principle of transfer of knowledge, rather than building understanding, i.e. considering the learning process as a construction (see, for example, Illeris 2007). This approach often results in programs that are stunningly boring and learning that is highly fragmented. Thus, it is not sufficient just to make available a series of computer training programs. A number of other factors must be in place at the same time before expectations for good results can be justified.

First, ICT must generally be conceived as an element in the work environment, that is, that all the constituent elements of the Åberg and Svensson model (Figure 6.1) must be in place; as described by Thång and Wärvik (2004), setting up a computer room and acquiring a number of software programs and then relying on the employees to do the rest is not a viable approach. Companies must design a structured situation that produces the commitment of the employees.

Second, there is the urgent question of which types of programs can be used for what purpose in these contexts. There *are* clearly many situations in which an instruction program can demonstrate precisely what to do in a specific context and no more. However, there are also, and as a rule far more often than many imagine, a multitude of learning and teaching contexts in which the participants need live interaction, two-way or network communication, and there are programs that are designed to provoke reflection and facilitate complex problem-solving.

For more than half a century, e-learning possibilities have developed from simple training programs to virtual learning environments. I will not go into detail here, but merely point out that, if ICT-mediated workplace learning is to live up to the great expectations frequently placed on it, then both the environmental and the design conditions must be right, and this seems to be the case today in only a small number of more advanced and experimental projects.

There are still an insufficient number of documented cases of the technology being used in such a way in practice for researchers to form a more general overview of what can actually be done with it on a broader scale. However, Åberg and Svensson's (2004) example can give us an idea about what is possible, and development will probably proceed rapidly.

Other important arguments in favour of ICT are that the more impersonal framework in many cases can make it easier for relatively low-skilled learners to avail themselves of training without exposing their weaknesses; also that there are good possibilities for differentiating training based on the prior qualifications and learning targets of the individual participant. This, however, applies only to learning courses that are structured as individual work or self-instructing training.

More generally, ICT-mediated learning processes are characterised by a high degree of transparency, that is, it is very easy to monitor the actions of learners. Furthermore, ICT support through network learning offers the opportunity for making a learning course a mixture of school-based tuition and workplace learning, for instance by combining situated, experience-based and problem-oriented material with general knowledge, distance and reflection. However, these forms of learning processes have usually presupposed a high degree of written activity. For those who have problems with reading and writing, this predominance of writing can be a serious problem. But the great emphasis on written activity/proficiency in relation to ICT can probably be considered a transitory phenomenon. ICT is precisely the possibility needed for developing educational material and communication and cooperation systems which in many different ways exploit the possibilities offered by combinations of colour, sound, images, speech, dynamic graphics and various degrees of interactivity.

ICT can contribute to mediating learning processes in new ways. For this to add new value and opportunities in the work situation, technological innovations must be combined with didactic and technological insight, even at the level of the very design of the ICT system.

Learning through conversations and interviews

Naturally, much workplace learning takes place through all the many informal conversations employees have in most workplaces, both directly in connection with work and in casual and more planned breaks, and generally whenever people meet. However, such conversations can also be employed systematically and thus encourage a more structured use of one of the most common, social and versatile ways in which to learn, which everybody knows and engages in.

In many workplaces this is done today first and foremost through set employee interviews or staff development interviews (SDIs). It should, however, be kept in mind that these interviews are primarily concerned not with learning but with the employee's situation and future in the workplace more generally, and that they have the status of a formal interview between an employee and his or her immediate superior, and the employee is therefore often tense and prepared for more negotiation than for learning.

However, in terms of learning, an advantage of SDIs is that they are, or should be, regular events, and ones for which both employee and manager are well prepared, for instance having previously completed a structured questionnaire. In addition, the manager will, or should, be listening and willing to enter into a dialogue about the employee's relationship with his or her work, and the interview should result in a written conclusion agreed by the employee and superior. All these factors help the employee to reflect thoroughly on his or her work situation, and therefore the employee should have more opportunity for relevant learning following the interview.

SDIs often also result in agreements that the employee should undertake a course or other kind of learning, but experience shows that it is far from certain that such agreements are actually implemented. There may be several reasons for this, including the identified courses being no longer available or available only in places and at times that are unsuitable. It may also be the case that the employee or his or her superior does not think that the time may be spared in practice or it can be because all requests for training are administered by a central training department that assesses them on the basis of some other, less person-oriented rationale, as part of a comprehensive and more strategically reasoned training plan.

Another and more widespread type of exchange from which one can learn much, but which is seldom formalised, is conversations between colleagues; systematising such conversations could unleash immense untapped potential. But this must be done to only a limited extent, because it is a kind of colonisation of the informal collegiality that has great significance for the social and cultural working environment. However, just as SDIs typically take place once a year, it might be possible to arrange annual systematic employee conversations, in which the employees talk to one another in pairs about questions of the same type as addressed in SDIs. The advantage is, of course, that, provided the pairs are appropriate combinations, there can be much more openness and creativity in these conversations because the participants are not subject to the same degree of 'vested interest'.

Because such conversations constitute a somewhat unknown approach, I shall here make a brief reference to a concrete example, i.e. the 'mutual interview about work', which was implemented by a Danish company in connection with a development project in public utility corporations. In this case, employee conversations were subject to a set of simple rules: pairs of employees interviewed each other for a maximum of 30 minutes using a set of prescribed questions. It was permissible to ask more questions, but the given questions *had* to be asked. The interviewer was allowed only to ask questions and not to make comments or evaluate the answers. The interviewer then presented the interviewee's answers in a plenary session. Interviewees were allowed to refuse to answer or to refuse to allow an answer to be quoted in the plenum or passed on to management (Clematide and Jørgensen 2003, p. 43).

In this example, the interviews thus formed part of a whole-day session for the employee group, and were used as input for a common discussion. Learning was promoted first by having the employees reflect and clarify their thoughts on particular issues of relevance to work, and subsequently by a common discussion that could lead to individual or joint development proposals.

In terms of learning, the formalised conversations and interviews described here have the great advantage of ensuring that everybody gets the chance to give their thoughts based on their own work conditions and experience and that there is some form of recapitulation of answers. The latter is important in terms of learning, because it increases the likelihood that the replies will result in individual or shared reflection and thereby open up the possibility of genuine competence development.

History workshops and future workshops

Workshops are meetings or seminars where the participants work together on a specific subject or issue. The concentration and focus implicit in this provide good opportunities for learning. If such a workshop is held internally in the company for an employee group, the subject or issue will most often be closely associated with the contents of the work or its organisation, and learning will probably be predominantly of a professional character. It may be done in an infinite number of ways, and the approach chosen will depend to a large degree on the subject of the workshop. However, a workshop can also be organised with learning in relation to the participants' attitude to the work or the workplace as the primary aim. In what follows, I shall go into a little more detail about two types of workshops that are important learning initiatives but which are not widely known and infrequently utilised. These are history workshops and future workshops.

History workshops take as their point of departure participants' common reconstruction of the history of the company or the workplace as the employees experienced it, and which they themselves to a greater or lesser extent have been part of. For employees who have been with the company for a long time, this can be an occasion for reliving experiences and reflecting. More recent employees can also gain a more systematic insight into the reasons why things are set up and function as they currently experience them. However, history workshops can also be the basis for looking forward on the background of earlier experience and may, for instance, be particularly important when the workforce is undergoing a generation shift, helping to avoid the risk that much, more or less tacit, knowledge and unformulated insight will be lost.

One way to structure such a history workshop is described in Clematide and Jørgensen (2003, p. 33ff.). The day starts with an introductory account of what is going to happen and the rules of the game. The participants are then given 'event cards', and asked to fill these in with brief descriptions of what they consider important events in the history of the company and the year when the event in question took place. These cards are then pegged on a line in chronological order, on which cards marking 'milestones' and their appropriate year may already have been placed. As each employee pins up the card, he or she gives a brief narrative about the event in question. Subsequently, the cards are grouped together into historical periods and thematic groups that can be used as bases for discussions about might happen in relation to these themes in the future. The general aim is thus that the employees, on the basis of their own experiences, become more conscious of key issues in the company in question and discuss them in a forward-looking perspective.

The future workshop approach, originally developed and described by Austrians Robert Jungk and Norbert Müllert (1981), is probably slightly better known and more commonly practised than the history workshop. It is more directly forward-looking and has, when used in workplaces, the prerequisite that both management and employees accept that the employees can in this way gain influence on the company's or organisation's future strategies. The following summary is based on Signe Berri's Danish text (Berri 2002).

A future workshop can be completed in a single day, but works better when it takes place over two or three days. One or two workshop leaders are needed to chair the proceedings, but it is the participants alone who produce the contents.

The workshop begins with an *introduction phase,* during which the aims and form of the proceedings are explained, and a number of practical rules are laid down. The most important rule is that participants should formulate statements in terms of keywords and refrain from adopting either a positive or a negative standpoint. Everything that springs to participants' minds is important, whether large or small, abstract or concrete, and everything is written on large sheets of papers pinned to the walls. It is strictly forbidden to criticise.

Then follows a *criticism phase,* during which the participants first take turns to suggest, and then contribute freely, keywords that encapsulate all the criticism they can think of concerning the subject under review. When the list is considered exhaustive, the keywords that refer to identical matters are consolidated, and each participant marks the three most important keywords so as to create a picture of what is generally considered the most important issues. Finally, the participants consolidate the keywords into themes of criticism, and in groups they produce critical images of the individual themes, so as to give them a sense of expression.

The next phase is the *utopia phase.* It starts by asking the groups to turn their critical image into a utopian vision, a wishful dream not constrained by current conditions. Then follows a round of producing keywords similar to the criticism phase, but the topic now is the limitless utopian vision. Once again the most important contributions are marked, and the participants formulate utopian themes that the groups rework into specific utopias about the imagined future.

Then comes the *realisation phase,* the longest phase in the process. It begins with a sharpening of the utopian themes based on the participants' answers to some open critical questions from the facilitators. After this, the groups formulate possible courses of action in relation to the individual themes. How can they be realised? What can be done first? The proposed courses of possible action are presented in plenum, and concrete action is discussed, planned and distributed among the participants. Processes are set in motion, and a follow-up meeting is agreed upon. After this, participants clear up the facility together and evaluate.

The future workshop thus moves from criticism of existing conditions via an imagined vision of the future to the initiation of an active process to move ahead in the direction the participants want to go. This can be a very strong and committing process. Participants may also find it frustrating when, during and after the workshop, they discover how difficult it is to change things. In terms of learning, the processes aimed at are to a high degree accommodative and possibly transformative, and a successful future workshop is something that leaves a lasting impression.

The process is based on radical democracy. Everybody is included and there are no demands of a character that requires special prior qualifications; everybody can join. However, it makes no sense to open up such processes if in reality the organisation is inadequate to support such a democratic approach.

Experience groups and internal networks

Whereas history and future workshops invite and build on great personal and emotional commitment, so-called experience groups and internal networks are generally more traditional approaches, in which the exchange of experience is largely limited to professional and organisational matters.

Experience groups typically comprise people with different types of experience but a shared field of interest. The term is often used with reference to groups comprising participants from different organisations who get together to exchange and share their experience. However, in larger organisations a sufficiently diverse range of experience may be found in various departments or groupings. The groups can be more or less formal in their organisation and practice, ranging from tightly organised and focused to the entirely informal and almost social framework. The groups can also be formed around a specific and possibly temporary issue, but they are most often broader in their outlook and without time limitations.

'Internal networks' is a more open term that may refer to limited groups similar to the experience groups, but is also used with reference to the patterns of informal contacts found in every organisation and to groups that, for instance, through a dedicated shared e-mail address keep each other mutually informed about various matters in and around the organisation.

Depending on the character of these organisations, they can to varying degrees provide the framework for relevant work-oriented learning. Especially for experience groups with a relatively firm organisation, for instance with a set frequency of meetings and clear agendas, the exchange of experience can be a significant source of learning, and it is precisely the participants' different backgrounds but common field of interest that enable the development of a broader understanding of the area. The groups may also invite guests who can contribute specific input of interest, but which cannot be obtained from among the ranks of its own members.

Most often, the members of such groups and networks participate because they possess a specific competence or position that others may benefit from sharing in. Thus, there is also a strong tendency for their members to be middle or top-level leaders, whereas lower-level and low-skilled employees are rarely included.

Conclusion and perspectives

In the above I have reviewed a number of different initiatives that may be used in workplaces to create and promote learning. The list is far from exhaustive, but I have included the types of initiatives that are most widespread, and some that I find particularly interesting, both in themselves and to substantiate an understanding of where the various activities can be used. Furthermore, I have not here included initiatives that have the character of guidance, or which to a significant degree aim further than the participants' current work functions and their further development, as these types of initiatives will be dealt with in the following chapters.

The perspectives of approaches that can be used in connection with learning initiatives in workplaces are thus very open. There are many possibilities and highly diverse opportunities. However, if the aim is appropriate and effective learning that goes beyond upgrading purely technical skills, then the learning process should satisfy certain general criteria, and this is certainly the case if the learning is to have any chance of being described as competence development. These criteria can be divided into four groups.

First, the approach must call for participant *activity* and *interaction*. It is only when the participants play an active role and indulge in exchange and cooperation that the advantages of learning taking place in the workplace are realised in earnest. This applies particularly to the low-skilled, who have little inclination to read books, and most of whom have had a discouraging experience with school-based learning, and who therefore, for these reasons, benefit particularly from learning in practice. As is also shown by the learning model in Chapter 4, it is only when employees are engaged in extension of their participation in work practice and get the opportunity to process this into experience and involve their work identity that the particular possibilities offered by workplace learning are achieved to their maximum extent.

Second, the approach must incorporate special *challenges*. There must be elements that go beyond business as usual while addressing problems relevant to employees' working life. It is necessary to gain commitment if the result is to be change or development. And the challenges and problems must not be limited to areas that are narrowly technical or immediately efficiency promoting. It is only when such matters are given full consideration, and particularly as they find expression and have an impact on the employees' work situation, that the proceedings open up the opportunity for competence development. In this regard, the workplace can offer special possibilities for providing learning for the low-skilled, who as a rule feel better when learning takes its point of departure in practice.

Third, the arrangement must offer the individual room and encouragement as well as shared *reflection,* that is, the time and opportunity for thinking about and processing the input which the various learning initiatives communicate, and thus arriving at a more coherent understanding. Shared reflection has a special mission here because it is easier to push reflection aside when one is alone than when it is being discussed with others, and because it can promote learning to experience how others react to the matters in question. And, again, the shared element is especially important for the low-skilled.

Fourth and last, it is important that learning has the possibility of generating or creating *consequences*. This is straightforward when the learning involves the acquisition of specific practical qualifications. But learning something new has no perspective if the new knowledge and skills cannot be put into practice. In addition, and more generally, it is important for employees' personal development that they are given the opportunity to use their new understanding and changed attitudes and methods in practical work. For this to happen, employees need a degree of freedom; it cannot take place if all activity is subjected to a tight matrix of functions and procedures. Neither an organisation nor its employees will benefit from investment in learning if what is learned cannot find expression.

The question of which learning initiatives to use must thus always be linked to the question of how the various initiatives are to and can be put into practice, and the four key criteria I have outlined here can provide a guideline for what must especially be emphasised.

Sparring and support schemes

Guided learning

Learning through various types of sparring and support for individual employees or groups of employees is a special form of workplace learning that takes place on a larger scale than the types of learning dealt with in the previous chapters. This type of learning is all about some kind of guidance, and in this first section this type of learning activity will be taken up in general and as an introduction to various more specific types of guidance in the following sections.

As the starting point I shall describe the ambitious attempt to set up a curriculum for workplace learning which has been made by Australian Stephen Billett (2001). On the basis of many years of well-documented experimentation and development work in many different trades, it is Billett's experience that guided learning is in general the most appropriate type and an absolutely key element of workplace learning.

For Billett, guided learning is something different from, and more than, co-worker training. It may often include technical instruction, but the important thing is that such instruction is placed and carried out on the basis of consideration of the learner's situation, i.e. is fitted in as an element of a more general learning process, and this process must in a holistic, well-planned and organised way encompass all the professional and the social elements of the work. Guided learning is conscious and goal-directed support for learners to enable them to get through the whole process which – in the sense of Lave and Wenger – leads them from being new and peripherally placed to being full participants in a community of practice (Lave and Wenger 1991; Billett 2001, p. 106).

Billett distinguishes between guided learning, described as support from an experienced co-worker during a process of training, and supervision, which is more in the nature of monitoring or control. It is true that a very important element of guided learning is that the guide should be professionally qualified and well integrated in the work, while the learner starts the process in a much weaker and more marginal position. But it is decisive that the relationship between the two is equal and friendly. Billett, therefore, contends that the way in which the guide is selected is very important:

Guides should:

- have expertise in the work area – be an expert other (can handle novel problems) and possess work-related knowledge to share with learners (must be viewed as being credible);
- understand the goals for performance – understand what is required for successful performance in the workplace;
- value guided learning – see a need for it and for the knowledge to be learnt by learners;
- have willingness to share knowledge with learners; and
- be a guide for learners rather than a teacher (making learners do the thinking and acting).

(Billett 2001, p. 189)

According to Billett, this approach works best if the learner chooses his or her own guide, but he acknowledges that this is not always acceptable to management. However, at the very least the learner should be able to freely express an opinion on the appointed guide, because, if learner and guide do not get on well, a reasonable learning process seldom gets under way.

In general, Billett says that

the roles of the expert other in the workplace are:

- securing access to experiences – determining readiness, sequencing of experiences and providing support for access;
- guarding against the learning of knowledge that is inappropriate – monitoring learners' experiences and outcomes;
- providing access to knowledge that is difficult to learn about – assisting access to knowledge that is hidden or opaque, or requires assistance to learn; and
- developing procedures through close interactions.

(Billett 2001, p. 117)

All of this is to take place through a gradual process of development managed in close interaction between the guide and the learner. Both parties are responsible for engaging in an interaction that promotes cooperative relations. In addition, there should be clear targets and expectations, and both the guide and the learner should know what they are trying to achieve and should be involved in deciding what the goals are. It is also important that the learner has on-going access to the guide, through both regular meetings and joint practical activities, and the culture and practice of the workplace must be open so that development processes such as guided learning form a natural part of it.

Billett thus sets up very large, ideal requirements concerning support from an experienced co-worker. It must be carefully planned and conducted with thoroughness, openness, preparation and responsibility by both parties. When this is the case the way is open for workplace learning that is generally the most appropriate, precisely because it builds on the qualities that are a consequence of learning being integrated in the daily work. Not least for low-skilled employees with a brief vocational training or none at all, and often also a sceptical attitude towards anything that reminds them of their schooldays, learning by means of guided learning is, in Billett's opinion, the best and most natural form of workplace learning, if the conditions are otherwise in order and it is conducted with the engagement of both parties.

At the same time, however, Billett is aware that there are also important learning elements of a theoretical and more general nature that are better learned in other contexts, usually outside the workplace, and it should be stressed that Billett's description concerns only the type of guided learning in which a more experienced employee guides a less experienced and, as a rule, new colleague.

Another possibility that may be beneficial is when employees who are on an equal level and who have related work areas follow each other's work for a period and provide mutual guidance and sparring. In this case also it is vital that the chemistry between the two is good, and it is best if they have chosen each other, or at least have had the possibility of expressing an opinion on the 'relationship', and that there is a prior agreement to which both are committed. If this is the case, then this can be a particularly instructive way of working. As mentioned earlier, one learns at least as much by being the one who 'gives' as by being the one who 'receives', and a successful period with mutual guidance can very easily be continued in a lengthy dialogue relationship, which could even develop into an internal network.

Mentoring schemes

Mentoring is closely related to collegiate guided learning. It also involves a more experienced guide supporting a less experienced employee, but, whereas guided learning is limited to relations between colleagues in a work context, mentoring can also be a supportive function in connection with education.

In general, mentoring may be defined as an interactive process of guidance and development between two parties and based on regular contact. The *mentor*, using his or her knowledge, skills and experience, contributes to the development of and supports the less experienced party, the *mentee,* in working towards his or her goals (Cohen and Galbraith 1995).

The mentor concept has its origin in Greek mythology. Mentor was Ulysses' trusted friend. Before Ulysses left for the Trojan wars, he asked Mentor to remain at home and take care of his son, Telemachus. In the myth, Mentor is wisdom personified, through whom the goddess Athena speaks, and it is his job to be Telemachus' teacher, guide, role model and father figure, so that when the time comes he will be able to take Ulysses' place. Thus, Mentor is somebody who contributes to a young person's growth and consciousness through protection and challenge. The mentor figure is connected with a transition phase, with personal growth and with the formation of identity (Carruthers 1993).

In modern parlance, a mentor is a person who guides, supports and challenges the mentee with the aim of reaching a goal. This is thus an *asymmetrical* relationship, where the more experienced mentor, by virtue of his or her wisdom and professional overview – not status, power or authority – supports and challenges the mentee in a process that is based on the mentee's gradual growth and liberation from the mentor towards equality. At the same time, the relationship is *formal* in the sense that mentor and mentee have been appointed to each other, in contrast to an informal relationship between partners who have chosen one another.

Formal mentoring can, for example, be established through a training department as part of a development process in an organisation. It is, naturally, crucial here that the parties accept one another. Formal mentoring often encompasses a lower degree of spontaneity and enthusiasm than guided learning, but, on the other hand, it is ensured through institutionalisation that the process is in fact implemented and that there is backing for the scheme in the organisation (Orpen 1997).

In the mentoring model of the myth, the emphasis is on the mentee's development and the mentor's benefit and development is without importance. However, if the scheme proceeds appropriately, experience indicates that both parties benefit from the joint process. Often by virtue of his or her position, knowledge and experience, the mentor will have access to key resources and information in the organisation, and the mentee will usually be an employee who is expected to have career potential. Therefore, the mentor will also feel satisfaction when the mentee develops to the benefit of the organisation; at the same time both become more aware of how they can communicate professional knowledge (Billett 2003). In addition, the mentor should be qualified with respect to tools and strategies to ask, explain and reflect, which is not something one automatically masters just because one is experienced in the job (Billett 2000).

The success and effect of a mentoring scheme is conditioned in particular by the mentor's understanding and development of the function as well as the possibilities and backing the mentor has in the organisation. Frequent contact between the parties and psychological support and attention help to strengthen the mentee's professional self-confidence and motivation. The mentor must be open, listen and question, and not dictate, judge or censure. It is about creating frames for reflection and facilitating learning processes on the basis of the mentee's perspective and vision concerning objectives and the future (Cohen and Galbraith 1995).

It may be said in general that the traditional mentoring model has its place in an organisation that seeks stability. It is a power–dependency relationship, the aim of which is to pass on established values and ideas from a powerful employee to one who is less powerful. Against this background, some critics have recommended that mentoring between equal parties should be established (Darwin

2000) or, more radically, that the one-to-one relation should be dissolved within a network structure (Pedersen 2004).

Mentoring can also provide support in connection with a course of training for, for example, low-skilled workers who experience the world of education as foreign to them. In this situation the mentor can help to introduce the mentee into the work and to navigate between the daily challenges, and at the same time positive attention and constructive feedback can strengthen the mentee's motivation to train.

What is crucial is that the mentoring takes place from the learner's perspective. Thus, the mentor must be conscious of his or her contribution, without taking over or dictating the learner's targets. To put it metaphorically, the mentee is on a journey together with his or her mentor, and not the reverse.

Coaching

If mentoring was the focus of workplace development in the 1990s, today the issue of coaching seems to be more to the fore, and often it goes far beyond learning, extending in the direction of career support and promotion. When the term 'coaching' is used in connection with counselling and learning, as a rule the emphasis is on some special conditions, even though the difference in relation to guided learning and mentoring is rather vague.

A coach is somebody between a trainer and a counsellor, and there are very many and quite different definitions of the concept. American Timothy Gallwey, who is usually regarded as the founder of the modern movement of coaching, has proposed the following short and essential formulation: 'Coaching is unlocking a person's potential to maximise their own performance. It is helping them to learn rather than teaching them' (Timothy Gallwey, after Whitmore 1996, p. 8).

But perhaps the aspirations of coaching today are better described by British professor and coaching psychologist Stephen Palmer in his preface to a recent broad presentation of the topic:

> Around the world, coaching has made in-roads into the personal and professional development arenas that were once the exclusive domain of therapists, consultants and trainers. [...] Coaching brings a greater emphasis on proactive approaches, real-time change, and long-term gains. As such, qualified coaches and multidisciplinary coaching teams are increasingly being called to enhance the levels of empowerment, development and performance in organizations and the broader society.
>
> (Palmer 2008, p. xvii)

The role of a coach may thus vary from that of a plain career guide to a psychotherapist, but in relation to workplace learning it can usually be described as a kind of mixture of an inspirer, a sparring partner and perhaps sometimes also a midwife. At any rate, it is decisive that it should not be someone who functions as a superior or as the one who has the solution to everything – and it is in these areas that coaching often becomes problematic because hidden power structures are not observed and recognised (Nitschke 2008).

As a rule, although the coach will usually be an expert in the area in question, this is not essential: the important thing is that coaches enable coachees to make progress. It is a matter of providing support and encouragement, of demonstrating that one believes it can be done, of giving good advice without taking control, of supporting the person's self-confidence and bringing out the best in him or her. (Much of this also applies to guided learning or mentoring , but the term 'coaching' is different by deliberately placing a strong and one-sided emphasis on these functions.)

The concept was originally developed in connection with competitive sport, not least through Tim Gallwey's almost legendary books *The Inner Game of Tennis*, *Inner Skiing* and *The Inner Game of Golf* (Gallwey 1975, 1979; Gallwey and Kriegel 1977). Today, coaching is particularly prevalent in team sport, when its aim is to get a team to function optimally and develop a spirit of solidarity without limiting individual performance.

Coaching as a means of workplace learning has, as mentioned, become very widespread in recent years, especially in connection with the development of selected employees' special abilities and talents; the term would rarely be used in connection with ordinary workplace learning for ordinary groups of employees. There must be a reason for an expert making a special effort in relation to a single employee or a small group of employees – an important need and confidence in the person(s) in question being able to do the job.

Thus, I am not going to dwell further on the concept here, but merely refer to the abundant literature devoted to this field (for example Drake *et al.* 2008).

Ambassadors, super-users and gardeners

The terms 'ambassadors', 'super-users' and 'gardeners' all came into being with the introduction of information and communication technology. In some companies, individuals so described are appointed as part of a strategy for introducing and supporting ICT applications in the workplace; in other cases individuals have 'appointed' themselves to the roles, or they have 'arisen' and functioned more or less informally as support persons or counsellors on the basis of their engagement.

The primary function of such ICT counsellors is to support users in their use of the technology in recognition of the fact that the integration and application of ICT is not just a technical problem, but also has a great deal to do with organisational change and learning. It is most important that ICT counsellors:

- are locally rooted (in contrast to a central IT support unit, for example), so that they are situated in the midst of those who are likely to need support and, above all, that they have insight into the working area concerned, which gives a greater deal of security in the counselling (Åsand *et al.* 2004);

- are not merely technical experts but distinguish themselves by their communicative competence, especially their ability to speak several 'languages', i.e. they can talk to technicians about technical problems and become familiar with new hardware and software as well as speaking the professional language of the users and the work domain and thus function as 'translators' (Mackay 1990);
- like to teach and find pleasure in seeing colleagues develop, in the same way as parents are proud to see their children grow up and become independent and resourceful – something that has also caused the term 'gardener' to be employed as an indication and in recognition of the fact that the individuals in question can get the users and organisation to grow (Nardi 1993; Christiansen 1997; Kanstrup 2004);
- and, finally, have a thirst for knowledge and are interested in the matters and insights they are to communicate and which give them the necessary legitimacy (Elkjær 2004).

Such ICT counsellors can have several or different functions in connection with workplace learning. In the case of the term 'ambassador', the emphasis is on their being able to promote the use of ICT (Elkjær 2004). In the case of super-users, the primary function is to support the users in applying ICT, and the focus here is primarily on learning concrete application possibilities (Åsand *et al.* 2004). The term 'gardener' introduces a further link to the communication of practice understanding, i.e. that it is not just a matter of knowledge of the concrete application but also, for example, knowledge of and opinions about ICT more generally and ICT application in the organisation (Kanstrup 2004).

Whichever term is used, it is important to remember that technologies and work practices change constantly, and the supporters will also often have a need themselves to be updated and supported, for example by entering a knowledge network with others. On the other hand, there is simultaneously a risk that they develop over time to being 'super-experts' and as a result become increasingly distant from local work practice. Some other problems may be that these types of support persons are not real experts so they may come to play a part in spreading ICT mistakes and wrong applications in the organisation (Mackay 1990) or lack the ability to step back and consider more radical changes instead of here-and-now solutions to technological problems (Bødker 2000).

These objections show how difficult it is to fulfil a function that has a foot in two camps, and at the same time points to the importance of maintaining the difficult middle position, or staying on the boundary, as Etienne Wenger has defined it in his description of 'brokers' who work to create connections between different communities of practice (Wenger 1998, p. 108 ff.).

Finally, it should also be noted that, even though these brokering functions have become topical, especially in the ICT field, conflicts also exist in other areas between technology application and the professional content of the work. Thus such brokering functions could perhaps also be used in other workplace learning areas when new developments are taking place, as they do so often nowadays.

Consultant-supported employee development

The forms of sparring and support schemes I have dealt with above mainly involve internal schemes with internal partners. It is the nature of guided learning, mentoring schemes, ambassadors, super-users and gardeners that they will normally involve different employees at the same workplace. In the case of coaching, however, the schemes can be both internal and external. This leads to the issue of working with external consultant support in connection with learning initiatives at the workplace.

Consultants are today used in very many contexts in both public and private workplaces, usually because the enterprise does not itself have the necessary knowledge and expertise to achieve the development desired, in general or in a more defined area.

There are, naturally, many different types of consultants and consultant services. For example, a consultant may be an expert in a certain area who performs a task that an enterprise cannot undertake itself and is not interested in doing so because it has only occasional need for this type of expertise. Examples include the development, maintenance and updating of ICT systems or conducting tests in connection with new appointments. In such cases, the expertise remains with the consultant; not much learning takes place at the workplace but this is not the intention.

However, in other contexts experts can be used to train managers and employees in their areas of expertise. This presupposes that, in addition to being a specialist in the field, the consultant has the ability to connect with the employees, whatever their professional qualifications and motivation. There is a risk that this type of training will fail, the most usual reason being that the expert talks over the heads of those who are supposed to be learning. Thus, this type of consultant support is in line with much other teaching in technical subjects at vocational schools, but at the same time it is aimed at a quite specific group of employees at a specific workplace and the instruction should therefore, at least to some degree, be tailor-made for the purpose.

The following will concentrate on two types of consultant support of special interest in connection with workplace learning, namely consultant assistance in relation to the learning environment of the workplace and forms of learning generally, and consultant support in relation to job-transcending learning initiatives.

External consultant support will often be appropriate if a workplace needs to evaluate or re-evaluate the manner in which a certain type of learning typically takes place, for example induction of new employees or professional upgrading or supplementary training. It can also provide advice on learning when a workplace is facing major new challenges such as a merger, changes in production workflow, installation of new production equipment, an imminent generation change or digitalisation of large sections of the administration.

In such cases, the external consultant support will primarily consist in more generally challenging and helping to change the workplace's usual ways of learning. In most workplaces, the way in which learning takes place develops over time, and changing these patterns requires a fresh look at things, which is easier to do when one comes from the outside (see, for example, Argyris and Schön 1996). This needs external consultant support within learning processes which is able to grasp the important challenges facing the particular workplace and identify the important aspects of the learning space of the workplace. Further, the support must have the capacity to evaluate what can be done and be able to challenge and expand the usual learning patterns. And if the central aim is to improve the learning possibilities, it must also be realised and accepted that the consultant support cannot be one-sided, directed only at management, but to a high degree must also be directed at and involve the groups of employees concerned.

However, not all external consultants meet these special demands, and in many cases the management of the enterprise which has hired the consultants is not really interested in making radical changes. Often both consultants and management fundamentally regard workplace learning in the same way as they regard production, i.e. as a technical matter that should be dealt with rationally in order to be run as effectively as possible and at the lowest possible expenses and costs. But learning is not a technical matter. It is a very complicated human matter, and therefore such human conditions as emotions, feelings, motivation, interest, self-esteem, social relations, aversions, resistance, defence, etc. must be taken into account. The mission of external consultants should first of all be to make allowances for all this and to make the management understand that this is necessary for a positive and satisfying result. However, many consultants do not fulfil these demands, and this is probably the main reason why Chris Argyris – one of the leading American experts in the field – after a review of literature concluded that 70 per cent or more of transformational consultant programmes in the US and Europe fail, and those programmes that succeed deal with relatively routine issues that do not involve challenging the status quo (Argyris 2000, p. 3).

These reservations apply not only to external consultants on general learning conditions and environment, but also, and even more so, to job-transcending arrangements, such as self-directed groups, projects, action learning, organisational development, external networks and internal and external job rotation. Such arrangements and changes are typically carried out in cooperation with external consultants, because it is in these cases obviously necessary to step back and distance oneself from the familiar everyday procedures and expand the horizon to encompass alternative possibilities of action. In such contexts qualified assistance from the outside is almost essential in order to become free of embedded and often unconscious habits and procedures and relate to new ideas without this being associated with hidden motives. There is an evident need for new forms of reflection that are based on development logic rather than production logic (Ellström 2004), and for double-loop rather than single-loop learning (Argyris and Schön 1996).

In such contexts the external consultant may also take on the role of process consultant, which implies, among other things, that there is mediation between different interests when the need arises, that a management-free room for reflection is made available for the employees, and an employee-free room is made abailable for the managers, to ensure that allowance is made for different perspectives, and that appropriate forms of dialogue are utilised.

In all cases in which external consultants are used, there remain associated risks. Furthermore, the particular role of mediator between different interests requires additional qualifications and skills that not all consultants, by any means, are able to offer. For instance, there is a risk that the external consultant pays more attention to the management than to the employees, or at any rate views the tasks more as sparring for the management than for the employees – after all, it is usually the managers who have hired them. Or the consultants may not be able to completely understand the unique conditions, traditions or power structures of the workplace. In any case, important changes in the basic workplace learning conditions usually imply serious organisational changes, which must be accepted and backed up by the management as well as those who are to carry through the learning processes and the changes that should be the result.

Conclusion and perspectives

In the above I have dealt with a number of different types of sparring, support and person- or group-directed guidance as procedures in the context of learning in working life. It is striking that, irrespective of what the different types are called and the nature of their special features, there is one recurring key characteristic: that the assistance must be provided at the recipient's premises, i.e. on the basis of the recipient's needs and situation. In some cases, and this is most pronounced in the case of coaching, it is this alone to which reference is made. Quite simply, coaching consists principally in helping the coachee or coachees to call on their own resources to find the way forward. It may also encompass some degree of teaching of content, but even in this case, the emphasis is on communication of content that takes place at the recipient's place of work and involves considerable personal interest and support on the part of the coach.

It is, thus, the wide-ranging individual- or group-directed personal support that constitutes the special characteristic and strength of these initiatives, as opposed to what we immediately understand by teaching, the core of which is the professional content.

There is, however, also a tendency here for these procedures to be regarded as a little 'extravagant', at least when applied to ordinary employees at shop-floor level. Coaching, in particular, and to a certain extent also mentoring schemes, are mainly used in the context of career development for employees whom the enterprise finds special reason to invest in as it is somewhat expensive for a highly qualified coach or mentor to spend a significant amount of working time supporting only one or few employees.

However, not least Stephen Billett's thorough work on guided learning shows that such schemes can to a high degree also be used widely and at all levels of the enterprise, and that they have some very key advantages concerning precisely direct, person-oriented support. What might at first seem expensive can be balanced by the possibility of establishing relevant learning more easily, more efficiently and to a greater extent on the content and personal levels through the close cooperation inherent in these modes of procedure. But as Billett also strongly emphasises, on the other hand it must be ensured that there really is cooperation, i.e. first and foremost that there exists mutual acceptance and a joint view of the goals.

Much of the learning that ordinary employees undertake by attending courses could usefully be replaced by guided learning of different types. Such schemes would enable combinations of guided learning and the gardener function to be developed. This could transfer significant parts of learning into day-to-day work, which would also greatly increase the chance of achieving genuine competence development. Not least for the low-skilled, who often find school-like initiatives difficult, this could become a relevant implementation of the possibilities referred to when one talks of learning in working life.

However, it is important to add that these methods also have a negative side, and that, at the same time as passing on the potential and experience of the workplace, they can also easily pass on limitations, bad habits and prejudices. For this reason, these procedures cannot stand alone. They must be combined with initiatives aimed at the communication of an overview and theoretical insight and with initiatives aimed at overcoming the existing and habitual state of affairs. I shall examine this more closely in the next chapter.

Job-transcending learning initiatives

Self-directed groups

The learning and guidance initiatives thus far considered have been predominantly directed at the employees' learning in relation to mastery and development of the job function they hold. This chapter will consider learning initiatives whose primary aim goes beyond the existing job function. This can take place in many ways, but all generally involve significant changes for the participants and thus also significant learning opportunities, even though learning is not always the primary aims of these initiatives.

Since the 1950s, it has been known that organisation of professional work in self-directed groups can, in many contexts, result in higher efficiency and greater job satisfaction than traditional organisation in individual, hierarchically organised jobs (Thorsrud and Emery 1976), although there are also examples of group organisation becoming a new routine and/or developing in ways that impose severe strain on the participants.

The first fundamental empirical research on, and the earliest development of theory of, self-directed groups were conducted at the Tavistock Institute of Human Relations in London. The research was principally carried out on the British coal-mining industry. Researchers found examples of workers organising themselves in working groups, and these groups were found to have a positive effect on, among other things, the individual worker's opportunities for personal development, general well-being and productivity. There was apparently no conflict between these elements of the work; they appeared to be realisable simultaneously.

It was fundamental to the Tavistock research that work processes were perceived to be determined by two basic factors: technology and the human/social factor, including psychological needs. This theoretical orientation was called socio-technological system theory, a designation which implies that the production of goods, services and information presupposes interaction between the social and the technological aspects as two independent systems that can be coupled and directed towards common goals (see Figure 4.1). A number of far-reaching perspectives follow from this:

- Group organisation points more generally to the possibility for development of ways to organise work that are substantially different from the traditional pyramid-shaped hierarchies.
- At the same time, it suggests the possibility of introducing 'democracy in the workplace', a possibility which in the Nordic context was implemented in two main models. In one employees gain formal representatives on the board and in the other they participate in daily work decisions (the Tavistock experience especially emphasises the latter).
- The complex thinking within socio-technical systems establishes a basis for thinking in terms of strategic models for the introduction of intentional and planned changes in the workplace.

One particularly well-known example in Scandinavia is the extensive use over many years of self-directed groups at the Swedish Volvo automobile factories (e.g. Berggren 1994; Sandberg 1995). During the 1990s, however, self-directed groups became a widespread practice in many more workplaces, including outside the industrial sector (see, for example, Procter and Mueller 2000).

Norwegian Jon Gulowsen has defined a self-directed group as a working group that is able 'to make decisions freely subject to the premise that it meets the obligations to the general system that the membership of this system imposes pursuant to the established target' (Gulowsen 1971, p. 43). Today, highly diverse types of self-directed groups with very different powers and framework conditions can be fond in different workplaces. At one extreme, there are groups that function within a narrowly defined area that is solely defined by management. At the other extreme are groups that are able to negotiate their framework conditions with management on a continuous basis. There are thus highly different degrees of self-direction within what is called self-directed groups, but it is common to them that external management control to some more or less limited extent is transferred to internal collegiate control.

The formation of self-directed groups is, of course, first and foremost an organisational change, but one of the arguments often presented in this connection is that the groups constitute an appropriate learning environment for employees. In a large number of areas, group organisation is able to promote the learning opportunities of the employees:

- Learning in groups can both increase challenges and reduce the routine element of the work, especially because it makes it easier to structure the individual jobs so that they encompass a wide spectrum of functions that are included in the working area of the group.
- Learning can take place through both individual and collective planning and problem-solving, which may include, for example, the design and implementation of experiments that provide experience and reflection that can lead to new perceptions and definitions of work functions.
- Learning can take place when employees exchange and share knowledge

and generate new knowledge through joint problem-solving and collective reflection.

- Learning is supported when individuals have the freedom to plan their activities, receive feedback and have the opportunity to reflect on the effect of their own actions.
- Learning is promoted when there is opportunity for reflection on unusual incidents at work and inclusion in development projects and processes of change.

Work in self-directed groups places new, broad demands on qualifications and competences. Often it requires more comprehensive technical and professional qualifications because the individual employee must be able to operate several different pieces of machinery or perform a wider range of work functions. In addition, there is a need for social and relational competences when work is to be performed in a field with mutual communication, cooperation, problem-solving, assistance and support and sharing of knowledge. It is also necessary to be able to see oneself and one's work functions as part of a larger context, and it calls for important personal competences such as initiative, responsibility and transparency, and value-oriented competences, e.g. being able to see oneself in new relations with colleagues and management or to relate the corporate values to one's own values.

To summarise, self-directed groups, when they function in an appropriate way and not as a new indirect form of control, constitute a learning environment that has the ability to be fruitful in two particular ways. First, they provide a framework that causes the work processes to unfold as social interaction within a group. This presents opportunities but also the need to be aware of each other, understand each other, help each other, inspect each other, coordinate activities among the group, take responsibility for larger units in the work, exchange knowledge and experience, solve problems together, etc. It becomes to a high degree learning in the form of *joint reflection in the course of the work process*.

Second, the organisation of self-directed groups sometimes, but not always, allows space and time to be set aside for *joint reflection before and after the work process,* e.g. in the form of planning and evaluation meetings. This form of reflection is not merely adaptation-oriented learning, concerned with becoming better at performing existing work routines, but is also learning through critical reflection so that things that are otherwise taken for granted, for example given structures, action patterns, norms and corporate culture, may be considered and revised.

Together these two types of joint reflection lead to learning that may often involve genuine competence development.

Projects

In Denmark in the 1970s, project work was taken up as a new work pattern, first in a number of education programmes, but eventually also in working life, as a form of organising work that is especially well suited for achieving one-off assignments within a limited period of time. In education programmes, the purpose of project work is to promote versatile, cross-discipline and problem-oriented learning in accordance with current competence needs, and this can also take place in projects in the workplace, even though it is not the primary aim in this context (Illeris 1986, 1999; Nielsen and Webb 1999).

A beneficial side-effect of project work in working life can be highly effective, relevant and up-to-date learning and competence development for employees, because learning in this context takes place in direct connection with current challenges and thus promotes precisely the learning that is most needed. However, this requires that this perspective is considered with specific goals in mind, so that the learning opportunities are acknowledged, made explicit, pursued in a systematic way, respected and appreciated, with the full support of the organisation and project management. This is, however, a relatively manageable task, because learning in projects takes place in interaction with the performance of an assignment that is to be discharged anyway (Illeris 1991).

Today, the word 'project' is considered a collective term for a number of highly diverse work activities that typically reach beyond daily work, demand cooperation across the boundaries between professional disciplines, involve several departments and often entail uncertainty or risk-taking. The scope of projects varies widely, ranging from solving a current practical problem in which many interests must be coordinated to a comprehensive project involving the entire enterprise or significant parts of it. For example, in Norway, each individual oil rig is viewed as a project that lasts from the time prospectors strike oil until the time the well runs dry and the oil rig is closed down. In major projects in particular, ordinary employees can easily experience a new form of more or less strenuous submission to changing project requirements rather than traditional hierarchical management.

Project literature distinguishes many different types of project, including negotiation projects, technical projects, product development, system development, planning project arrangements and research projects, as well as different types of project organisation: individual projects, project series, multiple projects, multi-projects and project companies (Keeling 2000). Learning opportunities in such major projects and project organisations are, of course, extensive and should be handled as an independent and equal dimension in the organisation. For instance, Ekstedt *et al.* (1999) include an extended discussion on differences in knowledge development between permanent organisations and organisations that are limited in time.

Here I shall, however, concentrate on learning opportunities in the classical form of less extensive projects, in which participants work with project groups to solve various cross-cutting assignments, i.e. groups of typically between three and 15 participants, with a limited time perspective and under conditions in which the goal is achieving the best possible result within the given framework.

Such projects are, as a rule, very goal oriented and subject to time constraints. Extraordinary performance is required, and this can teach much, but may also easily be stressful, diffuse, random and incoherent. It is therefore important that the educational goals of the projects are made clear in the same way as product requirements are made explicit, preferably jointly by the project management and employees, and it is, for example, agreed that the theoretical foundations or the overall context may be explored in more depth than is immediately necessary for the project in hand.

With respect to the composition of the project group also, it is important for exploiting the learning opportunities that planners think in broader terms than the project may immediately require. It may, for instance, in some cases be a good idea to add a few extra employees to a project with a special view to developing their competence.

It is as a rule implicit in projects as a work form that leadership is exercised in as democratic a fashion as circumstances permit, depending on the nature and scope of the project. Learning opportunities and competence development are to a large extent linked to participants being included in decisions and sharing part of the responsibility. It is also possible to appoint a project counsellor, i.e. an employee who is not a member of the project group, but who acts as external adviser with general experience in this work form and who can provide advice for the group both as regards the process and in relation to the educational goals. At the practical level, the involvement of a project counsellor is similar to that in education projects, i.e. the councillor is kept updated about the progress of the project, participates in regular meetings with the group and is on call if problems arise. However, it is crucial that everyone understands that the councillor's role is purely advisory: it is the project leader and the group who take decisions and carry the responsibility.

During the course of the project, there are many opportunities for learning. Typically, one may distinguish between the learning that takes place implicitly through participation in the project activities and particular initiatives with the explicit aim of upgrading skills. In the general busy work of a project, learning can easily be squeezed and become an overwhelming obstacle and apparently of little practical use. Thus, it is important to establish and secure some contexts that prevent the learning aspect from disintegrating.

The *starting phase* of the project is of particular importance in this connection. It will, of course, always encompass a number of initial activities, including specification of the aim and contents of the project and preliminary planning and distribution of work. However, it might also be a good idea to leave time for some professional impulses, something provocative and with the character of an overview, some input that can challenge the participants' habitual perceptions and patterns of action and open up new and perhaps more creative lines of thought. It might also be appropriate to provide an introduction to project work as a work form and allow the opportunity of mutual exchange of experience or professional orientation when people with different backgrounds are brought together. And it is important that everybody from the very start has a clear overview of the formal and informal framework that applies financially, in terms of time available, interaction, responsibility, etc., including the individual's scope for taking part in decisions and exercising influence. Finally, it might be a good idea at the outset to test the cooperation possibilities, e.g. through an initial 'pilot project' within a key constituent area of the project.

One technique that has become widespread in educational project work is the use of precise written *problem formulations*. This approach has some distinct advantages that can also be relevant for projects in working life. Problem formulation forces participants to clarify with complete precision and jointly what constitutes the problematic element in the task at hand. This also reveals possible differences between the perceptions of the various participants, and it is very important to bring these differences out in the open, have them made explicit and negotiated and, ideally, arrive at a common understanding from the beginning of the project. In interdisciplinary projects especially, participants often arrive with highly different perceptions of the problem, and this can give rise to many controversies, time-wasting and a tense and negative atmosphere. Furthermore, problem formulation can ensure that the project work is steered in the direction of dealing with and solving the actual problem with which the project is concerned.

Another approach that might be adopted from education projects is *continuous internal evaluations*. At regular, possibly predetermined, intervals, or at transition points between certain phases, the group takes time out to discuss how the work is progressing, possibly with assistance from the project counsellor, if there is one. The evaluations need not be very time-consuming, but it is important that everybody gets to contribute and that all aspects of the project are considered, including internal cooperation. With respect to learning, internal evaluations are, however, first and foremost a tool for securing the reflection that is decisive for coherent and conscious competence development (see Schön 1987).

It is also important that at the *completion of the project,* participants review and discuss as a group the outcome produced, what have been the most important gains, what may have gone wrong or could have been better, and what was learned by each individual and the group as a whole. Experience shows that this very important phase is often neglected, but it is particularly important for learning and competence development; to omit this final step would be like sowing vegetables in the garden, weeding the patch and watering the plants, and then forgetting to harvest them when the time comes.

There are, thus, some very strong learning opportunities inherent in the increased use of projects in the context of working life. There is, unfortunately, a tendency to mostly involve those employees that are already well qualified. However, it need not be so. There is a need for projects at all levels of work, and there is very often also a need for including people with practical experience at shop-floor level, so that the projects can also receive input from those who are involved in a concrete way in the practical work in the area in question.

A very large part of learning and education is concerned with motivation, and this is the main strength of project work. Projects are inherently innovative. Thus, they are, by definition, also motivating, and involve opportunities for innovative learning that is both broad and deep.

Action learning

Action learning is a work pattern that in many ways resembles project work, often including a number of more or less coherent projects, and ultimately a total restructuring of a company's organisation. However, whereas the term 'project work', at least in Denmark, often entails a relation to education-oriented projects, the term 'action learning' practically and historically originated in, and is connected to, organisational development.

The concept of action learning was first developed by Briton Reginald Revans, who was originally a nuclear physicist but abandoned this subject because he did not want to contribute to the development of nuclear bombs. During the Second World War he played a leading role in London's civil defence; later he carried out both theoretical and practical work on organisational development and management. His programme on action learning placed him in strong opposition to the Taylorist theories that dominated the field in the 1960s. For a period he had to move to the University of Brussels in order to continue his work, but he later returned to England and won great recognition. Revans formulated several definitions of action learning, the most recent with the following wording:

> Action learning is a means of development, intellectual, emotional or physical, that requires its subject, through responsible involvement in some real, complex and stressful problem, to achieve attended change sufficient to improve his observable behaviour henceforth in the problem field.
>
> (Revans 1982, pp. 626–627)

The key element of action learning is thus that learning, similar to what is the case in project work, takes place through the processing of actual problems, i.e. problems that exist in the organisation and its functions. Revans himself had a tendency to understand this in a somewhat sweeping fashion, and expressed himself often in terms of various simple mathematical formulae (see, for example, Revans 1970, 1978). Later, others developed the approach in various ways, and in 1999 the American Academy of Human Resource Development listed four different schools or interpretations within action learning (Yorks *et al.* 1999).

The *scientific school* is Yorks *et al.*'s designated term for Revans's original approach. It includes identification and reformulation of relevant problems and problem fields, problem-solving and implementation of solution proposals, and development and innovation in a learning process on the basis of experience in connection with the work with the problem. It is characteristic that problem-solving and learning are perceived to be simultaneous and necessary processes.

The *experiential school* has developed the approach further, especially on the basis of David Kolb's circle model of experiential learning, which includes the phases concrete experience, reflective observation, abstract conceptualisation and active experimentation, leading to new concrete experience, etc. (Kolb 1984; see

Illeris 2007). It is characteristic that against this background there is increased emphasis on personal development and personal learning style. Briton Alan Mumford is mentioned, among others, as an important representative of this approach (Mumford 1988, 1997).

The most radical approach, however, according to Yorks *et al.*, is the *critical reflection school,* which was largely developed by American Victoria Marsick (who is co-author of the account by Yorks *et al.*), in cooperation with Karen Watkins, among others (Marsick 1990; Marsick and Watkins 1990; Watkins and Marsick 1993), on the basis of Jack Mezirow's theory of transformative learning (Mezirow 1990, 1991, 2009), and with reference to, among others, Peter Senge's perception of the learning organisation (Senge 1990). The special emphasis is on personally and organisationally transcending learning through critical reflection in connection with the processing of the problem.

Last, Yorks *et al.* refer to the *tacit* or *incidental school,* which emphasises an informal process, in which learning takes place more or less 'automatically' when, in connection with the work on the problem, care has been taken to put together an appropriately composed group, and there is attention to team-building, and input from relevant experts (Downham *et al.* 1992; Dotlich and Noel 1998).

In addition to these four schools or approaches, I could mention an approach known as 'business-driven action learning' – a rather radical kind of action learning the principal emphasis of which is on action learning activities being closely connected to the financial gain produced by solving the problem (Boshyk 2000).

Although Revans considered the balance between problem-solving and learning to be the key issue, it is obvious that in the critical reflection approach the balance is tipped towards an increased emphasis on learning, whereas in the business-driven approach it is towards financially effective problem-solving, in that the financial incentive is considered to result in increased efficiency and focusing of the learning process.

Generally speaking, there is, as mentioned, both in the theoretical understanding and in the practical implementation, a considerable overlap between the project learning approach and the action learning approach. However, with its point of departure in organisational development and references to numerous examples from large concerns, action learning appeals more directly to companies, and this tendency is most noticeable in the business-oriented approach. There is also a tendency for action learning to be directed to an even greater degree than the project approach towards the management layers in the organisation, though one can also find examples of it being perceived as directed towards the organisation as a whole, and the endeavour is to get everybody involved.

On the other hand, the critical reflection approach, at least in theory, is not very different from the project approach, even though the language and thinking are clearly more business oriented. The emphasis on reflection and the relation to Mezirow's concept of transformative learning have, however, strong roots in current ideas about adult learning, and it is also characteristic that a key element of this approach includes a process and pedagogically qualified steering and coaching, and that the approach is typically structured as alternating between short intensive instruction phases that encompass relevant professional tuition and extended problem-oriented phases integrated in the daily work.

Job exchange and job rotation

Job exchange, job reshuffling and job rotation are initiatives that may have a number of different functions, including contributing to the learning and competence development of the employees involved. In Denmark, such arrangements are sometimes included in labour market agreements, for instance the general agreement on supplementary training and competence development between the unions and the municipal and county employers. An agreement on personnel policy at a large university hospital included the following arguments for job exchange and job rotation:

- Job rotation produces a higher number of qualifications, because employees learn new things and become more skilful.
- Job rotation can be part of further education.
- Employees can contribute inspiration and innovative thinking to both the new workplace and the old one when, or if, an employee returns.
- Job rotation produces skilful employees, which may mean greater job security for the individual employee.
- If employees want to be promoted, a great deal of experience is necessary.

Job exchange and job rotation can assume several forms, for example regular rotation of different job functions in the same workplace, typically in the same division, or rotation of tasks within a production group or a self-directed group. Usually, such job rotation schemes are introduced to relieve the monotony of the repetitive work that many low-skilled workers perform. In these cases, the basic motivation is more likely to be improvement of the working environment than of the learning environment, but the arrangement will, no doubt, at the same time also have a positive impact on learning possibilities.

Job exchange normally involves two or more employees swapping jobs, either within the same workplace or between different employers. Employees can exchange jobs for a period lasting anything from a few days to several months. Employees get the opportunity to learn by performing the tasks involved in the other job, and the workplace can benefit from reinvigorated employees returning to their original role with new experience and ideas.

Job exchange involves learning across different contexts or communities of practice and thus goes further than the theory of learning in communities of practice (Lave and Wenger 1991; Wenger 1998), because it opens new learning opportunities in the encounter between the different contexts. At the same time, however, it can cause problems and challenges because the continuous learning process and the coherent understanding of the learner is interrupted. Despite this, there are at least two good reasons in support of job exchange and job rotation, and thus learning across jobs and workplaces, in connection with learning in working life.

First, many jobs, particularly those of the low-skilled, consist of monotonous routine, and they do not offer much opportunity for learning and development. This is largely because for decades management philosophy has held that specialisation can increase efficiency, in other words the heritage of Taylorism. Particularly when the work does not require many qualifications, there is also a tendency for employees not to be oriented towards participation in supplementary training, a tendency which, for the low-skilled, is often amplified by negative experiences at school, and which contributes to locking them into a subordinate job. By participating in job exchange or job rotation, these employees are encouraged to learn new skills and move on without having to 'go back to school'.

Second, there are many engaged in active employment, and here again not least the low-skilled, who do not attach the same importance to what they can learn in an educational institution as to what they learn in practice, 'out there in real life'. Their experience is typically that in school one learns 'theory', and this is something entirely different from the reality that rules daily life in a workplace. For such employees, it can make a far greater impression to visit another workplace or hear employees from other companies tell about their experiences than to listen to to an instructor telling them the same things during a course. They consider school attendance and courses to have low value in terms of reality, and they attach more importance to what they learn through their own or other people's direct experience than to abstract and theoretical knowledge.

For example, by visiting another company, employees do not only learn in abstract form about new forms of organisation. They experience in a concrete way how such a form of organisation can function technically, socially and culturally, and, in particular, they learn that it can function in practice and not just in theory.

However, what an employee learns as part of a job exchange cannot, as a rule, be applied immediately to his or her own workplace, because it has been developed in another social and cultural context; there will be a so-called transfer problem (see Illeris 2009d). On the other hand, it will, to a greater degree, have the form of concrete practical and bodily experience that can be communicated in concrete stories and narratives on events and experiences that are convincing by virtue both of being subjective reality to the narrator and of being tried and tested reality in a functioning workplace.

Internal job rotation can immediately contribute to increasing employees' flexibility by enabling them to handle several different tasks in the workplace, and at the same time such rotation can counteract factional thinking and internal conflicts between the different departments of the company by creating increased mutual understanding and tolerance.

Job exchange across companies can result in employees bringing back entirely new ideas and suggestions. It may, of course, be a challenge for both leaders and colleagues to receive such ideas and they may easily react with, 'that can't be done in our workplace because it is obviously totally different'. With a little anticipation, such objections can, however, be counteracted through general openness and discussions in advance concerning the establishment, possibilities and purpose of the scheme.

There may also be other barriers to establishing job exchange and job rotation. Employees may, for example, have doubts about their ability to handle the new job, or possibly fear losing their close relationship with the group they work in. Or discord may arise within the group if its workload increased because a seasoned employee exchanges jobs with another who is new and inexperienced. In addition, management may have underlying concerns that good employees who exchange jobs with another company might be tempted to change jobs altogether.

Such barriers can make it appropriate to combine job exchange and job rotation with formalised education. In this way, employees become qualified to deal with both new professional tasks and the social and cultural conflicts that might arise. Experience of job rotation for those performing monotonous work shows that education can contribute to removing or reducing many of the barriers mentioned, among other things by creating space for the employees' doubts and hesitations to be processed in a more systematic and constructive way than can be done in the workplace.

Generally, job exchange and job rotation offer learning processes of a deeper character and emanating from practice, which makes these approaches particularly well suited to low-skilled employees.

External networks

In Chapter 7 internal networks were briefly mentioned as a possible means of promoting learning within an enterprise. In recent years, there has been increasing interest in external networks between organisations, which in many ways takes the principle even further. Today, network constructions are found in many different contexts and with different purposes. For example, they may take the form of constructions that resemble partnerships of suppliers, subcontractors and clients, or regional players on the labour market may work together to qualify job creation, guidance and education for the unemployed. Another type of network takes the form of close cooperation between companies and educational institutions with a view to strengthening education efforts. In this context, however, I shall focus on the network as a learning space, i.e. the possibilities for learning that might be involved in participation in an external, development-oriented network.

Today, networks are a pervasive organisational principle at many levels in society. Some even speak of today's society as 'the network society' (Castells 2000), with the ability to be part of social relations in different forms of networks being a key qualification for success. No company is an island; on the contrary, all companies are involved in a large number of relations with other companies and organisations, and it is the ability to act in these contexts that is decisive for a company's ability to operate profitably and to develop. Being part of networks is thus, according to this view, part of the daily operations of companies because they must acquire new knowledge and inspiration from many different places in order to develop, and networks constitute a key source of this. However, networks can obviously be of highly different characters.

Participation in networks is, among other things, a source of learning, a learning possibility and opportunity, for both those who participate and the organisations they represent. Networks can be seen as a means of creating organisational learning alongside the internal workplace initiatives and external offers such as courses, thematic meetings and project participation. At the same time, network constructions can be used to reinforce the work of formalised education, education planning and competence development. In some cases, schools with commercially oriented programmes are also included in such networks.

It is not possible to give one final definition of what characterises a network. A suggestion for a general and therefore somewhat loose definition might be that a network is a relatively stable assembly of persons/companies that meet repeatedly (virtually or physically) over an extended period of time to discuss a certain theme or with a particular purpose. The theme of the network may be broadly or narrowly defined, and the group can be more or less specifically composed, but mutual learning is typically one of several goals of a network.

One can consider networks a form of 'refuge', a meeting place governed by a set of rules different from those 'at home' or in the arenas of the competition-driven market. There is room to exchange opinions and experience with potential competitors as well as potential cooperation and sparring partners. The purpose is not to defeat each other in competition or blame each other for lack of success; quite the contrary, the purpose is to strengthen participants' ability to act in the current area, both individually and in community. There are things that can be said in this forum but nowhere else, because special rules have been defined or have arisen.

Participation in networks can, in terms of learning, be considered something between participation in education and workplace learning. The network is located outside the workplace and therefore involves, like participation in education, a transfer problem, i.e. the learning acquired must be transferred or translated into the context in which it is to be used (Illeris 2009d). On the other hand, in networks participants are, to a greater extent than in formalised education, able to contribute to defining goals, contents and working modes, which may in itself be an important part of learning, and no educator or expert is controlling the procedures. There may be persons who are administratively responsible, persons who are responsible for specific professional areas, persons who hold a special, formally powerful position, or persons who are more informally recognised as authorities. However, participants can also themselves take part in defining their role as procedures unfold, and this is also part of the learning process.

A number of factors influence the manner and extent to which learning processes can take place in networks, i.e. which learning space a network constitutes. Some of the most important factors are:

- What is the focus of the network's coherence, and how is it organised?
- Who participates, and what social relations are established?
- What qualifications do participants possess?
- Which resources are available, and what legitimacy does participation have in one's own organisation?

There is thus very great variation between different networks with respect to their concrete learning opportunities. The way in which the work within the network is organised is of great importance. Tight steering with very specific goals can create good opportunities for putting into words practices, routines and tacit assumptions that characterise daily work. In many networks, this will be a very important element. Conversely, early and strong focus on specific goals or outcomes may have the effect of excluding the rather unconventional angles and discussions that may offer fresh insights into and perspectives on practice. The participants' motivation and qualifications obviously also impose a framework on the possible learning processes, and appropriate participation is in itself a learning process. Participants have to invest effort to gain from the network; benefits are not a matter of course.

In relation to learning internally in the workplace, network participation can contribute new angles and ideas. It may, however, often be difficult to move beyond an exchange of practical tips and good ideas to handling of concrete issues. An overall analytical approach to one's own practice, a conceptualisation that may be required for rising above everyday life, will typically demand special input into the network, e.g. in the form of a coordinator who is capable of supplying relevant input and able to organise occasions for participants to take a fresh look at their own organisation.

Participation in networks is, to a great extent, concerned with being able to formulate one's own experience and communicate practice and viewpoints. This places great demands on communicative skills in a broad sense and can make it especially difficult for the low-skilled to benefit from this form of work. One of the challenges can be organising networks that are not only based on academic skills, but which invite exchange and processing of experience in ways that consider and accommodate to a greater extent the way in which the low-skilled typically work, experience and speak.

Conclusion and perspectives

In the above, I have looked at a number of different patterns in which work-related learning is linked with initiatives of a more far-reaching nature, which are concerned more with organisational development than with learning in a more limited sense. It is precisely this linking that causes these different initiatives to offer a unique learning potential and especially opportunities for learning to assume the character of competence development.

In these special types of organisation employees are placed in situations that reach beyond their daily work and its opportunities. This may, of course, involve uncertainty, and thus also resistance, but at the same time it is precisely this break with habitual thinking and practice that promotes the more challenging and far-reaching learning opportunities, both in the area of professional content and in personal and social areas.

It is, unfortunately, typical that most initiatives of this character entirely or predominantly involve the groups of employees that already have the most varied, interesting and challenging work. However, it is certainly possible to include all employee groups in these types of initiatives, and this can bring benefits for work-places, because it can bring into play new and hitherto neglected potential.

Both the elements of uncertainty and the specially developed opportunities in these initiatives have great significance in relation to low-skilled employees, who, as a rule, perform the more monotonous and routine functions and are less will-ing to accept that work can be challenging and involve demands for continuous learning processes. However, by implementing types of initiatives that require innovative thinking and adaptation without having the character of school attend-ance and teaching, it is possible for the low-skilled to fulfil their potential in ways that they find easier to accept and identify with. Extensive experience of self-directed groups of low-skilled employees at shop-floor level has shown that taking employees out of a subordinate position can be a way of releasing them from the socially and mentally marginal position they have traditionally had to accept.

However, it is important in this connection to be aware that the developing and transformative learning that may be inherent in these initiatives is closely linked to the organisational development perspective which, as a rule, is the basis of and rationale underlying such learning. It can very easily come to pass that the learning of the low-skilled becomes tied to and constricted by the new prac-tice and lacks broader foundations in the form of overview and more structural understanding.

Thus, there may be a reason for also including elements of professional training and a technical and theoretical dimension in connection with such initiatives. This may be done in many ways and need not always have the character of teaching, but may also be an opportunity for the commitment concerning organisational development to be precisely the incentive that gets those who are reluctant to undergo education to break through their barriers in this area.

It was mentioned above how Yorks et al. (1999) recommend the inclusion of a minor course of education in connection with action learning. It was also mentioned that a course of education may be a good idea in connection with job exchange and job rotation, and that networks can involve a sort of mutual instruction. In terms of learning, it is well known that transcending forms of learning cannot in the long run stand alone, but must be part of an interaction or alternation with more traditional learning of contents. This applies also to transcending learning connected with courses of an organisational development and restructuring character.

Interaction between workplace learning, courses and education

Interaction between learning environments

This chapter deals with the interaction between learning in the workplace and learning through vocationally oriented educational activities at schools and on courses. Typical examples of this are, of course, training/work experience programmes, for example apprenticeships, and a number of professional educational programmes, such as nursing training, that provide elementary training for a particular vocation and which involve a combination of school and practical learning. However, such interaction also takes place when employees take part in work-oriented courses or programmes of training at a school or arranged by another external provider.

Although the learning potential in such interaction would seem to be very great, experience shows that realising this potential is not so easy. It is clear that there are some special learning possibilities inherent in such interaction. In the workplace, the possibility for training exists in direct connection with the work by means of a number of different types of learning initiatives. In the case of learning outside the workplace, daily work can be set at a distance, enabling the learner to take a more general, overall view of the workplace, and to acquire the background theoretical insights of importance for understanding various work functions, the learning environment and social functions of the workplace, and to put work in perspective in relation to the surroundings.

However, there is a great deal of evidence showing that it is often difficult for the employees to make the connection between the formal school/course learning and workplace practice. The background of this is that schools and workplaces provide two different types of learning spaces based on very different rationales, cultures and existential conditions: the learning-oriented environment of the schools and the production-oriented environment of the workplaces. In addition, the participants themselves function on the basis of yet a third rationale: they prioritise their learning from the point of view of their own interests and situation. In practice, these different rationales fight against each other, and targeted efforts are needed if they are to be brought to interact in such a way that the advantages of the two learning spaces enter into a fruitful interaction and mutual relationship instead of remaining an unmediated relationship of tension. The intended interaction does not just take place by itself, and a number of barriers must be overcome for the interaction to be transmitted into appropriate, coherent learning.

Both the possibilities for interaction and the barriers can, naturally, be very different in character depending on the participants, workplaces and types of educational institutions or courses that are involved. In some cases the interaction can be such that it is impossible for the participant to directly apply what is learned during the course to a specific work function. But it can also be the case that the training course contributes to changing and developing the workplace, for example by challenging employees' ideas and inspiring them to change their work practice. Education can provide the professional skills necessary for the employees to participate actively in a project of change, and education can also provide time and space for discussion and clarification of attitudes between different groups of personnel. Thus, interaction can be about utilising the school and workplace as different learning environments as part of a continued process of development.

Another important perspective is that education can provide qualifications for broader work tasks in a trade or occupation, and not merely for performing a certain work function. This is, typically, the expectation of vocationally oriented training/work experience programmes, whether they are youth or adult programmes, particularly in modern organisations that break with the Taylorist division of labour and create more wide-ranging jobs that allow employees to independently organise, perform and control their own work. This requires a broader competence profile so that the staff can handle unfamiliar situations and grasp a total work process.

Yet another angle on the interaction can be that the training should prepare the employees for new and future work tasks, and therefore should not be planned only on the basis of already known qualification requirements. But this begs the question of how to plan more future-oriented education when the future is becoming more and more unpredictable. For example, should the teaching be principally personally relevant and motivating, should it be aimed at the current needs of the individual enterprise, or should it aim at broader and future requirements in the labour market and in society?

In order to answer the question of what constitutes good interaction, one must also look at the objective of the training for the different actors. If it consists in learning the finer points of a new computer program or operating a new machine, then the objective is normally clear and reasonably unambiguous for all. But if the aim is to improve cooperation and change attitudes among the employees, then this is more complicated. Changes in an organisation often trigger unexpected social-psychological forces. On the one hand, insecurity, resistance and power battles can emerge and, on the other hand, new alliances and room for the development of hidden resources and new initiatives can be created.

One of the primary questions that must be answered to create good interaction is therefore who and what – actors, expectations, learning processes, etc. – are to interact in the individual project, and it is important to consider the way in which this process can take place as an open dialogue and negotiation in which all relevant actors are allowed to play a part. Is it a large orchestra that is to play together with a conductor and according to a score, or a smaller group that lets the music develop freely and by ear? Who sets the tune and how is the rhythm to be found?

An important point in relation to schools and workplaces as learning environments is that, although they could be described as special systems, each with its own rationale, ultimately it is the learner's experience of the two worlds and the interaction between them that determines the type of learning that occurs – or if any learning at all takes place. There are, thus, always three parties or actors involved in a course of interaction: the school/course, the workplace and the learner. In the following these three parties shall be described as they basically function in relation to learning.

Three rationales of learning

The school rationale

Public schools and educational institutions have traditionally had teaching as their central rationale and their main condition of existence. But the 1990s, in particular, perhaps influenced by slogans such as 'lifelong learning' and 'the knowledge society', saw a remarkable change in focus from teaching to *learning*. This involved not only schools and other educational institutions but all kinds of education and training efforts and activities in a very thorough and comprehensive way, and encompassed the general understanding that there is no automatic link between teaching efforts and learning outcome.

However, although this was the most immediate and striking change, another, but related, development has been occurring at a higher level: the general perception of schools and education has changed from one of respected cultural and democratic institutions to a much more practical and economic one which ultimately places the institutions as producers of societally usable qualifications and competences and consequently to be regulated by a cost–benefit rationale.

This tendency has been supported mainly by policy-makers and international agents such as the OECD and the World Bank (see, for example, Rubenson 2009), but at the same time has been strongly opposed by the community of educators, who have on numerous occasions referred both to public statements and object clauses about the general and generic aims of schooling and education and to learning and educational theory and research. In any case, it is obvious that the general rationale of schools and education as estimated cultural institutions of central importance for well-functioning democratic societies has been fundamentally challenged by a much more business-oriented conception which has included modern management, production plans, control, tests, calculations and cut-downs or requests for increased outcome inside unchanged budgets.

Adult education and vocational training have also been affected by these tendencies. At the theoretical level, concepts such as 'situated learning' (Lave and Wenger 1991) and 'practice learning' (Chaiklin and Lave 1993) can be seen as important contributions to the shift of focus from teaching to learning and also as challenging the educational system as the main supplier of learning. And the increased interest in the very concept of 'workplace learning' is undoubtedly also associated with this. In real life, however, the situation seems to be more complex (as briefly discussed in Chapter 1) because learning activities in the workplace are both beneficial for and place strain on the enterprise. But the emergence of more private providers of courses and other learning initiatives is certainly linked to changes in the views of public education.

Thus, in general, the central rationale of schools and courses is to create learning and competence development. In public education programmes this tends to be interpreted in a broad and inclusive sense that encompasses more than just what employers tend to accept as relevant labour qualifications. And in current educational policy there is a tendency to regard learning processes as a kind of production which should be regulated according to the rationales of efficiency and productivity.

The workplace rationale

Workplaces in the private sector are ultimately driven by the rationale of maximum economic output, and in the public sector by a corresponding aim of maximum output in relation to the economic input (although it is not always quite clear what this actually means in practice).

However, as suggested by the Swede Per-Erik Ellström, these general rationales include two subrationales that are largely in harmony but quite often are to some degree in conflict: the rationale of production and the rationale of development (Ellström 2001). These two rationales are of significant importance in relation to workplace learning because the production rationale tends to reduce this to what can be learned directly through coping with the production processing without any extra time or economic input, whereas the development rationale will attach great importance to the learning and competence development of the staff. This also implies that the production rationale is oriented towards learning that is immediately needed and applicable, whereas the development rationale implies a much broader approach to what should be learned, placing more emphasis on general and theoretical orientation, generic skills and competence development.

So the workplace rationale of learning is clearly related to the production and output of the organisation, but at the same time ambiguous in relation to learning needs and investments. A general tendency seems to be that large organisations with advanced technology and which are producing for the global market are dedicated to creating top-notch learning possibilities for their employees, and many of them establish their own educational courses, school or academies. In contrast, smaller enterprises and those with more traditional work processes will tend to exhibit lower commitment to special workplace learning arrangements and to spend less. Public sector organisations will usually have a closer relationship with the public education system and in some cases will have a say in the retraining and updating courses provided by the various professional organisations of which their employees are members.

Further, across all kinds of organisations and enterprises there is the impact of the so-called 'Matthew effect' that 'for whoever has to him shall be given and he shall be caused to be in abundance' (Matthew 13:12), i.e. that those who already are the best educated participate in learning activities to a much greater extent than those who have received less education and schooling.

The learner rationale

Workplace learners are, as adults, usually interested in learning and competence development if they personally find it relevant and meaningful (Illeris 2005, 2009e). Their rationale in relation to workplace learning is therefore closely related to their personal experience of the work situation and the organisation in which they are employed.

As learning is generally believed to lead to improvements in individuals' work situation and in some cases even to promotion and/or a wage increase, one would normally expect employees to view workplace learning possibilities and activities positively, but two types of conditions may stand in the way of this: there may be personal or collective conditions inside or outside the workplace that reduce or prevent the commitment, or the learning content or activities may not be experienced or understood as relevant and meaningful. In both cases there will be a lack of motivation, which will probably lead to incomplete or low-quality learning, no learning at all, or even unintended negative learning or reinforcement of negative attitudes.

In the case of learning programmes involving an interaction between workplace learning and school learning, there is a further risk that the learner may well find both kinds of learning meaningful and interesting, but is unable to see the connection between the two, and that the teachers or instructors are unable to see or understand this and interpret it as the learners' own inadequacy and responsibility and do nothing to improve or explain the connection. Indeed, an overwhelming body of evidence indicates that this lack of connection is the most widespread barrier to the commitment and effective learning of participants in such interaction learning programmes.

So, although the learning rationale of employees and workers in relation to workplace learning is usually positive at the outset, there may be both individual and collective reasons why it is not always so, and these reasons seem to occur more frequently in relation to interaction programmes than in relation to separate workplace or school learning programmes.

The battle and interaction of the rationales

Three different rationales in the learning interaction between the school, the workplace and the learner have now been outlined. In practice, the interaction can take as its starting point any of these rationales. To illustrate this I shall refer to some recent trends in Danish educational policy that have in turn taken each of the three angles of approach and thereby pulled in different and even conflicting directions.

Traditionally, discussions about learning and the interaction between schools and practice have been based on youth and adult vocational training programmes. It was typically held that learning is the result of tuition and education. Hence, the difficulty became the transfer of the acquired knowledge from education to the workplace where it was to be used, and where routine and experience were to be achieved (see Illeris 2009d). This was largely left up to the learners themselves and to conditions and initiatives at the workplaces.

The curriculum to be learned in the schools was primarily determined by the education system and broken down into individual subjects, possibly within a framework laid down by politicians and professionals in the trade. The general idea was that education should provide nationally recognised qualifications within recognised occupations. Publicly financed education should not be primarily aimed at specific enterprises or individual personal interests and development. This was considered important with respect to mobility and transparency in the labour market.

The drawback of this rationale is that, when the contents of the education programmes are determined in this way, they can easily deviate from what the participants find personally relevant and from what is relevant in relation to enterprises. The interaction is limited because the point of view is dominated by one of the three parties.

Subsequently, during the late 1980s the school rationale was seriously challenged by another trend that followed the workplace rationale by emphasising the practical applicability of education to the labour market. This resulted from, among other things, political demand for a stronger labour market focus of education programmes, so that their content and practice should be based to a greater degree on the needs of enterprises. This also led to a change in the management of supplementary education from supply management to demand management, while the focus of the players in the labour market shifted from education and courses to competence development directly in the workplace.

At the same time, the education system was developing a growing pedagogical interest in 'situated learning' and 'practice learning' and, inherent in this, a criticism of school-based general and theoretical knowledge, and an emphasis on workplace learning and the significance of this learning for the motivation of both employees and enterprises. This approach was also believed to be beneficial for those who are not oriented towards formal education, but who find it important to learn things that are clearly relevant in relation to their workplace.

The problem in this case was that the acquired knowledge would not necessarily lead to acknowledged competences of general value in the labour market. Furthermore, such education might not be perceived to be personally relevant if it was seen within a narrow enterprise horizon with which the learner might not necessarily identify. If enterprises focused one-sidedly on internal learning, it might lead to the practical qualification acquired in the workplace becoming disjointed from relevant theoretical knowledge, and part of the workforce obtaining only limited and application-oriented qualifications tied to the specific jobs in the enterprise in question.

During the 1990s, however, the trend for individualisation made its mark on the education system. This relates mainly to the learner rationale and places individuals' personal career goals and learning and development requirements at the centre. It is a general trend attributable to the increasing differentiation among learners as well as their expectations that the teaching should be personally relevant. It thereby mirrors the increased reflection both in society and among participants, who have become less inclined to accept tuition that is justified in targets outside of themselves (see Beck and Beck-Gernsheim 2002).

In addition, the trend towards individualisation is in line with the aims of current education policy – increased flexibility, a higher completion rate, a lower dropout rate and fewer participants switching to other education programmes – all of which are primarily based on economic considerations. Against this background, education programmes are increasingly organised according to the principles of modularisation, flexible entry and leaving opportunities, merit for real competences and open opportunities for combining and composing subjects and contents.

Each of these three trends in educational policy may form the basis for interaction between school and workplace. All three rationales are in practice involved in learning and competence development in interaction between workplace learning and formal education. But the emphasis can be very different and different parts of the education system and political interests prioritise the first, second or third rationale – or some combination of them.

The discussion above indicates that learning through interaction between practice and educational activities must be regarded as a multidimensional and continuous process, taking place in different types of learning environments that promote different types of learning processes, depending on how the learner experiences the learning environments and utilises them on the basis of his or her interests, experience and life situation.

Learning at school and at the workplace cannot and must not be the same. On the contrary, it is necessary to exploit the differences that exist to create a greater range of possibilities. But this means that it must be possible for the learner to experience coherence, that is, a connection and reciprocity between what is taking place in the two learning spaces. Good interaction between school and workplace thus presupposes that the two parties are familiar with each other's conditions and practice. The parties, together with the learners themselves, each has its role to play, but there must be clear connections if coherent learning processes are to be created. Close, continuous cooperation can strengthen the interaction and clarify what each party can contribute in particular and where their strong and less strong sides are. Without such cooperation it is the learners themselves who must create the context, and much experience shows that this can lead to significant problems.

Educational institutions and workplaces must stop regarding each other as client and supplier, or contractor and customer, and rather see each other as partners in a common project that aims at creating relevant competence development for employees. If this is to work, both partners must open up and allow the other party to legitimately intervene in areas that they previously controlled.

Educational institutions, teachers and consultants must permit workplaces to intervene in the organisation of the teaching activities, and the representatives of workplaces must accept the interference of the educational institutions in internal matters to do with work and its organisation. But this does not mean that everything thereby becomes a common matter. There are still two parties, each of which has its special tasks, competences and requirements of each other. Therefore, both the representatives of the enterprises and teachers/consultants must be aware of their own limitations and their own competences, and both parties must be clear about the requirements and expectations they have of each other.

For example, networks between schools and enterprises can help to ensure that small and medium-sized enterprises, in particular, receive better counselling, have an easier time filling classes, adapt their courses and exchange experience. They can also contribute to larger investments in education, broader educational programmes and less competition for the qualified workforce as well as helping to develop the way in which the teaching and interaction are organised. This is a form of cooperation that makes it easier to translate knowledge to everyday life, because it creates connections and cooperation interfaces that are closer to the every day of the workplace than the traditional teaching situation. There are examples of such closer forms of cooperation having developed along the way into a type of partnership that does not merely coordinate concrete learning processes but is also used to exchange experience and viewpoints about broader issues.

Anyway, it is necessary to realise that the central learning problem of the learners is to experience coherence between school learning and practice learning. This is unlikely to be solved without extra effort, which also means allocation of extra resources, mainly in the form of extra time for staff members in both areas to follow developments in the partner organisation, to come to know people and their ways of thinking and acting and, as a result, to be able to facilitate the interaction for the learners.

The generally poor results of almost all attempts to solve this interaction problem so far strongly suggest that the cooperation has not been sufficient. The differences between the school rationale and the workplace rationale are so great and mutually excluding that it takes daily effort by the agents involved to bridge them. And without such bridging all the promises and possibilities of such interaction – which should be able to function as the optimal version of workplace learning – will be missed, and the learners will be left to create the coherence themselves, which only very few can achieve.

The organisation and practice of the interaction

The increasing interest in workplace learning has also resulted in increasing interest in vocational courses and education programmes and how they interact – or do not interact – with everyday workplace practice and more special needs for learning and competence development. Most vocational training and many courses by various providers have traditionally been offered as products that are developed in advance, in some cases with a great deal of competence, insight and experience on the part of the provider, but nonetheless ready-made commodities on which the workplaces as consumers have no immediate influence, even though there may be a high degree of participant influence during the process.

There will, naturally, always be a market for such courses in a great number of areas, and if one, for example, needs to learn something about statistics for beginners or elementary welding, one will usually be only too pleased to leave the arrangement in the hands of an experienced course provider. But if it is a matter of courses that are broader, more complex and perhaps more personally oriented in nature – and that type of course is in steadily greater demand on the market in connection with vocationally oriented continuing education – then there are some fundamental problems involved in ready-made courses. This is partly because the degree to which the contents of the courses in fact meet the participants' needs is uncertain, and partly because the enterprises and participants can learn a great deal by being involved in the design and programming of the activities and in an interaction with the school or other provider that reaches further than the simple participation in a ready-made course.

Thus, courses and other learning activities that function in direct interaction with workplaces and users and seek to develop forms of cooperation, taking as their starting point the needs of enterprises and participants, will usually result in better and more relevant learning than ready-made packages. This does not mean that the content and the activities should be a copy of what takes place at the workplace. Interaction is not achieved by trying to make the teaching resemble the workplace to the greatest possible extent. Experience from many development projects shows that it is not least by making a break with the environment at the workplace, by being together in quite different surroundings and by working together across the boundaries with quite different subjects that participants learn something new and important and a better climate of cooperation and greater openness towards changes are created.

In external courses learners are freed from the daily demands for efficiency and the usual roles and hierarchies. This can free up both the time and energy to go beyond defensive routines and other limitations of the workplace environment and practice. Learning during external courses contributes to change and development processes in ways that are different from workplace learning, and the aim should be to create a fruitful balance between proximity and distance and between identity and difference in the two learning environments. If the distance and difference are too great, the interaction will be insufficient and experiences from the two environments will not be linked. If, on the other hand, there is too little difference and too much identity, there is no challenge and no new inspiration that can pave the way for transcending learning processes and change.

The content of external education must therefore strike a balance between, on the one hand, relevance to participants' experience and conditions at their workplace and, on the other, providing new impetus, challenging participants' opinions and creating cohesion and perspective in their everyday understanding. Participants must be stimulated to see how conditions at the workplace could be organised differently – for example by meeting participants from other related enterprises with different experience. The teaching should develop a critical and self-critical perception by giving participants the opportunity to shift perspective. But at the same time such learning-transcending processes must be associated with the practical possibilities for action at the workplace and in other aspects of participants' lives.

In practice, this is typically achieved by delivering course content not just through traditional teaching methods, but also by means of videos, company visits, excursions, activities such as role play and projects in which the participants form groups and discuss important issues and problems that they experience in connection with their work. It is often appropriate – as is typically the case in action learning, for example – to structure the course into an initial period, typically of two to five days, during which project groups are formed and projects are decided on, structured and further developed, with the course instructors acting as advisors, and another period, usually of about three to six weeks, during which participants are at work and try to integrate the project problems into their practice.

There is now, in Denmark at least, a great deal of experience of such courses – including for low-skilled workers. They take many different forms, but what they have in common is that the projects tie together the course element and the work element. It is a crucial precondition that the workplaces involved, including both management and colleagues, are aware of, and accept, the need for participants to spend some of their working time on the projects. It is also of decisive importance that the learners have in advance been involved both in discussions concerning their own educational needs and in organising the activities they are to take part in – and as ordinary employees are not usually particularly well qualified to contribute to such activities, they must be given the time and opportunity to acquire the qualifications they need.

If these conditions are provided, learners' commitment will usually be very strong, and by taking part in group work they will benefit from the experience of others, thus acquiring new ideas and a fresh perspective that they can take back to their own workplace. Learning processes that include both learning in the workplace and learning, including activities, in educational institutions clearly have the potential to be better than learning at the workplace alone. But for this potential to be realised it is essential that the learning arrangement engages and involves interaction between all three parties, that the different interests of the three are acknowledged and respected, and that it is recognised that there is a considerable common interest in establishing relevant learning processes and promoting competence development.

Conclusion and perspectives

Learning activities and programmes that include an interaction between workplaces and public or private providers of vocational education and training generally offer some of the best possibilities for work-related learning processes aimed at broad, all-round learning that also includes both professional qualifications and personal competence development.

But the practical realisation of these possibilities depends on many different matters, because they involve different parties with different angles of approach, qualifications and direct interests, and, if they cannot be made to cooperate in an appropriate way, the learning can easily become disjointed and of little practical use. A great number of conditions must be met for these advantages to be converted into important learning processes.

In practice, the problems are concentrated on getting what happens at the workplace and what happens in school-based or course-based education to function in such a way that the participants experience it as a coherent process, at the same time as the learning differences and the special advantages and potentials of the two different learning spaces are fully considered. This is generally a matter of the different logics or rationales that control the workplace, the school or the institution and of uniting the participants in a fruitful interaction. Psychologically, it is a matter of how the learning that is established in one context can take place in such a way that it can also be utilised in another context – the so-called transfer problem. And in daily activities, it is a matter of getting the cooperation itself to function in such a way that it is relatively frictionless, while simultaneously allowing time and space for the creation and practice of mutual understanding.

Whereas the previous chapters went into detail about the many different ways in which learning in the workplace can take place, the focus in this chapter has been on the nature and practice of the interaction, because it is in the part of this interaction that occurs at the workplace that it is possible to make use of most of the procedures already described, and detailed descriptions of the many different types of procedure that can be utilised in school and course activities can be found elsewhere (see, for example, Illeris 2004). The key possibilities and problems in interaction processes have to do less with these procedures than with the interaction itself and its framework conditions.

First and foremost it is important to recognise that appropriate interaction does not arise just because a process takes the form of alternating between time in the workplace and periods of course or school attendance: it is up to the learners themselves to make things work. The classical problem of institutionalised training/work experience programmes, whether apprenticeships or in the professions, is that participants do not immediately experience such a connection and even, very often, regard the interaction as not merely disjointed but contradictory and counterproductive.

If it is to be made to function as more than a practical arrangement, if the great learning potentials in the interaction between practice learning and school learning are to be realised, it is necessary that genuine cooperation is established around the project and *that resources are allocated to it.*

In terms of timescales, this cooperation should include a concrete preparatory phase that encompasses clarification and identification of the needs and interests of the parties involved in the process, a learning/teaching phase, which can be subdivided into workplace and school/course activities in an alternating fashion over a lengthy period, if necessary, and a subsequent implementation phase at the workplace.

From the point of view of content, the cooperation should include the whole range of didactic matters that are at play in every educational context (even though all its facets are by no means always made explicit) – i.e. formulation of objectives, identification of the participants' qualifications, establishment of framework conditions, distribution of management and responsibility, learning environment, counselling, forms of activity, materials, professional content, ICT use, community, control, assessment and evaluation (Illeris 2004).

Many of these conditions are, of course, already established to a greater or lesser degree in educational institutions, and some of them are also in place in the case of training in the workplace and in relation to course series. But in the case of the interaction processes, the established conditions *always* enter into a new context and must therefore be re-evaluated – because it is when, among other things, such matters have not been harmonised that clashes and a lack of coherence come into the picture. Thus, the current framework and regulations often function as an obstacle to the cooperation, and it becomes necessary to dispense with some of them, thereby perhaps slaughtering some sacred cows.

But – again – 'harmonised' does not mean equalised. An important part of the productive potential in interaction processes is found precisely in the differences that exist between workplace learning and school or course learning. Coherence does not necessarily imply evening out contradictions, but just as frequently making the contradictions visible. It must be clear to the participants that there *are* two different learning environments with different conditions, potentials and terms – and that dealing with these contradictions in both practice and theory is something that is most productive from the point of view of learning and competence development. This occurs when, for example, one is brought to see and understand conditions for the workplace from the outside and on the basis of general and theoretical perspectives, or is brought to see and understand relevant theories in the light of concrete work experience.

It is by virtue of the tension between the two types of learning areas that interaction processes have their special learning possibilities and potentials. This may not be a new perception, but has been a pillar of training/work experience for a long time, even though there have constantly been problems with the practical implementation of the interaction.

In connection with the current interest in workplace learning, practice learning and whatever other terms are used, there is renewed interest in interaction processes – and at the same time the problems involved in actually getting the interaction to work have been made clear and taken more seriously.

There are great perspectives in developing interaction programmes, not least for the low-skilled, for whom work experience can be the starting point for learning processes that go further than technical-practical updating. For this group in particular, it will often be appropriate for the interaction to take a point of departure in the workplace with experience gathering and questioning concerning the work issues with which they are familiar, and it should be recognised that these matters must be seen in a larger context, which is best achieved by moving the process outside the learning space of the workplace.

But this requires innovative thinking and practical development that is probably more radical and demands greater and more permanent investment of resources than most people imagine. Thus, cooperation between the parties – the education provider, the workplace and the participants – is the absolutely crucial key condition in this education and learning concept, and the necessary resources and time and the necessary will and understanding among all parties must be present for this cooperation to develop.

These are considerable demands, and in practice it has been found that serious problems can easily arise – so serious that it is not advisable to embark on the interaction process unless there is reasonable certainty that all parties are prepared for what is necessary – both economically and from the point of view of cooperation.

On the other hand, the opportunities for learning are great, and they can be taken up in many ways that can be adapted both in general and in detail according to the conditions in the individual case. The potentials in the interaction process are obvious, not least for the low-skilled, because they are based on experience from daily work but nevertheless contain possibilities for further professional development and a personal competence perspective.

Part III

Cross-cutting perspectives

Chapter 11: The general conditions of workplace learning

In the third and concluding part of the book some important general and cross-cutting issues of workplace learning will be pointed out and discussed. This chapter first returns to the importance of the learning environment and then proceeds to the selection of learning activities and learning strategies for different purposes. Further, the responsibility and non-responsibility of the management in relation to workplace learning are discussed, and the questions of cooperation with outside partners and what can be done to support learning as competence development are taken up from a general perspective.

Chapter 12: Special learner groups

In this chapter attention is drawn to some groups who have some special learning problems which must be addressed and solved if any significant learning is to take place. The most important of these groups are undoubtedly the low-skilled and others who have a poor learning experience dating right back to their school days. However, members of the young so-called generation Y also often have special attitudes to learning, which are certainly not poor but may be very different from what is expected. Further, there are some groups who for various reasons do not want to engage themselves in workplace learning, for example housewives who make family life their first priority, and older people who do not feel they need or want any more workplace learning.

Chapter 13: Some general conclusions

In this final chapter of the book, some general conclusions are drawn in relation to workplace learning on both the theoretical and the practice levels. Against this background some wider perspectives, possibilities and more or less utopian ideas are formulated, and discussion centres on how the issues of workplace learning can be dealt with in the future when employees, employers, enterprises, nations and even supranational organisations can be expected to take increasing interest in the possibilities of professional as well as personal workplace learning.

The general conditions of workplace learning

The workplace as a learning environment

In relation to workplace learning there seems to be a broad agreement that the most important general condition determining the realisation of learning possibilities is the learning environment offered by the individual workplace. Ever since the publication of Marsick and Watkins' now classic book *Informal and Incidental Learning in the Workplace* (Marsick and Watkins 1990), it has been an underlying understanding in most of the literature that the quality of the workplace learning environment is directly decisive for the everyday learning and thereby also indirectly has a strong influence on more specific and goal-directed learning initiatives. This has been discussed from many perspectives in several publications (for example Garrick 1998; Boud and Garrick 1999; Rainbird *et al.* 2004; Billett *et al.* 2008), and the concluding chapter of the book *Improving Workplace Learning* includes a very useful description of how more expansive learning environments can be developed through a process of five stages (Evans *et al.* 2006, p. 169ff.). In the following I shall discuss what essentially characterises a good and supporting workplace learning environment.

The first requirement of a good workplace learning environment is, without doubt, that it is experienced as essentially confident and safe. Specifically, this refers to the fundamental nature of the environment, the everyday atmosphere and feeling, rather than to every possible situation. Confidence and safety are key because the first condition for good, important and creative learning is a general feeling of security. Any accommodative or transformative learning process requires the learner to take an element of risk and, if the environment is basically experienced as doubtful or uncertain, learning opportunities will typically generate defence and evasion. Any learning that takes place under such conditions will tend to be weaker, less significant and accurate, easier to forget and more difficult to recall.

Having said that, safety is just the general mode of the learning environment, the background that enables challenges and assignments to be taken up, commitment to be developed and curiosity to be acknowledged and deployed whenever new situations and tasks are presented or arise. An environment that is safe just because it is always the same, i.e. one day passes as the previous and the next, does not provoke much learning. It is the challenging possibility of capturing new insights, skills and potentials which can drive transcendent and transformative learning when the background conditions are safe and confident. So the interaction between basic security and inspiring challenges is the first and most fundamental balance of a good workplace learning environment.

But there are also other conditions and balances that are essential for a good workplace learning environment. It is very important that the environment is one of community and cooperation with mutual helpfulness and support. As described in Chapter 2, learning starts with the impulses from the individual's interaction with the environment, and particularly with the social environment. It is therefore extremely important that the social environment is experienced as positive and supporting – in line with the general experience of safety and confidence which was mentioned above. There must be an underlying team spirit which, for example, allows the individual to ask questions, even 'silly' questions, without feeling ashamed or inadequate, and which also makes it natural to ask for help, reasons and explanation, and to work together on tasks and problem-solving when needed.

On the other hand, the community feeling must not be so exclusive that it prevents individual thinking and initiatives. Although people are to be regarded and treated as equal, allowance must be made for individual differences and strengths and weakness, which will always be present in a group of people. Individual ideas and initiatives may be of benefit to all, and it is important for individuals, especially the younger generation, to be recognised as the persons they are and feel accepted and appreciated as individuals. So again there is a balance which is of fundamental importance for the workplace learning environment: the balance between community and individuality.

In close relation to this balance is the question of solidarity and competition. This can be observed most distinctly in team sports such as football. When should a player pursue his or her own chances and achievements, and when should that player pass the ball to a team-mate who is perhaps in a better position? It is very difficult to give definitive answers or rules for such situations, but it is easy to see that neither of the extremes of total selfishness or total self-sacrifice is beneficial for anybody. Further competition can be a two-edged sword – it can be a strong motivation for some, especially those who are in a strong position, but for others it can be the opposite and activate all sorts of defence. Competition always produces both winners and losers, and losers often also lose their motivation, whereas winners find that competition is highly motivating – and it is usually winners who are in the position to determine the environment. Again there is a balance to be found and established. And, just as in professional sport, the situation becomes even more tense when money, opportunities or positions are involved.

Finally, there is also a balance between on the one side rules, regulations, guidelines, directions and fixed procedures and on the other side individual freedom to do as one feels right and most appropriate in all the different and often unforeseen situations that may arise in the workplace. Here also it is evident that neither of the extremes is very useful, but it is obvious that there must always be some common framework that everybody accepts and follows and a degree of room for individual judgement and initiatives.

Thus, rather than describe the ideal workplace learning environment in terms of certain characteristics or qualities that should be provided, I think it is more appropriate and fruitful to deal with this topic as a set of balances that should be established in relation to various issues which are different and appropriate for the individual workplace, depending on the kind of work it performs, its position in society, its specific history and traditions, the people and groups involved and other conditions that may be relevant.

I have mentioned and briefly described four types of balances which I think are of a general and always important nature, but no doubt there could be others that are just as important and significant at specific workplaces. The advantage of thinking of these matters in terms of balances is that this implies a recognition and understanding that there are always contrasts and different interests involved, and there is no final or common solution; it is not possible to describe the ideal workplace learning environment that will fit anywhere.

However, there seems to be a general trend in today's late modern societies and enterprises that the balance is tipping in a specific direction: from more safety and confidence towards celebrating more challenges, from more commitment to the community towards more individuality, from more solidarity towards more competition, and from more common rules and guidelines towards more space and freedom for individual initiatives and solutions. These movements seem to be a consequence of a general orientation towards more liberal attitudes and often supported by the ideas of human resource management – and, not to forget, a belief that a movement in this direction in the end will lead to better economic outcomes in both the private and the public sector.

Better economic outcomes may well be achieved if these tendencies are maintained at an appropriate point in the different areas. But there are certainly also enterprises where this trend has gone too far. In Denmark I know of two organisations in which this has obviously been the case (Tynell 2001; Thomasen 2008). The consequence has been that the employees have come to work much more than they have been paid for and that many have suffered stress, breakdown or burnout. And in the public sector such cases seem to be still more widespread in the wake of new public management implemented during the last decade (Prætorius 2004, 2007; Hjort 2008, 2009).

Thus, the need to establish the right balance between what may today appear to be traditional qualities and new apparently more humanistic and democratic trends, which are ultimately driven by economic forces, is an urgent one – at least, although not only, from a learning and competence development point of view.

Workplace learning activities and strategies

In the previous chapters a broad variety of workplace learning activities have been presented and discussed. It is obvious that such activities can be very different in nature, ranging from the incidental learning of everyday working activities to projects and networks without any fixed time limits, and from a single learner to all members or employees of an organisation or an enterprise. The activities can also be aimed at everything from very specific and limited goals to the general development of the workforce's potentials and the organisation of the work. Thus, workplace learning activities should be chosen with care and in accordance with which kind of learning is needed or wanted.

However, it is important to realise that targeted workplace learning that goes beyond the incidental level always implies to some degree the direct or indirect inclusion of activities and forms of interaction that wholly or in part have a different rationale than the basis and aim of the work – something with a learning-oriented goal must also be involved or intended.

In cases of directly learning-oriented processes, this means that there is an overall increase in activity, i.e. there is something more to be done, which requires more time and resources. This is usually immediately visible; for example, courses, network meetings and other similar initiatives require time and resources for planning, preparation, execution and often also some kind of subsequent processing.

In cases where learning is to be promoted by means of changes in the working environment and work organisation, this is not always a matter of increased activity – on the contrary, there is often a notion that the measures in question will not only lead to wide-ranging learning processes that are directly integrated in the work, but simultaneously will result in a better working environment with greater job satisfaction and ideally also increased productivity. Such ideas lie, for instance, behind the concept of 'the learning organisation', and it certainly cannot be excluded that such a happy union of changes in the work organisation and increased and improved learning can sometimes take place. But at the same time it can also mean a considerable amount of extra stress as in the above-mentioned cases described by Tynell, Thomason, Prætorius and Hjort.

In any case, in the larger context – but perhaps not always directly in the individual case – it will not be without cost to increase and qualify learning directly in working life, and it must be maintained as an important point of departure for the question and the debate about workplace learning, that if this learning, qualitatively and quantitatively, is to extend beyond the ordinary and random learning that will always take place, then to some extent or other it means an extra burden on the workplaces and the employees.

There are both advantages and disadvantages in this, which from the point of view of burdens and economy can be compared with the advantages and disadvantages of the same learning being conducted outside the workplaces in the form of courses and institutionalised education. However, such weighting cannot solely be based on economy. Important questions also include the nature and quality of the learning, and the impact on the work, the employees and the workplace in general.

A more varied and deeper understanding of the relation between work orientation and learning orientation in working life can be found in the work of the previously mentioned Swedish researcher on working life, Per-Erik Ellström, who operates a distinction between adaptation-oriented and development-oriented learning (in particular, Ellström 1992, 2004) and a distinction between production rationale and development rationale (in particular, Ellström 2001, 2002).

The difference between adaptation-oriented and development-oriented learning largely corresponds to Americans Chris Argyris and Donald Schön's distinction between single-loop and double-loop learning (e.g. Argyris and Schön 1996), and also in many ways to the distinction between cumulative and assimilative learning on the one hand and accommodative and transformative learning on the other, as described in Chapter 2. But in Ellström the concepts are directly inscribed in a work context.

Adaptation-oriented learning 'means that the individual (the group) learns something with a point of departure in given (or taken for granted) goals and preconditions without questioning or trying to alter the task, the goal or the preconditions' (Ellström 1996, p. 151). The aim of the learning is that one is able to perform work tasks that form a part or component of a larger context, can solve problems of a kind with which one is already familiar, e.g. perform a measurement or control, and can take responsibility for specific work tasks.

Development-oriented learning means 'that the individual (the group) learns to formulate problems and not just to solve given problems. Instead of only and merely asking the question: How?, the questions: What? and Why? come to the fore' (ibid.). The aim of the learning is that one is able to perform work tasks that concern a whole or a system, formulate problems and analyse the way in which they arise and how they can be dealt with or solved, that one can critically judge measurement values and deal with them appropriately, and also take responsibility for larger areas or processes.

The main point in the present context is that appropriate, up-to-date learning in working life must include both adaptation-oriented and development-oriented processes. If the learning is only adaptation oriented, the work becomes routine, and if the learning is only development oriented it becomes too demanding and lacks stability and anchorage.

Adaptation-oriented learning typically dominates if the work primarily follows the production rationale, where the main emphasis is on 'efficient action on a routine or regulation based level, problem resolution by means of adaptation of given rules or instructions, uniformity and habitual ways of thinking, stability and security, learning that aims at mastery of procedures and routines' (Ellström 2002, p. 341).

Development-oriented learning typically dominates if the work mainly follows the development rationale, where the main emphasis is on 'thought and reflection, alternative thinking, experimentation and risk-taking, toleration of difference, insecurity and faulty action as well as development oriented learning' (ibid., p. 341).

Here the main point is about the establishment of a suitable balance. One must be aware that this balance is to be established between two different rationales: the rather short-sighted production rationale, which – whether it has to do with material production or services – focuses on efficiency and thus also on minimisation of time, and the rather long-term development rationale, with its focus on continued competitiveness and thus constant development of products, processes and employee competences, which taken together imply a potential demand on non-production-oriented use of time.

The optimal balance must thus be established on the basis of a conflictual relation that peaks around use of time, but to a large degree also concerns the consumption and orientation of human and other resources, and in practice there will almost always be a tendency for the production rationale to predominate. Thus, consideration of the development rationale – and thereby also, indirectly, an appropriately balanced learning process – requires a continued willingness and awareness to ensure that the development-oriented and more long-term rationale is not pushed into the background.

The responsibility and non-responsibility of management

It is evident that the management of the enterprise has a large role to play and great responsibility to carry in connection with learning initiatives at the workplace. The active efforts and contribution of management are the most important factor when it comes to providing the time, space, resources and backing for learning. And wholehearted engagement on the part of the management is of great importance for the learning possibilities: it has to be something management really wants, has thought through, has decided in favour of and follows up. Ellström (2003) has pointed out that if the management's perspective is embedded in 'opportunistic' motives, such as access to economic support schemes or an idea that the enterprise should appear as modern or advanced, the foundation will hardly be sustainable in relation to larger-scale learning initiatives.

But it is equally significant that important initiatives neither appear to be nor are implemented as the management's project alone. Adults do not complete meaningful and demanding learning processes if they are not underpinned by strong, internalised motivation, either because they find learning directly rewarding or because they have realised that learning is necessary for something they want to achieve (see Illeris 2004).

In addition, one of the most important factors influencing whether learning initiatives at the workplace have any practical impact is the presence of what Ellström terms a good 'education and learning culture'. It can be assumed that this culture is formed 'inter alia by the ideas held by management and the trade unions of the value of education, but also by the need experienced by the employees for competence development and motivation for participating in education' (Ellström 2004).

It is very important precisely in connection with such a 'culture' that the management's learning efforts do not assume the character of a top-down project. On the contrary, in this context it is first and foremost the function of management to make sure that employees are part of, and having genuine influence on, all planning, decision-making and evaluation activities, so that they really have an influence on and co-responsibility for the processes. After all, it is they who individually and together must become involved and complete the learning programme. This presupposes confidence and belief in having an impact, that one is really listened to and taken seriously – and this is not just as a matter of form. It also presupposes that one is actually able to think for oneself and transcend one's daily work horizon and the known patterns from earlier learning processes. And these things are to a large extent also conditional on the manner in which the learning culture of the workplace functions and is experienced. It is not enough for education and learning initiatives to be discussed in a joint consultation committee or other groups that include employee representatives. Co-influence and co-responsibility must extend to those who are to carry out the processes. One learns in a completely different, radical way when one has taken co-responsibility for learning.

For this reason, the responsibility of management is to a considerable degree about *taking responsibility for delegating responsibility*. It is a rather awkward, unfamiliar and perhaps, therefore, for many, difficult form of behaviour, the importance of which has attracted an increasing amount of attention in adult education programmes (e.g. Illeris 1998, 2004; Wildemeersch 2000). But it is, after all, completely accepted and has been practised for many years in the case of, for example, self-directed groups.

In connection with learning initiatives, 'not taking' responsibility applies to all management levels right down to teachers and instructors at shop-floor level. It is not merely a matter of delegating responsibility so much as ensuring that this takes place in a way that those who are to carry through the learning processes really understand and experience that within the existing framework they themselves can take decisions on the basis of their own needs – and respecting this in practice, even when the manager responsible does not agree. The immediate result may be a certain degree of perplexity for all parties, because it is a radical break with habitual ideas of power and responsibility, but once established this practice can really make participants' own self-managed learning flourish – and it can also, in the longer term, lead to the existing framework having to change in nature.

It is important to understand here that both individual and social learning processes are human processes that follow a rationale different from the technical and economic processes to which we are used to relating – that it is engagement that is decisive for the scope and quality of the learning, and that engagement is linked to one experiencing influence, responsibility and respect.

Cooperation outside the workplace

Regarding courses of interaction, the necessary framework conditions are somewhat more complicated. It has already been stated that it is crucial that the interaction is based on close and mutual cooperation between the parties involved. This applies at management level and among those who carry out the concrete planning of the initiative. However, experience from training/work experience courses of education shows that this is not sufficient at a general level, at any rate not if such courses of interaction are to function and meet expectations to a greater extent and on a broader societal level than individual instances of cooperation between a company and an education provider. In such cases there are some conditions which must of necessity be made available and secured at a general level.

The most comprehensive experience with regard to courses of learning that combine initiatives in and outside work is found specifically within apprenticeship and professional training programmes, as such schemes have been developed and practised for a number of years. Here, however, the most significant general experience seems to be that the schemes concerning the interaction aspect have seldom functioned in a satisfactory way. A considerable drop-out rate has often been a feature of vocational training programmes and remains a dominant complaint from the participants and other parties involved.

In Denmark, the field of adult and supplementary vocational training has a special focus on work, with courses of interaction linked to work-related education programmes for low-skilled and unemployed adults through a number of initiatives that go all the way back to the beginning of the 1960s. Some years ago, independent consultant Bruno Clematide described and discussed this whole development (in a Danish language version), and concluded, *inter alia*:

> This means that there is a fair amount of experience to build on [as concerns] the interaction between learning at work and learning in business related adult education and training [...]. If, in this development, one wants to build on more recent discoveries from the world of research, and at the same time work with elements in the interaction which in earlier efforts received a less prominent position, the key is not least to develop the teaching itself in a way so the participants experience direct proximity in practice. Elements in this development will be attention to the ways in which participants usually learn, and an ability to read signals in the learning spaces of the workplaces that are able to promote or obstruct successful learning. These are quite difficult and vast subjects. This kind of challenge requires a major effort in the field of teacher training, which is rooted in and interacts with the organisational development of the schools. This is required to avoid losing the thread.
>
> (Clematide 2004, p. 52)

Clematide, as might be expected when development is analysed from the perspective of the educational institutions, points out weaknesses in the part of the interaction that is the responsibility of the educational institutions, including the teaching itself, teacher training and school organisation, but also the ability to find and analyse what things take place in the workplaces that have significance for the interaction.

If one looks at the same interaction from the perspective of the workplaces, other weaknesses can be found. Do workplaces provide enough resources for the interaction? Is it not the case that the organisation and structuring of work in the workplaces are assumed to be given entities that the interaction must take as its point of departure? Are employers willing to accept that their employees, individually and collectively, take the opportunity for improving and making demands concerning the interaction that is to promote their learning? Are employers willing to accept that their employees' learning is something that can be used in practice and must result in reflections on changes in the work conditions?

Finally, one may view the interaction from the perspective of employees and learning. What does it take for employees to view the courses of interaction as an opportunity to gain qualifications and develop, as something they can use both in their daily work and in their personal development and self-perception? If there is no acceptance and commitment from employees, relevant learning will be a rare occurrence indeed, and then major investments from both employers and institutions will have produced few or no significant results.

These are in truth what Bruno Clematide calls 'rather difficult and vast subjects', not least when one considers the magnitude of the problems they cause when training/work experience education courses rest on established traditions and the efforts have been of far greater dimensions than the initiatives here referred to. If such courses of interaction are to be a decisive part of the response to the current situation regarding adult and supplementary education programmes, something that many factors would suggest is necessary from a learning point of view, it is clear that both employers and institutions (the government) must give the commitment and resources needed to get the interaction to work, including ensuring that relevant employees, both in workplaces and in institutions, have the time to establish and maintain the ongoing cooperation.

One main conclusion of the above, that broader work-related learning generally functions best on a background of interaction between goal-oriented learning at work and broadly conceived initiatives of an educational nature outside work, thus turns out to presuppose that there is the political will, on the part of both enterprises, private as well as public, and government, as providers of the framework for education policy and for institutions, to provide the preconditions and resources needed to strengthen considerably the interaction between learning in work and learning in educational institutions.

Support for competence development

As a last topic in this chapter I shall return to the challenge of competence development that was presented in Chapter 5. That chapter concluded with a very simple formula for what it is central to take into account if workplace learning shall have optimal possibilities of functioning as competence development: *commitment–practice–reflection*.

In relation to the many different kinds of workplace learning activities which have been discussed in the previous chapters it is clear that some have a better chance than others of being described by these keywords. Generally speaking, meeting the demand for *commitment* depends on many conditions other than the learning activity itself, for example the workplace learning environment and, probably most of all, the relationship between employees, individually and as a whole, and the enterprise.

But also certainly of considerable importance is the kind of learning activity in question: How is it introduced? How much influence is assigned to the learners, i.e. is the learning voluntary or directly or indirectly compulsory? What is the intended learning content and how is it related to the various jobs carried out in the organisation? What incentives are involved and how will learners experience their position in the process: are they just passive receivers of teaching and instructions or are they to a minor or major degree active partners with influence and responsibility? In particular, some of the more advanced and complex kinds of learning activities of some duration, such as action learning, project work, external interaction and networking, tend to involve a high degree of commitment on the part of learners, but this may also be true of shorter and more limited activities if they are experienced as meeting the current interests and needs of the learners in relation to their work tasks or in a broader context.

As to the keyword *practice*, there is a more distinct boundary: do the learning activities, partly or wholly, take place as integrated elements of the work activities, or are they entirely located and happening outside the field of practice, for instance in the form of teaching, coaching, meetings, etc.? If the latter, the possibility of competence development will strongly depend on how closely the direct connection to practice is experienced by the learners – whereas when work and learning are partly or fully integrated the demand for practice involvement is met more or less to the same degree as practice is involved.

The keyword *reflection* probably indicates the most vulnerable demand. A great deal of workplace learning could have been turned into competence development if serious reflection activities had been planned and carried out, but this did not happen, perhaps because no one thought of it, or there was no time left for it, or the participants did not engage themselves sufficiently in such unaccustomed processes. In particular, workers with a brief or no professional or academic education often experience systematic reflection as an unusual and awkward kind of activity.

However, during recent years the importance of reflection has gained considerable influence in the literature on workplace learning and learning as a whole because it has been realised how central it is for an extensive and useful learning outcome – and thereby precisely for learning to have the quality of competence development. In fact, probably all kinds of learning activities could be arranged in ways that would ensure that reflection is included. But this is something that has been recognised only gradually and, not least in the busy environment of workplaces, appears to be difficult to maintain in practice.

Overall, it can be concluded that almost all workplace learning activities can be planned and carried out in ways that afford good opportunities for competence development. It is usually much easier to achieve competence development through workplace learning than in schools and other educational institutions, because it is so much easier to find opportunities to practise. But it takes insight and determination to keep going in circumstances in which production, and not learning or competence development, has first priority.

Special learner groups

The low-skilled and other vulnerable groups

Throughout this book workplace learners have generally been referred to as 'employees' or 'workers', and only in special cases have I referred to more specific groups of learners. The one special group that I have mentioned most often is undoubtedly 'the low-skilled'. This is partly because this is, from a learning point of view, by far the biggest group meriting special attention, but also because this group is very often overlooked in connection with workplace learning initiatives, or there is a failure to appreciate that their background for learning is fundamentally different from that of other groups.

The result is that the low-skilled are generally little engaged in workplace learning: they do not learn very much, with the result that the gap in qualification level compared with other groups is actually widened. This is very bad, both for the low-skilled themselves, whose feeling of inferiority is reinforced and who also become more vulnerable to organisational changes or staff reductions, but also for their employing organisations, which fail to fully utilise the resources at their disposal. It is commonly believed that the economic success of the Scandinavian countries, despite their relative lack of natural resources, can be attributed to the fact that they have invested more than most other countries in workplace learning, reskilling courses and general adult education for the low-skilled.

The low-skilled have traditionally been understood or defined as all whose formal education consists only of primary and lower secondary education and perhaps some short training courses. But if the issue is approached from the angle of who is vulnerable and at risk of being marginalised in society and in the labour market, two other groups should also be included. First, many adults with solid skills and recognised educational qualifications are in a vulnerable situation because the vocational area for which they have been trained has been forced to radically reduce its workforce, and therefore the skills they have are not in demand. Second, a growing group of young adults have never had a permanent job, although they may have developed considerable and often untraditional qualifications through their own winding routes. Some of these young adults are definitely not low-skilled in the traditional sense, but many seem to lack the stability and perhaps other social competences that today are necessary for a lasting occupation.

Naturally, in addition to the main groups outlined here, there are also others who must be regarded as vulnerable in the present context. These are, for example, those who have completely given up trying to break into the official labour market and muddle through on a mixture of cash benefits, a low level of consumption, mutual services and perhaps some petty crime at times – or those with health problems or a handicap.

Thus, the problems traditionally related to the low-skilled have developed in scope and content, and the field has become more complicated and varied, requiring particularly differentiated, flexible and sensitive policies and services. So when I use the term 'low-skilled' it is with the clear reservation that this term is on its way to becoming obsolete, and that, although my deliberations do not cover all low-skilled learners, they apply also to a great number of people who are skilled, educated and/or trained but, nevertheless, are not in demand in the labour market.

In many countries much effort has been put into increasing the work qualifications of this part of the workforce as this is obviously an important way in which countries can raise their general competitiveness and at the same time reduce social costs and strengthen coherence. However, any such initiatives have usually taken as their starting point the labour market situation and economic considerations, and there is generally little understanding of or interest in the personal and motivational situation of the people in question. For example, they have often been sent to courses to prepare them for jobs in which they are not at all interested, and this has not led to much genuine learning.

Therefore, I shall here try to approach this problem from the perspective of the low-skilled adults' feelings and opinions in relation to education and training, to uncover the psychological processes that tend to keep them away or reduce their motivation and, finally, I shall try to point to some practical measures that could help to overcome these barriers, i.e. what to do and what not to do if the low-skilled are to be attracted to joining work-related learning activities to a greater extent.

The complex psychological background

In relation to any kind of formal education or training it is characteristic of most of this group that they are subjectively deeply *ambivalent* (see Chapter 2). They want and do not want to participate at one and the same time. When my colleagues and I have interviewed members of this group, whether it has been at workplaces or in educational settings, we have generally found that they know very well that what they need in order to achieve a stable job situation is formal education or training. But at the same time they strongly wish that this were not the case (Illeris 2005, 2006c,d).

Those in this group who are formally low-skilled are usually so because they did not do very well at school. They have nine or more years of everyday experience of not being good enough, of being humiliated and marginalised, and of wanting to leave school as soon as they possibly could. Very few of them feel any desire to return to a situation that would remind them of all their failures and humiliations – and probably also repeat them. On the other hand, it becomes more and more obvious that this is the only way out of their vulnerable situation.

The situation is somewhat different for those who are skilled or trained, but in unmarketable areas. The reason why they are often reluctant to be retrained or re-educated has to do with their strong need to maintain their self-respect. Typically, they have for many years held a decent and respectable job by which they have earned their living and social position, and they have built up an identity as a valuable employee and a useful citizen who has contributed his or her share to society. They are therefore eager to defend this identity, and they feel it somehow misplaced, unfair and infantilising to have to go back to school and to the subordinate position of a pupil. But they also know that this is their only chance to find a way back to a life on the level they used to have.

In the case of the young unemployed adults (roughly, those under 30), the reason for their ambivalence is also slightly different. They do not find it humiliating to go back to school because they have grown up in a society devoted to lifelong learning, and thus they have always known that it would somehow be their fate. But this does not mean that more schooling is an attractive prospect to them. They typically see it as something boring and restricting, which places them in an unwanted subordinate position. However, they also know that it is their only chance (Simonsen 2000).

There is no doubt that the various groups of low-skilled or vulnerable people on the labour market nearly always have a rather clear awareness of their need for more education, not least in general areas such as reading, written skills, arithmetic and mathematics, foreign languages, computer skills and general social and cultural orientation. But the forces pulling in the opposite direction – the lack of self-confidence in terms of education and the unpleasantness of going back to school again – are often stronger.

For this reason there must be a special incentive, a relevant opening that links up with the needs they have experienced and implies some circumstances that reduce social, practical and financial barriers. And at the same time it is of decisive importance that initiatives deliberately avoid all arrangements, rules, formulations or references that can in any way be experienced as humiliating, disrespectful, infantilising or the like, as this is not only offensive but may easily be taken as a most welcome excuse, both to oneself and to others, to withdraw.

For adults who already have a vocational or other qualifying education, but who have become victims of structural unemployment and therefore must readjust and be retrained to get back on the labour market, the main psychological problem is identity defence. In this situation it is very understandable that they have a more or less unconscious urge to cling to the professional identity that has hitherto been the basis of their self-respect and dignity, although it is now irrelevant and worthless. Thus, the challenge, for themselves and for those who are trying to help them, is how to overcome or circumvent these defensive tendencies. Continuing education or retraining must be offered and conducted in ways that respect the wounded work identity at the same time as a new identity is gradually built up. The present counselling and educational systems do not seem to be geared to this or to adequately understand it (see Illeris 2003, 2004).

Young unemployed adults are strongly marked by the widespread individualisation of late modern market society (Beck and Beck-Gernsheim 2002). They have usually been constantly presented with personal choices in all possible areas from earliest childhood, they think that free choices exist in all areas and should exist and that it is important, the very core of life itself, that they always make the right choice and thereby create themselves as what they want to be. Therefore, when they start an education or training course, it is typically to see if this might be something that 'turns them on' and could be a way to fulfil their often sky-high expectations. So what they need is support for holding on to a goal, not to give up at the first hint of problems, and the support must sometimes also include an element of 'dream crushing', which carefully and surely can help them to realise what is out of their reach. Not everyone can become a rock star, host a TV show or become a designer.

For others in this group the problem is to find anything that 'turns them on' or to be enthusiastic about. They cannot live up to the expectations of society and educators to 'feel' their own innermost motivation, and at the same time they cannot bring themselves to go for the jobs with least status, for example in the health or retail sectors. Young men, especially those from an ethnic minority background in less industrialised societies, usually want to get an unskilled manual job as quickly as possible so that they can get good wages and avoid the endless choices that they cannot handle.

To meet these various psychological situations and barriers there is, at a general level, a need to create special initiatives, both to make workplaces involve this group in, for example, projects, action learning, learning-oriented networks, job exchange and job rotation schemes that offer learning opportunities of another nature than teaching, and to initiate and provide funding for relevant contacts and outreach activities from schools and training centres.

Simultaneously, it is of crucial importance to provide opportunities and incentives that directly relate to the scepticism of and barriers facing the low-skilled in relation to general learning and upgrading of skills, particularly in such areas as reading and writing, arithmetic and computer skills, but also in relation to general information about work-relevant and social subjects.

However, many of the low-skilled who need training are not employed, and their contact with working life is usually established by various counselling agencies. In fact, the majority of adult education participants in Denmark today have been placed, referred or sent to attend the education programme in question by public authorities or agencies, and this has usually not been a positive experience.

In the course of my research I have been rather shocked to observe the proportion of participants in adult education programmes who felt they had been 'placed' there and who had no reasonable prior knowledge of what the course aimed to achieve (Illeris 2003).

The time, place and context of education and training activities

When planning learning activities for the low-skilled and other vulnerable groups it is important to constantly take into account and respect the strained relations that many of them have with schools and educational activities. At the start especially, both physically and from the point of view of content, everything must take place as close as possible to the daily work, and it also creates security if the training involves co-workers whom the learner knows well and trusts.

For those who are employed in larger enterprises, it will often be possible to provide education activities in locations at the workplace, sometimes even combined with training directly connected to production or other work activities. In other cases, if participants are unemployed or come from mixed backgrounds, it may be useful to base the course in a variety of locations at school and relevant workplaces, which will allow the participants to experience a range of work environments.

In general, it is always important to take into account the fact that, for participants who may often be fundamentally ambivalent, such practical features as time and place may easily be decisive for their attitude. It is very easy to use practical problems or inconveniencies as an excuse for not participating, and it is much easier to put up with long travel times and give up one's time when attending a course that one has chosen voluntarily and perhaps even with enthusiasm.

In Denmark, there are several examples of vocational training courses taking place at or close to the workplace at the end of the working day; typically learners are paid by their employer for half the time, relinquishing their leisure time for the other half. This is considered a 'fair deal' and thus provides a good starting point and climate for the learning.

In the case of programmes for the unemployed, it is a very good investment to ensure that the practical circumstances are such that potential participants have no excuses for not attending. Many just need a threshold to get started in a positive way, and providing the psychological conditions that can help them cross this threshold is often one of the most crucial challenges of the planning.

Learning content and methods

With respect to the content and methods of learning activities, it is important to provide a wide variety. Part of the problem for low-skilled workers is often to see and understand the work in a larger context, to experience that it is performed in other ways at other places, to gain insight into what triggers and determines the changes that take place, to have the opportunity of asking questions and expressing doubt and resistance, to try for themselves – for example through projects – to be active in relation to their own work situation and work function, and to see that the experience and qualifications they have can be important and used as a starting point for learning more. It can be an almost euphoric experience for this group to realise that learning initiatives can also be something that allow one to make active use of one's experience, to play a part in making decisions and to make a contribution that is not irrelevant.

One Danish example is a teaching programme at a large sugar factory, where the participants prioritised teaching in the 'soft' subjects such as communication, active listening and coaching. At the same time the participants typically emphasised being allowed to deal with subjects and problems from their own everyday work life as something positive and different from what they previously had experienced during their time at school. That anyone 'could be bothered doing something just for us' was quite a different and surprising experience that strengthened the self-confidence and self-awareness of many.

In the case of the unemployed, it is generally not possible to establish direct links to workplace conditions. It is therefore of decisive importance in other ways to make the relations to the labour market visible whenever possible. For a great majority of the unemployed, admission to the labour market is the predominant reason for participating in educational and training activities, and they must constantly be able to see how the training activities relate to work openings which they can experience as realistic.

However, today this does not just mean training in practical knowledge and skills. In one of the surveys in which I have been involved, it was a remarkably clear conclusion that the unemployed experience personal qualities as more important for getting a job than practical skills. Courses and instructors are usually primarily focused on the practical content of training activities. Of course, this is also important, but participants often feel that it must somehow be related to the personal qualities that are so necessary today, so it should be compulsory to find ways to include these essential issues. This is not easy to do in ways that are neither superficial nor offending; it often requires techniques such as role playing, for which most teachers and instructors have only incidental qualifications, so there is a strong need for training and discussion in this area.

But it must also be remembered that the most important qualification needs of the low-skilled are generally in basic subjects such as writing, reading, languages and computer skills. This is usually also recognised by the learners themselves. But the more school-like teaching that is a necessary part of these subjects is precisely what they more or less consciously try to avoid. It was therefore a remarkable feature of the example mentioned above that once the participants had 'broken the ice' by taking part in projects closely connected to their work situation, it was easier for them later to come to terms with a more traditional teaching situation and take up the more school-like subjects.

At the pedagogical level, the most important feature seems to be a genuine participant direction, i.e. that the learners control the process in interaction with the teachers' qualified and loyal assistance and support. Another important peda-gogical principle is problem orientation, i.e. that the point of departure for the learning activities is broadly defined thematic areas and problem fields that will help participants achieve their educational goals. This increases the possibilities for active, relevant learning. In general, participant direction and problem orien-tation are best practised through such pedagogical forms as action learning (Yorks *et al.* 1999) and project work (Illeris 1999, 2004).

Monitoring, evaluation and implementation

During and at the end of education courses there is, as a rule, some kind of monitoring and evaluation of the participants' activities and qualifications. Such monitoring and evaluation is in its source and essence a societal necessity; society must ensure that individuals have specific skills to handle specific functions or to be accepted into further education. At the same time, it can be very important for individuals to have their qualifications formally approved, both for practical reasons, as concerns status, and for psychological reasons, as an acknowledgement of achievement that can provide identity and generate self-confidence.

However, it is also well known that monitoring and evaluation may have a very forceful and controlling influence on the education course and on the behaviour and consciousness of both participants and teachers down to even the smallest details. It is therefore important that ways and means of practice in these areas are chosen carefully and in accordance with the participants' attitudes and preferences.

In Denmark today, adult education participants generally want some sort of documentation to prove that they have satisfactorily participated in education programmes, and to testify to the qualifications they have acquired. This shows that they recognise the need to be tested, but there is widespread reluctance for this to take place by means of an examination in the traditional sense. Many low-skilled participants have painful experiences of taking exams, believing, among other things, that it involves heavy and unnecessary psychological pressure, that the evaluation is unfair, that too much depends on luck or coincidence, etc.

However, it is not easy for the participants to give clear expression to possible alternative ways of monitoring and evaluating, as must be done to make it pos-sible to document the competences acquired. However, it is a widely held view that evaluation must be carried out by the teachers with whom the students have daily contact because, although there are both good and less good teachers, only they can assess what the student actually knows and is able to do and understand. Furthermore, it is claimed that only in exceptional cases, where the focus is on highly specific practical skills, is a test or exam relevant. The great majority of participants want the evaluation to be based on daily work and the minor and major assignments and projects that form part of the course.

Based on the assumption that participants are responsible adults and that the aim of the education programmes is generally to develop competences, there is every reason to respect the attitudes here expressed. In terms of learning, the concern is to find monitoring and evaluation forms that support, rather than inhibit, participants' independence, responsibility, cooperation, etc., and thereby also their competence development.

The traditional forms of monitoring and evaluation must be considered an obsolete reflection of industrial society. With attendance monitoring and exams, the participants are placed in opposition to the 'system' as a powerful adversary in the same way as in the labour conditions seen in industrial employment. The concern here is conformity and submission to external power-based demands and not the joint promotion of personal development and having it realistically evaluated.

Naturally, the power aspect cannot be eliminated, but it is not impossible to find methods that assume a less dominant character and which accord more respect to adult participants' experience, even if they exhibit a certain duality between the desire for self-direction and the desire to obtain formal approval.

The need for subjective anchorage

In general, educational initiatives for the low-skilled and other vulnerable groups seem to be becoming more varied but less clear. If this is to be addressed there is a need for radical initiatives that consistently take their starting point in and respect the situation as it is experienced by those whom it concerns. Nothing will be improved if those who are to learn are not met with something that is meaningful for them on the basis of their own premises (Illeris 2004).

For these groups it is this subjective anchorage that is the key to activities and measures that can provide a broader breakthrough. Despite their different situations, what the various groups mentioned have in common is that they are not directly open to traditional educational and training initiatives. They do not really believe in them, they have bad experiences of not being able to live up to what is expected, and they have usually repeatedly experienced what it means to be rejected, to feel that they are not respected. An anchorage or a point of departure in this psychological experience and interpretation of the situation is an unavoidable necessity in these contexts.

But, simultaneously, relevant initiatives are also about coming further, because it is precisely the current situation and the way in which the individual relates to it that is the problem. A sustainable solution thus presupposes some type of breakthrough, an educational angst that must be dealt with, an identity defence that must be overcome, some unrealistic dreams that must be brought down to a realistic level, or perhaps some dreams and goals that must be found somewhere in what is experienced as a great unstructured vacuum.

These are processes that psychologically go deeper than what is generally understood as education. Nevertheless, learning initiatives in the great majority of cases are the best way forward, because the development of better and more practically relevant competences is an important part of what is necessary to escape from the situation. However, if we want to tackle the problems of the low-skilled and other vulnerable groups in the breadth and complexity they have today, we must realise that it does not help to invest in minimum solutions. We have to go into depth and take the psychological aspect seriously. Highly qualified people are needed to undertake the key functions. It must be ensured that the labour market parties involve themselves actively and disregard narrow interests. Relevant workplaces must also be involved, even though in some cases this might mean financial compensation or other similar incentives.

Generation Y

Another and quite different special group in relation to work-related learning is the young generation, which can generally be understood as those who are born after 1985, although the boundary is more a psychological than a chronological one. This is the generation which until the current financial crisis has experienced nothing but progress; until now everything has in principle been possible, and the great individual problem and challenge has been to make the right individual choices in all dimensions of life.

In the end it is a question of choosing and forming precisely the personal identity that meets the deepest hopes, wishes and ambitions of the individual – and this is not a simple matter, but something that seems to take, on average, about 20 years of selecting, testing, adjusting and retesting relevant possibilities of all kinds, a task which is extremely engaging, sensational, but also demanding and sometimes embarrassing (see, for example, Giddens 1991; Furlong and Cartmel 1997; Baumann 2001; Beck and Beck-Gernsheim 2002; Illeris *et al.* 2009). This group has been called generation Y, partly because it comes after the insignificant generation X, and partly because it is the generation which meets any statement and any proposal with a 'why?' – and does not accept anything without a satisfactory explanation.

In relation to learning this is also the generation which has grown up with the perspective of lifelong learning as a matter of course. They have right from their early childhood experienced learning as a life condition, a necessity and almost the meaning of life, and they are far from the traditional understanding that goal-directed learning is finished when one has completed a qualifying education. This, on the one hand, makes workplace learning a quite natural matter – of course one must learn something everywhere, including at work – but, on the other hand, it also makes it quite natural to make inquiries and claims about the kind and quality of the learning possibilities which are offered at the workplace.

Against this background, the young members of generation Y cannot stand routine work: they hate slow and dull processes, they oppose hierarchies and they avoid definite choices because they will shut off some possibilities, and all possibilities should be kept open. All this is immediately and strongly against the expectations and opinions of most of their older colleagues, their superiors and often also the management, who think and feel that young newcomers should be modest, respectful, adapting and listening, and experience their pushy behaviour as misplaced, self-promoting and demanding.

On the other hand, the young people ask for clear educational perspectives: they want to be visible, and they flourish and quickly become valuable employees with new ideas and resources if they experience a good social climate, personal visibility and a positive attitude to their integration and career. They are generally prepared to adjust, work hard, learn a lot and do their utmost if they have a feeling of being accepted, appreciated and treated as equals with a specific individuality which is respected.

In many cases, the attitudes of such young and insistent employees, apprentices or trainees are so greatly in contrast to the workplace environment that clashes are inevitable, and if the young feel that they cannot prevail, that they are disregarded, not wanted or disliked, they are very quick to get out and find something else, because they have been in demand and it has always been possible for them to get another job or another opportunity. However, with the financial crises and increasing unemployment this last condition has changed, at least for the foreseeable future, and it is not easy to predict how this will influence the situation. The young generation will certainly not stop asking and demanding, but to some extent they will have to react differently and swallow some disappointments and hardship – which will not be easy for them, and for some will probably lead to a rejection of the normal labour market and attempts to find other ways of existence over a broad scale ranging from very creative and innovative projects to occasional jobs of all kinds, idleness and sometimes also criminality.

So, in general, generation Y constitutes a very big challenge, and also a very big chance of renewal, to workplace traditions – a challenge that strongly appeals to new, extensive, untraditional and creative workplace learning initiatives, involving the whole gamut of possibilities described in the previous chapters and probably also new ways which are to be discovered and developed with the young newcomers as innovative and dynamic tractive forces. Enterprises that want to aim at and prepare for future conditions and possibilities should really try to overcome the troubles and conflicts that the entry of the generation Y may cause in order to benefit from the inspiration and new ideas they also bring with them.

Housewives and other limit-setting groups

There will always on the labour market be some individuals and groups who are in a specific situation in which the workplace, for some reason, is not their top priority, not even during working hours.

For example, in some workplaces I have visited, and which are characterised by a rather large component of routine work, I have observed the group of housewives whose first priority is running their household and looking after their family, but who have to take a part-time or full-time job to keep the family economy in balance, often because they have bought a house which demands a certain level of income.

These housewives form a very important part of the labour force at these workplaces because they are reliable, obliging, punctual, very careful, with an often extremely low rate of errors, and they are also – in diametric opposition to generation Y – extremely adaptable: they want clear instructions and do precisely as they are told. This is because they are normal people who want nothing more than to keep their job and attract no trouble that could disturb their more important functions outside the workplace. But, on the other hand, the limits of their contributions and responsibility are sharply defined. They do as they are told, but nothing more. They invest their labour, but not themselves. Work, to them, means earning a wage: they are prepared to do what they are paid for, and to do it carefully and satisfactorily, but nothing more.

Their understanding of learning is learning to do the job and nothing more. They tend to draw a mental limit, and they are not inclined to cross this limit, not even for money or other rewards – because doing something extra, achieving more than what is agreed upon, is reserved for the first priority of private life.

As an example, consider a company I know that produces hospital equipment that must be absolutely faultless and antiseptic. The factory is placed close to a new housing area, dominated by young families with children. The majority of workers are housewives from this area. The factory manager, having observed how conscientious these housewives are in their work, had the idea of offering them a specially developed course of competence development so that they could work more independently and perhaps develop and improve their work functions. But they completely refused, and even though the manager brought in two female psychologists to convince the workers and he offered to adjust the course to meet their needs and wishes, the manager finally had to give up and drop all of his plans.

In such cases I think that all advocates of workplace learning meet their Waterloo, and there is nothing more to say. Learning may be useful, but, after all, people must have some kind of interest and openness if it is to be meaningful and worth the efforts that it will always involve. The housewives and other limit-setting employees must be respected – and, if not, they seem to have the power to stand by the limits they have.

After the life turn

The final group of special workplace learners I shall deal with here are elderly workers, or to be more precise, those who have passed the so-called life turn, which is a psychological phenomenon implying a personal perception and acknowledgement that one's remaining lifetime is not unlimited. This happens to everyone, usually some time between the ages of 45 and 65, sometimes as a consequence of a specific event, in other cases more gradually over a span of two to three years (see Jensen 1993; Illeris 2007).

The experience of the life turn is usually not immediately very strong, but it has a strong influence on the individual's attitude to learning, releasing a kind of unconscious recognition that it is no longer worthwhile engaging in everything

– one must reserve remaining learning capacity for what really has a personal meaning and value; one has to be selective.

In relation to workplace learning this selectivity usually means learning as well as possible what is necessary to manage one's position and perform daily tasks, and applying sufficient motivation and application; however, anything that does not fall into this category is ignored or considered insignificant stuff that does not really affect the learner.

Thus, the subjective experience of one's situation and position at work becomes even more important for attitude to and motivation for learning. Employees who feel that their efforts and opinions are appreciated and influential may be as good learners as they have always been, or even better because their total experience and understanding of their job may still be increasing. But employees who expect to spend the rest of their working lives doing what they have always been doing may be demodulated, putting no effort at all into learning or trying to develop or change anything – they may end up as the 'sour old men' behaving as 'reinforced concrete', as two of my colleagues jokingly described the most contrary segment of the male working population, aged between 40 and 60 years, that they had been studying (Dupont and Hansen 1997).

Of course, most workplace learners who have passed the life turn will be somewhere between these two extremes. What is generally to be understood and taken into account is that there is a quite big section of elderly workplace learners whose attitudes to learning are distinctly selective with a yardstick for their selectivity which is narrowly dependent on their subjective experience of the importance and influence of their job, how they manage it, and how it is appreciated by their colleagues and superiors.

When everybody at a workplace is expected to take part in common learning initiatives, it will often be important to take into account that some workers will join with a negative attitude that may influence the possible engagement and enthusiasm of their colleagues and actually cause considerable damage to the project.

Some general conclusions

Main points on the level of theory

In this concluding chapter I shall briefly sum up some main conclusions. On the theoretical level I have presented a general perspective that encompasses some overall terms of reference for the understanding and further development in the field of workplace learning and a model depicting the interaction between some main features of learning and also of the workplace as a learning environment.

Workplace learning – like all other learning – is fundamentally always taking place simultaneously on two levels. First, it takes place in an interaction situation: learning is always *situated* in a certain context, which can be, for example, a workplace, an educational institution, the home or any place whatsoever. Second, learning takes places within the individual as a mental and bodily acquisition process, where the impulses triggered by the interaction are processed and coupled with the results of prior learning, by which learning acquires its individual form and significance. Learning is thus both a social and an individual process at one and the same time.

On the social level, workplace learning takes place in an environment where there are some occurrences, something happens, people say something to each other, do different things, there is a specific culture and in the end the workplace is part of a society that influences and frames the nature of the occurrence. For workplace learning it has special significance that the work is at one and the same time part of a short-term production process and a long-term development process, and the learning demands made by these two processes are different and can even be contradictory in nature.

At the individual level, it is a case of learning something specific, that the learning always has a content with the character of knowledge, skills, attitudes, perceptions, patterns of reaction, etc. At the same time, this learning is influenced by the way the individual relates to what is taking place, emotionally and motivationally, including the fact that there can be difficulties, distortions or barriers in the form of defence mechanisms or resistance to learning. All of this is important for the quality, sustainability and application potentials of the learning. For example, the nature of the learning is significantly different if the learner is engaged or reluctant vis-à-vis what is learned – and for workplace learning it is central that the work is at one and the same time a necessity and a substantial part of the learners' life and personal development.

Workplace learning always involves the practical, social and cultural context of which it is a part as well as the learners' qualifications and relations to both the learning situation and the content of the learning. One must therefore relate to the content of the work, its nature and organisation, and to the working environment in the broadest sense, including the basic social conditions (which can be summed up in the concept of *work practice*), and to the way in which the employees and workers, individually and socially, relate to the work (which can be summed up in the concept of *work identity*).

Although the major focus has been on the individual side of learning (the acquisition process) as it usually is in traditional learning psychology and school learning, in the context of learning in working life in recent years there has been a tendency to focus first and foremost on the social side (the interaction process), for example with concepts such as situated learning, organisational learning, the learning organisation and social constructionism. It is, therefore, a main point of theory in connection with workplace learning that along with the practical, organisational, social and cultural sides of the working environment and the organisation of the work, one must also examine the employees' subjective experiences and situation in relation to work, individually and collectively.

Throughout the whole book I have tried to maintain the double view of learning outlined by examining all the different initiatives that can contribute to promoting targeted learning processes in the workplace while simultaneously relating to the different initiatives from the perspective of the learner. Further, I have tried to define and make special references to how workplace learning can be carried out in ways which can qualify it as competence development.

Main points on the level of practice

With respect to initiatives that promote learning on the practical level, I have found it suitable to crave a basic distinction between, on the one hand, initiatives that have to do with developing the learning environment in general, including such concepts as 'the learning organisation', and, on the other hand, more specific initiatives that have to do with a certain learning content and/or application of certain forms of learning.

Of course, the learning environment is of fundamental importance both for the nature of the more or less informal and unintended learning that always takes place at work and for what comes out of the more specific learning initiatives, which have been dealt with on four levels.

First, there are the more traditional types of initiatives aimed at specific dissemination or training in relation to the content of the work, its relations and professional processes. This has typically to do with instruction, training and teaching that can take place in direct relation to work, for instance through

ICT-mediated learning processes, or at meetings, internal courses, seminars and workshops at the workplace. More experience-processing contexts can also be established, such as experience groups and networks.

Second, one can work with different types of sparring and support schemes for the individual employee or certain groups of employees. These schemes may take the form of guided learning and mentoring schemes, appointment of super-users etc., coaching or consultant support, and the content can deal with specific work functions, typically such as utilisation of ICT or more personal sparring and support.

Third, there are the more development-oriented initiatives that reach beyond the known work processes and job functions and often are connected with broader organisational development. Typical of these is the establishment of self-directed groups, internal projects or action learning, but internal and external job exchange or job rotation schemes or external networks and communities of practice can also be included.

Fourth, and finally, interaction schemes can be established between work-places and education providers, such that learning is established in a process of alternation between more broadly structured educational initiatives outside the workplace, *inter alia* in the form of more overview-oriented and theoretical com-munication, and practice processing and experience-oriented processes at the workplace. What is crucial in this connection is that genuine learning interaction is established, both individually and collectively, which would seem to presuppose the development of close cooperation and mutual understanding between the workplaces and the education providers.

There is, of course, a considerable degree of overlap among these four levels of initiatives and between the various concrete modes of procedure at each of the levels, and it is quite possible to combine the different options, just as one can work simultaneously with general development of the working environment. The accounts given of the many different kinds of learning initiatives have primarily been aimed at providing an overview and thus facilitating the choice of suitable activities in a given context.

It is particularly important to distinguish between initiatives aimed mainly at training and upgrading in relation to the existing work organisation, and thus also primarily in relation to work as a production process (the first two main levels), and initiatives mainly aimed at further development of the employees involved, the organisation and content of the work, and thus primarily work as a process of development (the last two main levels). Despite the distinction, there is again a considerable degree of overlap and it is by no means the case that both kinds cannot be aimed at simultaneously.

It would seem to be decisive that the initiatives should be chosen with care on the basis of the intended learning, and that they should be practised wholeheart-edly and receive the backing and allocation of resources necessary at both the individual and the community level. If workplace learning on a broader political and social level is to be developed as an important supplement to, and even to some extent take the place of, institutionalised education and training, it is crucial that there is targeted investment in the learning initiatives utilised, in the same way as in educational institutions.

At the workplace, it is the responsibility of management to ensure that the fundamental resources, relations and working environment are put in place and respected, and that learners have practical responsibility for the implementation of the various initiatives, so that it matches their qualifications and meets their needs and interests.

Utopias and perspectives

With the last conclusion in the section above, we are on the way to a more general discussion of the long-term perspectives and thus also of more general and political angles of approach.

There would seem to be some critical conditions from a learning point of view. First, agreement and cooperation among all involved parties is essential, i.e. the state as overall framemaker, labour market organisations, workplaces, education providers and participants. Second, the necessary resources must be made available and there must be the political commitment that is a fundamental precondition for learning in general to achieve the quality and sustainability, both individually and socially, that is necessary to meet the intentions and aspirations underlying investment in workplace learning.

On the basis of these assumptions, workplace learning is or should be the most appropriate arena for directly work-related learning and competence development, if necessary supplemented by short, targeted, practical courses. In the case of more long-term and more broadly oriented learning processes and competence development that encompass general understanding and personal and democratic development as well as overview and theoretical insight, it must generally be regarded as most appropriate to aim at interaction between learning initiatives in and outside work. In the case of the low-skilled and other particularly vulnerable groups, it would seem to be particularly important that the key elements of their learning take place at functioning workplaces, and thus it is essential for workplaces to be open to such learning initiatives, which often take place on a special basis that exceeds the normal market conditions.

However, if future development is to head in the direction of these general and somewhat utopian terms of reference, the different parties involved must fulfil a number of conditions.

In the case of the state, this means deliberately favouring and practising a policy in the area of work-related education and training that is built on learning rationales as much as on economic and administrative rationales. It is not unlikely that a policy that puts more emphasis on the important parts of work-oriented learning taking place directly at work will prove to be economically advantageous in the long term. At bottom this means that the necessary changes in the framework conditions must be primarily based on learning insights and rationales, and that the state does not start with economic calculations, which in any case are fundamentally unable to account for the value of greater engagement in learning and the qualitatively better learning that results from this.

The great political question of how the costs of such increased investment in workplace learning are to be distributed among the different parties is, naturally, a subject that must form part of negotiations when the necessary reforms are being developed. This process is essentially different in different countries with different political and cultural traditions, forms of understanding and political systems. For this reason I shall present only some very general reflections in this area.

On the one hand, it could be argued that it is entirely appropriate for state, workplaces and participants to share the financing because this is a substantial expression of involvement while simultaneously legitimising co-influence. However, from a social perspective direct individual participant payment for work-related education must consistently be kept at a symbolic level that does not prevent anyone from taking part nor cause interest in participating to become dependent on the financial situation of the individual. Similarly, collective co-financing via employees' organisations must not be at a level that places a serious burden on members through their subscriptions.

On the other hand, it is obvious that if workplace learning is to be a broad social project, the distribution of costs and responsibility can by no means be left to market mechanisms, quite simply because experience shows that this will result in the so-called Matthew effect: 'those who have (education) shall be given more'. The low-skilled and other vulnerable groups will be the greatest losers, resulting in social and economic marginalisation, and in the final analysis polarisation will take place, leading to human tragedies and social destabilisation.

When the issue of financing must thus necessarily become a matter of negotiation, there is all the more reason to concentrate on parties' interests and engagement as the key starting point. The challenges inherent in considerably upgrading workplaces as a learning arena make some very far-reaching demands on different parties.

The state cannot pursue a minimum policy, but it must provide and guarantee the necessary framework conditions and underwrite the reasonable costs of doing so. If it wants to increase the emphasis on workplace learning, it must also demonstrate its belief that developing more and better workplace learning is a societal matter of such great importance that it provides the necessary resources (which in the longer term will probably be a particularly profitable use of resources).

For workplaces, private as well as public, the principal requirement is to be open to learning initiatives and to provide the time and place needed to allow both current employees, and other groups who need work-related learning but have no job, to participate in them. Training of the latter group is both a practical and economic problem in a market society, and workplaces should not be expected to bear the financial burden alone. Both the state and the labour market parties must play their part if a sustainable solution is to be found.

Educational institutions could experience an immediate reduction in activities to the same extent as learning initiatives transfer to the workplaces. But substantial investment is needed to develop sustainable interaction processes, and the staff of educational institutions could play an important role here provided they can adjust to the changed conditions. There will also be an increase in demand for employees who can help to undertake the additional learning functions at the workplace. If educationalists take up these challenges proactively, the result will be more a readjustment and relocation than any reduction in employment opportunities.

Finally, for learners themselves, fulfilment of the above conditions will open up new possibilities and conditions that both require and allow them to become engaged in learning processes that do not have the nature of school learning and which should be more immediately satisfying. For many, such readjustment will at first cause serious problems. There will be a threshold to cross and it must, of course, be possible to receive qualified support and counselling for such a process. More appropriate and satisfactory learning processes from the point of view of society, the workplaces and the participants will very quickly address this.

Thus, in general, there can be a certain identity of interests: that all interested parties in the area can have an overall interest in targeted and simultaneous expansion of the workplace learning possibilities. But it should not be forgotten that there are also important differences between the parties when it comes to the more concrete issues of what learning should be aimed at and how, about who is to have what influence, and not least, who is to pay what. There will also be different interests within the different parties – for example between the state and the municipalities, between different types of workplaces and education providers, and between different groups of participants.

If workplace learning is to be something other and more than a political slogan, it is therefore of fundamental importance that all the involved parties engage themselves in a process of readjustment that will reach deeply into habitual modes of understanding and patterns of work and thinking. Through my work in this area I have come to the conviction that it *can* become an important and large-scale process with significant potential to benefit all parties. I have set up some central terms of reference here as a kind of utopia. But I do not think it is utopian to believe that, if the parties involved are to take their own declared objectives seriously, they must also be able to pull themselves together to find sustainable compromises and to invest the necessary engagement and the necessary resources.

At the same time it should be borne in mind that these are matters whose significance extends far beyond the labour market and the education sector. It is no accident that the large supranational organisations such as Unesco, OECD, the EU and even the World Bank time and again draw attention to the fact that concepts such as 'lifelong learning' and 'workplace learning' are of vital importance for the internal stability, social balance and democratic development of societies.

Broad efforts concerning education and training that are organised in accordance with participants' needs and interests can, first and foremost, help to counteract the far-reaching polarisation that is increasingly manifesting itself as an inevitable consequence of the freeing and globalisation of market mechanisms.

Greater emphasis on workplace learning – and it must be learning that is in agreement with up-to-date competence requirements and therefore cannot be limited to technical-professional upgrading – will of necessity lead to increased co-influence and democratisation of the workplace. Learning that encompasses overview, understanding and the development of personal competences cannot be implemented without increased respect for those who participate in the learning processes, for their situation, interests and needs and, ultimately, for themselves.

In a wider perspective, the most important effect of more emphasis on workplace learning can perhaps be that it can play a part in forcing and accelerating a democratisation process within a very large sector of society. As pointed out by the large supranational bodies, this process can also be important for society in general, in that more people will feel that they are respected, engaged and also responsible, and therefore can make a significant contribution to democratisation 'from below'.

How do we proceed from here?

I have now outlined the contours of a development that can place a greater part of the social education and competence development effort more directly at the workplaces than is the case at present. I have also identified key matters in what such reform must imply as well as the far-reaching demands made on all the parties involved, their cooperation and their engagement.

The line in such development is very much an extension of a number of initiatives and readjustments that have taken place over the last decades in connection with work-related adult education and training. But it also proposes that a great step forward must be taken if we seriously wish to realise the learning potentials that workplace learning can imply.

In my opinion such a project does not have to merely be a utopia, but it neither can nor should be realised directly by means of large-scale reform. The changes that would be needed for this are too radical and untried in a larger context. What can be done in single cases carried by reformers and enthusiasts cannot simply be transferred to a larger scale.

As I see it, the way forward must therefore be by means of more broadly structured development projects, with the initiative firmly anchored in the relevant public authorities, and involving a wide range of different workplaces – private and public, small, medium-sized and large, industrial, trade and service enterprises. Both employees and other participants undergoing upgrading or requalification should be included and a professional expertise and follow-up function for learning and education must be guaranteed.

There is no need to go into more detail here about such a development initiative – that is up to the parties who are directly involved. But there is a need to stress that, if we are to make any decisive progress, there must be a broad and well-founded emphasis with a clear perspective in the direction of working towards a development and readjustment that is more than just an updating of the educational thinking that currently predominates.

Throughout the centuries there has been an unbroken trend for more and more work-related learning to be transferred from workplaces to the education system. Today there would seem to be good reasons for attempting to reverse this trend. But this is not something that can merely be decided and arranged overnight. It will require engagement, goal direction and resources.

References

Åberg, C. and Svensson, L. (2004) Arbejdspladsen – en arena for uddannelse og læring? [The workplace: an arena for education and learning?]. In Kanstrup, A.M. (ed.) *E-læring på arbejde*. Copenhagen: Roskilde University Press.

Alheit, P. (2009) Biographical learning – within the new lifelong learning discourse. In Illeris, K. (ed.) *Contemporary Theories of Learning*. London: Routledge.

Andersen, V. and Jørgensen, C.H. (2002) Det båndstyrede bageri og den ustyrlige styrelse. In Illeris, K. (ed.) *Udspil om læring i arbejdslivet* [*The Assembly Line Directed Bakery and the Unruly Governmental Agency*]. Copenhagen: Roskilde University Press.

Andersen, V., Illeris, K., Kjærsgaard, C., Larsen, K., Olesen, H.S. and Ulriksen, L. (1992) *Qualifications and Living People*. Roskilde: The Adult Education Research Group, Roskilde University.

Andersen, V., Illeris, K., Kjærsgaard, C., Larsen, K., Olesen, H.S. and Ulriksen, L. (1994) *General Qualification*. Roskilde: The Adult Education Research Group, Roskilde University.

Andersen, V., Illeris, K., Kjærsgaard, C., Larsen, K., Olesen, H.S. and Ulriksen, L. (1996) *General Qualification*. Copenhagen: Roskilde University Press.

Argyris, C. (2000) *The Next Challenge in Organisational Learning, Leadership and Change*. Harvard University, draft presentation, 1 November 2000.

Argyris, C. and Schön, D.A. (1978) *Organisational Learning: A Theory of Action Perspective*. Reading, MA: Addison-Wesley.

Argyris, C. and Schön, D.A. (1996) *Organisational Learning II – Theory, Method, Practice*. Reading, MA: Addison-Wesley.

Åsand, H.-R.H., Mørch, A. and Ludvigsen, S. (2004) Superbrugere: En strategi for ikt-omstilling [Super-users: a strategy for changing to ICT]. In Kanstrup, A.M. (ed.) *E-læring på arbejde*. Copenhagen: Roskilde University Press.

Baron-Cohen, S. (2003) *The Essential Difference*. London: Penguin.

Baumann, Z. (1998) *Globalisation: The Human Consequences*. Cambridge: Polity Press.

Baumann, Z. (2001) *The Individualised Society*. Cambridge: Polity Press.

Bechtle, G. (1994) Systemische Rationalisierung als neues Paradigma industriesoziologischer Forschung? [Systemic Rationalisation as a New Paradigm of Industrial Sociological Research?]. Göttingen: *Soziale Welt* (special issue).

Beck, U. (1992 [1986]) *Risk Society: Towards a New Modernity*. London: Sage.

Beck, U. and Beck-Gernsheim, E. (2002) *Individualisation: Institutionalised Individualism and its Social and Political Consequences*. London: Sage.

Becker-Schmidt, R. (1982) Modsætningsfyldt realitet og ambivalens [Contrasting reality and ambivalence]. *Udkast* no. 2, 164–198.

Beckett, D. (2004) Embodied competence and generic skill: the emergence of inferential understanding. *Educational Philosophy and Theory* 36, 497–508.

Beckett, D. (2009) Holistic competence: putting judgements first. In Illeris, K. (ed.) *International Perspectives on Competence Development*. London: Routledge.

Beckett, D. and Hager, P. (2000) Making judgements as the basis for workplace learning: towards an epistemology of practice. *International Journal of Lifelong Education* 19, 300–311.

Beckett, D. and Hager, P. (2002) *Life, Work and Learning: Practice in Postmodernity*. London: Routledge.

Berger, P.L. and Luckmann, T. (1969) *The Social Construction of Reality*. New York: Doubleday.

Berggren, C. (1994) *The Volvo Experience*. London: Macmillan.

Berri, S. (2002) *Forskning som demokratisk læreproces [Research as a Democratic Learning Process]*. Roskilde: Roskilde University.

Billett, S. (2000) Guided learning at work. *Journal of Workplace Learning* 12, 272–285.

Billett, S. (2001) *Learning in the Workplace: Strategies for Effective Practice*. Crows Nest, NSW: Allen & Unwin.

Billett, S. (2003) Workplace mentors: demands and benefits. *Journal of Workplace Learning* 15, 105–113.

Billett, S., Harteis, C. and Eteläpelto, A. (2008) *Emerging Perspectives of Workplace Learning*. Rotterdam: Sense Publishers.

Bødker, S. (2000) Coordinating technical support platforms. *Communications of the ACM* 43, 215–222.

Boshyk, Yury (ed.) (2000) *Business Driven Action Learning: Global Best Practices*. London: Macmillan.

Boud, David (2003) *Combining Work and Learning: The Disturbing Challenge of Practice*. Keynote speech at the International Conference 'Experiential: Community: Workbased – Researching Learning Outside the Academy', Glasgow Caledonian University, 27–29 June 2003.

Boud, D. and Garrick, J. (eds.) (1999) *Understanding Learning at Work*. London: Routledge.

Bourdieu, P. (1977 [1970]) *Reproduction in Education, Society and Culture*. London: Sage.

Bourdieu, P. (1998 [1980]) *Practical Reason*. Cambridge: Polity Press.

Boxall, P., Purcell, J. and Wright, P. (eds.) (2008) *The Oxford Handbook of Human Resource Management*. Oxford: Oxford University Press.

Braverman, H. (1974) *Labour and Monopoly Capital*. New York: Monthly Review Press.

Brookfield, S.D. (1987) *Developing Critical Thinkers: Challenging Adults to Explore Alternative Ways of Thinking and Acting*. Milton Keynes: Open University Press.

Brookfield, S.D. (1996) *Understanding and Facilitating Adult Learning*. Buckingham: Open University Press.

Brown, J.S., Collins, A. and Daguid, P. (1989) Situated cognition and the culture of learning. *Educational Researcher* 18, 32–42.

Burr, V. (2003) *Social Constructionism*. London: Routledge.

Carruthers, J. (1993) The principles and practice of mentoring. In Caldwell, B.J. and

Carter, E.M.A. (eds.) *The Return of the Mentor: Strategies for Workplace Learning*. London: Falmer Press.

Castells, M. (2000) *The Rise of the Network Society*. Oxford: Blackwell.

Cecchin, D. (ed.) (2000) *Børns kompetencer [Children's Competences]*. Copenhagen: BUPL.

Cedefop (European Centre for the Development of Vocational Training) (2003) *Lifelong Learning: Citizens' Views*. Luxembourg: Office for Official Publications of the EU.

Chaiklin, S. and Lave, J. (eds.) (1993) *Understanding Practice: Perspectives on Activity and Context*. Cambridge, MA: Cambridge University Press.

Christiansen, E. (1997) Gardening: a metaphor for sustainability in information technology-technical support. In Berleur, J. and Whitehouse, D. (eds.) *An Ethical Global Information Society – Culture and Democracy Revisited*. London: Chapman & Hall.

Clematide, Bruno (2004) Historien om samspillet. In Bottrup, P. and Jørgensen, C.H. (eds.) *Læring i et spændingsfelt – mellemuddannelse og arbejde [The History of the Interplay – Between Work and Education]*. Copenhagen: Roskilde University Press.

Clematide, B. and Jørgensen, E. (2003) *Inspiration til måder at lære på [Inspiration for Ways of Learning]*. Copenhagen: Learning Lab Denmark.

Cohen, N.H. and Galbraith, M.W. (1995) Mentoring in the learning society. In Galbraith, M.W. and Cohen, N.H. (eds.) *Mentoring: New Strategies and Challenges*. San Francisco: Jossey Bass.

Colley, H., Hodkinson, P. and Malcolm, J. (2003) *Informality and Formality in Learning*. London: Learning and Skills Research Centre.

Damasio, A.R. (1994) *Descartes' Error: Emotion, Reason, and the Human Brain*. New York: Grosset/Putnam.

Damasio, A.R. (1999) *The Feeling of What Happens: Body, Emotions and the Making of Consciousness*. London: Vintage.

Danish Ministry of Education (2008) *Bekendtgørelse om uddannelse til professionsbachelor i sygepleje [Departmental order on the education of bachelors of nursing]*. 24 January 2008. Copenhagen: Undervisningsministeriet.

Darwin, A. (2000) Critical reflections on mentoring in work settings. *Adult Education Quarterly* 50, 197–211.

Dirckinck-Holmfeld, L. (2004) Et europæisk perspektiv på eLæring [A European perspective on e-learning at work]. In Kanstrup, A.M. (ed.) *E-læring på arbejde*. Copenhagen: Roskilde University Press.

Dotlich, D.L. and Noel, J.L. (1998) *Action Learning*. San Francisco: Jossey-Bass.

Downham, T.A., Noel, J.L. and Prendergast, A.E. (1992) Executive development. *Human Resource Management* 31, 95–107.

Drake, D.B., Brennan, D. and Gørtz, K. (eds.) (2008) *The Philosophy and Practice of Coaching*. San Francisco: Jossey-Bass.

Dreyfus, H. and Dreyfus, S. (1986) *Mind over Machine*. New York: Free Press.

Dupont, S. and Hansen, L. (1997) *En undersøgelse af nogle 40–60-årige mænds motivation og barrierer i forhold til deltagelse i voksenuddannelse [A Survey of Some 40–60-Years-Old Males' Motivation and Barriers Towards Participation in Adult Education]*. Copenhagen: Danish Ministry of Education.

Easterby-Smith, M., Burgoyne, J. and Araujo, L. (eds.) (1999) *Organisational Learning and the Learning Organisation*. London: Sage.

Easterby-Smith, M. and Lyles, M.A. (eds.) (2003) *Handbook of Organisational Learning and Knowledge Management*. Oxford: Blackwell.

Edwards, R. (1979) *Contested Terrain: The Transformation of the Workplace in the Twentieth Century*. New York: Basic Books.

Ekstedt, E., Lundin, R.A., Söderholm, A. and Wirdenius, H. (1999) *Neo-Industrial Organising: Renewal by Action and Knowledge Formation in a Project-intensive Economy*. London: Routledge.

Elkjær, B. (1999) In search of a social learning theory. In Easterby-Smith, M., Burgoyne, J. and Araujo, L. (eds.) *Organisational Learning and the Learning Organisation*. London: Sage.

Elkjær, B. (2004) Organisatorisk læring i et organisationsudviklingsprojekt [Organisational learning in an organisational development project]. In Kanstrup, A.M. (ed.) *E-læring på arbejde*. Copenhagen: Roskilde University Press.

Ellström, P.-E. (1992) *Kompetens, utbildning och lärande i arbetslivet* [*Competence, Education and Learning in Working Life*]. Stockholm: Publica.

Ellström, P.-E. (1996): Rutin och reflexion. Förutsätningner och hinder för lärande i dagligt arbete. [Routine and reflection: preconditions and impediments to learning in everyday work]. In Ellström, P.-E., Gustavsson, B. and Larsson, S. (eds.) *Livslångt Lärande*. Lund: Studentlitteratur.

Ellström, P.-E. (2001) Integrating learning and work: conceptual issues and critical conditions. *Human Resource Development Quarterly* 12, 421–435.

Ellström, P.-E. (2002) Lärande – i spänningsfeltet mellan produktionens och utvecklingens logik. In Abrahamsson, K., Abrahamsson. L., Björkman, T., Ellström, P.-E. and Johansson, J. (eds.) *Utbildning, kompetens och arbete* [*Learning – in the Tension Field Between the Logics of Production and Development*]. Lund: Studentlitteratur.

Ellström, P.-E. (2003) *Kompetenceutveckling på arbetsplatsen: Forutsättningar, processer och effekter* [*Competence development at the workplace: Preconditions, processes and effects*]. Lecture at the Danish University of Education, 18 November 2003.

Ellström, P.-E. (2004) Kompetenceudvikling på arbejdspladsen: Forudsætninger, processer, resultater [Competence development at the workplace: conditions, processes, results]. In Andersen, V., Clematide, B. and Høyrup, S. (eds.) *Læring på arbejdspladsen – udfordringer til læreprocesser på arbejdet*. Copenhagen: Roskilde University Press.

Ellström, P.-E. and Kock, H. (2009) Competence development in the workplace: Concepts, strategies and effects. In Illeris, K. (ed.) *International Perspectives on Competence Development*. London: Routledge.

Engeström, Y. (1987) *Learning by Expanding: An Activity-Theoretical Approach to Developmental Research*. Helsinki: Orienta-Konsultit.

Engeström, Y. (2009) Expansive learning: towards an activity-theoretical reconceptualisation. In Illeris, K. (ed.) *Contemporary Theories of Learning*. London: Routledge.

Erikson, E.H. (1971) *Identity, Youth and Crisis*. New York: Norton.

EU Commission (2000) *Memorandum on Lifelong Learning*. Brussels: EU.

Evans, K. (2009) *Learning, Work and Social Responsibility*. Dordrecht: Springer.

Evans, K., Hodkinson, P. and Unwin, L. (eds.) (2002) *Working to Learn: Transforming Learning in the Workplace*. London: Kogan Page.

Evans, K., Hodkinson, P., Rainbird, H. and Unwin, L. (2006) *Improving Workplace Learning*. London: Routledge.

Freud, A. (1942 [1936]) *The Ego and the Mechanisms of Defence*. London: Hogarth Press.

Freud, S. and Breuer, J. (1956 [1895]) *Studies on Hysteria*. London: Pelican Freud Library.

Furlong, A. and Cartmel, F. (1997) *Young People and Social Change: Individualisation and Risk in Late Modernity*. Buckingham: Open University Press.

Gallwey, T. (1975) *The Inner Game of Tennis*. New York: Random House.

Gallwey, T. (1979) *The Inner Game of Golf*. New York: Random House.

Gallwey, T. and Kriegel, R. (1977) *Inner Skiing*. New York: Random House.

Garrick, J. (1998) *Informal Learning in the Workplace: Unmasking Human Resource Development*. London: Routledge.

Garrick, J. (1999) The dominant discourses of learning at work. In Boud, D. and Garrick, J. (eds.) *Understanding Learning at Work*. London: Routledge.

Gergen, K.J. (1994) *Realities and Relationships*. Cambridge, MA: Harvard University Press.

Giddens, A. (1990) *The Consequences of Modernity*. Stanford, CA: Stanford University Press.

Giddens, A. (1991) *Modernity and Self-Identity*. Cambridge: Polity Press.

Goldberg, E. (2001) *The Executive Brain: Frontal Lobes and the Civilised Mind*. New York: Oxford University Press.

Goleman, D. (1995) *Emotional Intelligence: Why it can Matter More than IQ*. London: Bloomsbury.

Gulowsen, J. (1971) *Selvstyrte arbeidsgrupper* [*Self-Directed Work Groups*]. Oslo: Tanum.

Habermas, J. (1984) *The Theory of Communicative Action*, Vol. I: *Reason and the Rationalisation of Society*. Cambridge: Polity Press.

Hager, P. and Beckett, D. (1995) Philosophical underpinnings of the integrated conception of competence. *Educational Philosophy and Theory* 21, 1–24.

Han, S. (2009) Commodification of human ability. In Illeris, K. (ed.) *International Perspectives on Competence Development*. London: Routledge.

Harvard Business Review (2001) *On Organisational Learning*. Harvard: Harvard Business School Publishing Corporation.

Herling, R.W. (2001) Operational definitions of expertise and competence. In Swanson, R.A. and Holton, E.F. (eds.) *Foundations of Human Resourse Development*. San Francisco: Berrett-Koehler Publishers.

Hjort, K. (2008) What's new, Doc? – old tensions or new knowledge on professions and organisations? In Aili, C. and Nilsson, L.-E. (eds.) *In Tension between Professions and Organisations*. Stockholm: Nordic Academic Press.

Hjort, K.(2009) Competence development in the public sector: development, or dismantling of professionalism? In Illeris, K. (ed.) *International Perspectives on Competence Development*. London: Routledge.

Hodkinson, P., Hodkinson, H., Evans, K. and Kersh, N. (2004) The significance of individual biography in workplace learning. *Studies in the Education of Adults* 36, 6–24.

Horton, S. (ed.) (2006) New public management: its impact on public servants' identity. *International Journal of Public Sector Management,* 19 (special issue).

Illeris, K. (1986) The use of projects in university education as inspiration for project management. In Gabriel, E. (ed.) *New Approaches in Project Management*. Zurich: Internet.

Illeris, K. (1991) Project education in Denmark. *International Journal of Project Management* 9, 45–48.

Illeris, K. (1998) Adult learning and responsibility. In Illeris, K. (ed.) *Adult Education in a Transforming Society*. Copenhagen: Roskilde University Press.

Illeris, K. (1999) Project work in university studies: background and current issues. In Olsen, H.S. and Jensen, J.H. (eds.) *Project Studies: A Late Modern University Reform?* Copenhagen: Roskilde University Press.

Illeris, K. (ed.) (2000) *Adult Education in the Perspective of the Learners*. Copenhagen: Roskilde University Press.

Illeris, K. (2002) *The Three Dimensions of Learning: Contemporary Learning Theory in the Tension Field between the Cognitive, the Emotional and the Social*. Copenhagen: Roskilde University Press/Lancaster: NIACE/Malabar, FL: Kriger Publishing.

Illeris, K. (2003) Adult education as experienced by the learners. *International Journal of Lifelong Education* 22, 13–23.

Illeris, K. (2004) *Adult Education and Adult Learning*. Copenhagen: Roskilde University Press/Malabar, FL: Krieger Publishing.

Illeris, K. (2005) Low-skilled workers learn at the workplace. *Lifelong Learning in Europe* 10.

Illeris, K. (2006a) A comprehensive understanding of human learning. In Jarvis, P. and Parker, S. (eds.) *Human Learning: An Holistic Approach*. London: Routledge.

Illeris, K. (2006b) What is special about adult learning? In Sutherland, P. and Crowther, J. (eds.) *Lifelong Learning: Concepts and Contexts*. London: Routledge.

Illeris, K. (2006c) Lifelong learning and the low-skilled. In Antikainen, A., Harinen, P. and Torres, C.A. (eds.) *In From the Margins: Adult Education, Work and Civil Society*. Rotterdam: Sense Publishers.

Illeris, K. (2006d) Lifelong learning and the low-skilled. *International Journal of Lifelong Education* 25, 15–28.

Illeris, K. (2007) *How We Learn: Learning and Non-learning in School and Beyond*. London: Routledge.

Illeris, K. (ed.) (2009a) *International Perspectives on Competence Development*. London: Routledge.

Illeris, K. (2009b) Competence, learning and education: how can competences be learned, and how can they be developed in formal education? In Illeris, K. (ed.) *International Perspectives on Competence Development*. London: Routledge.

Illeris, K. (2009c) A comprehensive understanding of human learning. In Illeris, K. (ed.) *Contemporary Theories of Learning*. London: Routledge.

Illeris, K. (2009d) Transfer of learning in the learning society. *International Journal of Lifelong Education*, 28, 137–148.

Illeris, K. (2009e) Lifelong learning as a psychological process. In Jarvis, P. (ed.) *The Routledge International Handbook of Lifelong Learning*. London: Routledge.

Illeris, K. and associates (2004) *Learning in Working Life*. Copenhagen: Roskilde University Press.

Illeris, K., Katznelson, N., Nielsen, J.C., Simonsen, B. and Sørensen, N.U. (2009). *Ungdomsliv – mellem individualisering og standardisering [Youth Life – between Individualisation and Standardisation]*. Copenhagen: Samfundslitteratur.

Jarvis, P. (2006) *Towards a Comprehensive Theory of Human Learning*. London: Routledge.

Jarvis, P. (2009a) Learning to be a person in society: learning to be me. In Illeris, K. (ed.) *Contemporary Theories of Learning*. London: Routledge.

Jarvis, P. (ed.) (2009b) *The Routledge International Handbook of Lifelong Learning*. London: Routledge.

Jarvis, P. (2009c) Learning to be an expert: competence development and expertise. In Illeris, K. (ed.) *International Perspectives on Competence Development*. London: Routledge.

Jensen, J.F. (1993) *Livsbuen: voksenpsykologi og livsaldre* [*The Life Arch: Adult Psychology and Life Ages*]. Copenhagen: Gyldendal.

Jensen, P.E. (2000) Kapabiliteter og kompetencer som ledelsesværktøj [Capabilities and competences as a tool of management]. In Andersen, T., Jensen, I. and Prahl, A. (eds.) *Kompetence i et organisatorisk perspektiv*. Copenhagen: Roskilde University Press.

Jørgensen, C.H. and Warring, N. (2003) Learning in the workplace: the interplay between learning environments and biographical learning trajectories. In Jørgensen, C.H. and Warring, N. (eds.) *Adult Education and the Labour Market VII B*. Copenhagen: Roskilde University Press.

Jørgensen, Per Schultz (1999) Hvad er kompetence? [What is competence?]. *Uddannelse* 9.

Jungk, R. and Müllert, N.R. (1981) *Zukunftswerkstätten* [*Future Workshops*]. Hamburg: Hoffmann und Campe.

Juul, J. (2001 [1995]) *Your Competent Child*. New York: Farrar, Strauss & Giroux.

Kanstrup, A.M. (2004) Læring bag facaden: om værdien af lokale gartnere [E-learning behind the surface: the value of local gardeners]. In Kanstrup, A.M. (ed.) *E-læring på arbejde*. Copenhagen: Roskilde University Press.

Keeling, R. (2000) *Project Management – an International Perspective*. London: Macmillan Business.

Kern, H. and Schumann, M. (1970) *Industriearbeit und Arbeiterbewusstsei* [*Industrial Work and Workers' Consciousness*]. Munich: Beck.

Kern, H. and Schumann, M. (1984) *Das Ende der Arbeitsteilung?* [*The End of Labour Division?*]. Munich: Beck.

Knights, D. and Willmott, H. (1990) *Labour Process Theory: Studies in the Labour Process*. Basingstoke: Macmillan.

Kolb, D.A. (1984) *Experiential Learning*. Englewood Cliffs, NJ: Prentice-Hall.

Lahn, L.C. (2004) Udvikling af netbaserede læringsomgivelser i arbejdslivet [The development of net-based learning environments in working life]. In Kanstrup, A.M. (ed.) *E-læring på arbejde*. Copenhagen: Roskilde University Press.

Lane, J.-E. (2000) *New Public Management*. London: Routledge.

Lave, J. (2009) The practice of learning. In Illeris, K. (ed.) *Contemporary Theories of Learning*. London: Routledge.

Lave, J. and Wenger, E. (1991) *Situated Learning: Legitimate Peripheral Participation*. Cambridge, MA: Cambridge University Press.

Leithäuser, T. (1976) *Formen des Alltagsbewusstseins* [*The Forms of Everyday Consciousness*]. Frankfurt a.M.: Campus.

Leithäuser, T. (2000) Subjectivity, lifeworld and life organization. In Illeris, K. (ed.) *Adult Education in the Perspective of the Learners*. Copenhagen: Roskilde University Press.

Leontyev, A.N. (1981 [1959]) *Problems of the Development of the Mind* (collected manuscripts from the 1930s). Moscow: Progress.

Lucio, M.M., Skule, S., Kruse, W. and Trappmann, V. (2007) Regulating skill formation in Europe. *European Journal of Industrial Relations* 13, 323–340.

Mackay, W.E. (1990) Patterns of sharing customizable software. In *Proceedings of the Conference on Computer-Supported Cooperative Work,* Los Angeles, 7–10 October 1990.

McLaughlin, K., Osborne, S.P. and Ferlie, E. (eds.) (2002) *New Public Management: Current Trends and Future Prospects.* London: Routledge.

Marsick, V.J. (1990) Action learning and reflection in the workplace. In Mezirow, J. and associates (eds.) *Fostering Critical Reflection in Adulthood: A Guide to Transformative and Emancipatory Learning.* San Francisco: Jossey-Bass.

Marsick, V.J. and Watkins, K.E. (1990) *Informal and Incidental Learning in the Workplace.* London: Routledge.

Mayo, E. (1949) *The Social Problems of an Industrial Civilisation.* London: Routledge & Kegan.

Mezirow, J. (1978) *Education for Perspective Transformation.* New York: Teachers College, Columbia University.

Mezirow, J. (1990) How critical reflection triggers transformative learning. In Jack Mezirow *et al.* (eds.) *Fostering Critical Reflection in Adulthood.* San Francisco: Jossey-Bass.

Mezirow, J. (1991) *Transformative Dimensions of Adult Learning.* San Francisco: Jossey-Bass.

Mezirow, J. (2009) An overview on transformative learning. In Illeris, K. (ed.) *Contemporary Theories of Learning.* London: Routledge.

Morsing, M. (1995) Organisatorisk læring af anden orden – fra en struktur til en proces-orienteret teori om læring [Organisational learning of second order: from a structure-oriented to a process-oriented theory of learning]. *Virksomhedens strategi og ledelse* 5.

Mumford, A. (1988) *Developing Top Managers.* Aldershot: Gower.

Mumford, A. (ed.) (1997) *Action Learning at Work.* Aldershot: Gower.

Nardi, B.A. (1993) *A Small Matter of Programming: Perspectives on End User Computing.* Cambridge, MA: MIT Press.

Nicolini, D., Gherardi, S. and Yanow, D. (eds.) (2003) *Knowing in Organisations.* New York: M.E. Sharpe.

Nielsen, J.L. and Webb, T.W. (1999) Project work at the New Reform University of Roskilde: different interpretations. In Olesen, H.S. and Jensen, J.H. (eds.) *Project Studies: A Late Modern University Reform?* Copenhagen: Roskilde University Press, 00–00.

Nitschke, H. (2008) Fanget i selv-reflektionens spejlkabinet [Caught in the mirror gallery of self-reflection]. In Kim Gørtz, K. and Prehn, A. (eds.) *Coaching i perspektiv.* Copenhagen: Reitzel.

OECD (1996) *Lifelong Learning for All.* Paris: OECD.

OECD (2000) *Knowledge Management in the Learning Society.* Paris: OECD, Centre for Educational Research and Innovation.

OECD (2001) *Cities and Regions in the New Learning Economy.* Paris: OECD, Centre for Educational research and Innovation.

OECD (2010) *The OECD Programme for the International Assessment of Adult Competencies (PIAAC)*. Paris: OECD Publication No. 88999.

Olesen, H.S. (2001) Professional identity as learning processes in life histories. *Journal of Workplace Learning* 13, 290–297.

Orpen, C. (1997) The effects of formal mentoring on employee work motivation, organizational commitment and job performance. *The Learning Organization* 4, 53–60.

Palmer, S. (2008) Foreword. In Drake, D.B., Brennan, D. and Gørtz, K. (eds.) *The Philosophy and Practice of Coaching: Insights and Issues for a New Era*. San Francisco: Jossey-Bass.

Parker, B. and Walters, S. (2009) Competence-based training and National Qualifications Frameworks in South Africa. In Illeris, K. (ed.) *International Perspectives on Competence Development*. London: Routledge.

Pedersen, K. (2004) Mentoring – et bidrag til bedre samspil? [Mentoring: a contribution to improved interaction?]. In Bottrup, P. and Jørgensen, C.H. (eds.) *Læring i et spændingsfelt – mellem uddannelse og arbejde*. Copenhagen: Roskilde University Press.

Prætorius, Nadja U. (2004) Livet som undtagelsestilstand [Life as a state of emergency]. *FOFU-NYT* 1, 13–26.

Prætorius, N.U. (2007) *Stress – det moderne traume* [*Stress – the Modern Trauma*]. Copenhagen: Dansk Psykologisk Forlag.

Procter, S. and Mueller, F. (eds.) (2000) *Teamworking*. London: Macmillan.

Rainbird, H., Fuller, A. and Munro, A. (eds.) (2004) *Workplace Learning in Context*. London: Routledge.

Raven, J. and Stephenson, J. (eds.) (2001) *Competence in the Learning Society*. New York: Peter Lang.

Revans, R.W. (1970) The managerial alphabet. In Heald, G. (ed.) *Approaches to the Study of Organizational Behaviour*. London: Tavistock.

Revans, R.W. (1978) *The a.b.c. of Action Learning: A Review of 25 Years of Experience*. Salford: University of Salford.

Revans, R.W. (1982) *The Origin and Growth of Action Learning*. London: Chartwell Bratt.

Rogers, C.R. (1951) *Client-Centred Therapy*. Boston: Houghton-Mifflin.

Rogers, C.R. (1969) *Freedom to Learn*. Columbus, OH: Charles E. Merrill.

Rubenson, K. (2009) Lifelong learning: between humanism and global capitalism. In Jarvis, P. (ed.) *The Routledge International Handbook of Lifelong Learning*. London: Routledge.

Rychen, D.S. and Salganik, L.H. (eds.) (2003) *Key Competencies: For a Succesful Life and a Wellfunctioning Society*. Cambridge, MA: Hogrefe & Huber.

Rychen, D.S. and Tiana, A. (2004) *Developing Key Competencies in Education*. Paris: Unesco International Bureau of Education.

Sandberg, Å. (1995) *Enriching Production: Perspectives on Volvo's Uddevalla Plant as an Alternative to Lean Production*. Aldershot: Avebury.

Schein, E. (1986) *Organisational Culture and Leadership*. San Francisco: Jossey-Bass.

Schön, D.A. (1983) *The Reflective Practitioner: How Professionals Think in Action*. New York: Basic Books.

Schön, D.A. (1987) *Educating the Reflective Practitioner*. San Francisco: Jossey-Bass.

Senge, P.M. (1990) *The Fifth Discipline: The Art and Practice of the Learning Organisation*. New York: Doubleday.

Sennett, R. (1998) *The Corrosion of Character*. New York: Norton.

Simonsen, B. (2000) New young people, new forms of consciousness, new educational methods. In Illeris, K. (ed.) *Adult Education in the Perspective of the Learners*. Copenhagen: Roskilde University Press.

Skule, S. (2004) Learning conditions at work: a framework to understand and assess informal learning in the workplace. *International Journal of Training and Development* 1, 8–20.

Swanson, R.A. and Holton, E.F. (2001) *Foundations of Human Ressource Development*. San Francisco: Barrett Koehler.

Tennant, M. (1999) Is learning transferable? In David Boud and John Garrick (eds.) *Understanding Learning at Work*. London: Routledge.

Thång, P.-O. and Wärvik, G.-B. (2004) Produktionsnær uddannelse med IT-støtte for erhvervsaktive i den svenske industri [IT-supported production-based education of employees in Swedish industry]. In Kanstrup, A.M. (ed.) *E-læring på arbejde*. Copenhagen: Roskilde University Press.

Thomasen, J.G. (2008) Kan vi lære at nå det, eller kan vi nå at lære det? – om medarbejdertrivsel når arbejdspladsen sætter fokus på læring og kompetenceudvikling [Can we learn to achieve it, or can we achieve to learn it?: on job satisfaction when the workplace focuses on learning and competence development]. Copenhagen: The Danish School of Education.

Thorsrud, E. and Emery, F.E. (1976) *Democracy at Work: The Report of the Norwegian Industrial Democracy Program*. Leiden: Martinus Nijhoff.

Toulmin, S. and Gustavsen, B. (eds.) (1996) *Beyond Theory: Changing Organisations through Participation*. Philadelphia: John Benjamins.

Trier, U.P. (2001) *12 Countries Contributing to DeSeCo – A Summary Report*. Neuchâtel: University of Neuchâtel on behalf of the Swiss Federal Statistical Office.

Tynell, J. (2001) *Da medarbejderne blev en ressource. Magtrelationer i en virksomhed, der profilerer sig på at pleje og udvikle medarbejdernes menneskelige ressourcer. [When Employees Became a Ressource: Power Relations in an Enterprise Raising its Profile by Supporting and Developing the Human Resources of the Employees]*. Roskilde: Roskilde University.

Tyson, S. (2006) *Essentials of Human Resource Management*, 5th edn. Oxford: Butterworth-Heinemann.

Volmerg, B., Senghaas-Knobloch, E. and Leithäuser, T. (1986) *Betriebliche Lebenswelt. Eine Sozialpsychologie industrieller Arbeitsverhältnisse [Life World at Work: A Social Psychology of Work Conditions in Industry]*. Opladen: Westdeutscher Verlag.

Volmerg, U. (1976) Zur Verhältnis von Produktion und Sozialisation am Beispiel industrieller Lohnarbeit [Conditions of production and socialisation in industrial wage labour]. In Leithäuser, T. and Heinz, W. (eds.) *Produktion, Arbeit, Sozialisation*. Frankfurt a.M.: Suhrkamp.

Vygotsky, L.S. (1978) *Mind in Society: The Development of Higher Psychological Processes*. Cambridge, MA: Harvard University Press.

Vygotsky, L.S. (1986 [1934]) *Thought and Language*. Cambridge, MA: MIT Press.

Watkins, K.E. and Marsick, V.J. (1993) *Sculpting the Learning Organisation: Lessons in the Art and Science of Systemic Change*. San Francisco: Jossey-Bass.

Weil, S.W., Wildemeersch, D. and Jansen, T. (2005) *Unemployed Youth and Social Exclusion in Europe: Learning from Inclusion?* Aldershot: Ashgate.

Wenger, E. (1998) *Communities of Practice: Learning, Meaning and Identity.* Cambridge, MA: Cambridge University Press.

Wenger, E. (2009) A social theory of learning. In Illeris, K. (ed.) *Contemporary Theories of Learning.* London: Routledge.

Wenger, E., McDermott, R. and Snyder, W. (2002) *Cultivating Communities of Practice: A Guide to Managing Knowledge.* Cambridge, MA: Harvard Business School Press.

Whitmore, J. (1996) *Coaching for Performance: Growing People, Performance and Purpose.* London: Nicholas Brealey.

Wildemeersch, D. (2000) Lifelong learning and the significance of the interpretive professional. In Illeris, K. (ed.) *Adult Education in the Perspective of the Learners.* Copenhagen: Roskilde University Press.

Willis, P.E. (1977) *Learning to Labour: How Working Class Kids Get Working Class Jobs.* Farnborough: Saxon House.

Yorks, L., O'Neil, J. and Marsick, V.J. (eds.) (1999) *Action Learning – Successful Strategies for Individual, Team, and Organisational Development.* Baton Rouge, LA: Academy of Human Resource Development.

Index

Note: page numbers in *italics* refer to Figures.

utopia phase: future workshops 86–7

variety of opportunities 71
vertical division of labour 33
visits to other companies 110
vocational training 116, 123;
    cooperation outside the workplace
    138–9; time and place 146
Volmerg, Birgit 33, 36
Volmerg, Ute 33, 71
Volvo automobile factories: self-directed
    groups 102
vulnerable groups 142–3; elderly
    workers 152–3; generation Y 150–1;
    housewives 151–2; learning content
    and methods 146–8; monitoring
    and evaluation 148–9; psychological
    background 143–6; subjective
    anchorage 149–50; time, place and
    context of activities 146; *see also* low-
    skilled workforce

Warring, Niels 37
Watkins, Karen 108
Wenger, Etienne 8, 26, 36, 70, 96
work content 32–3

work experience 116
work identities 19, 27–8, 39–40, 155;
    identity defence 144–5; overlap with
    work practice *43–4*; and retraining
    144
work practice 155; involvement in
    competence development 60–1;
    overlap with work identities *43–4*;
    relationship to workplace learning
    39–41, *40*
working memory 20–1
workplace communities 36–8
workplace learning: difference from
    childhood learning 38; differences
    between different types of work 29;
    fundamental elements 30–*1*; locations
    29; rationale 3–6; relationship to
    work practice 39–41, *40*; theoretical
    approaches 6–9
workplace rationale of learning 118–19
workshops 85–7

young generation 150–1; expectations
    145
Your Competent Child (Juul 2001) 53